AF581267

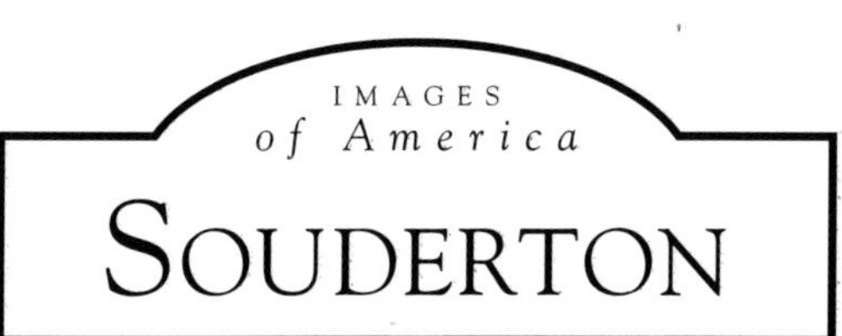
IMAGES
of America
SOUDERTON

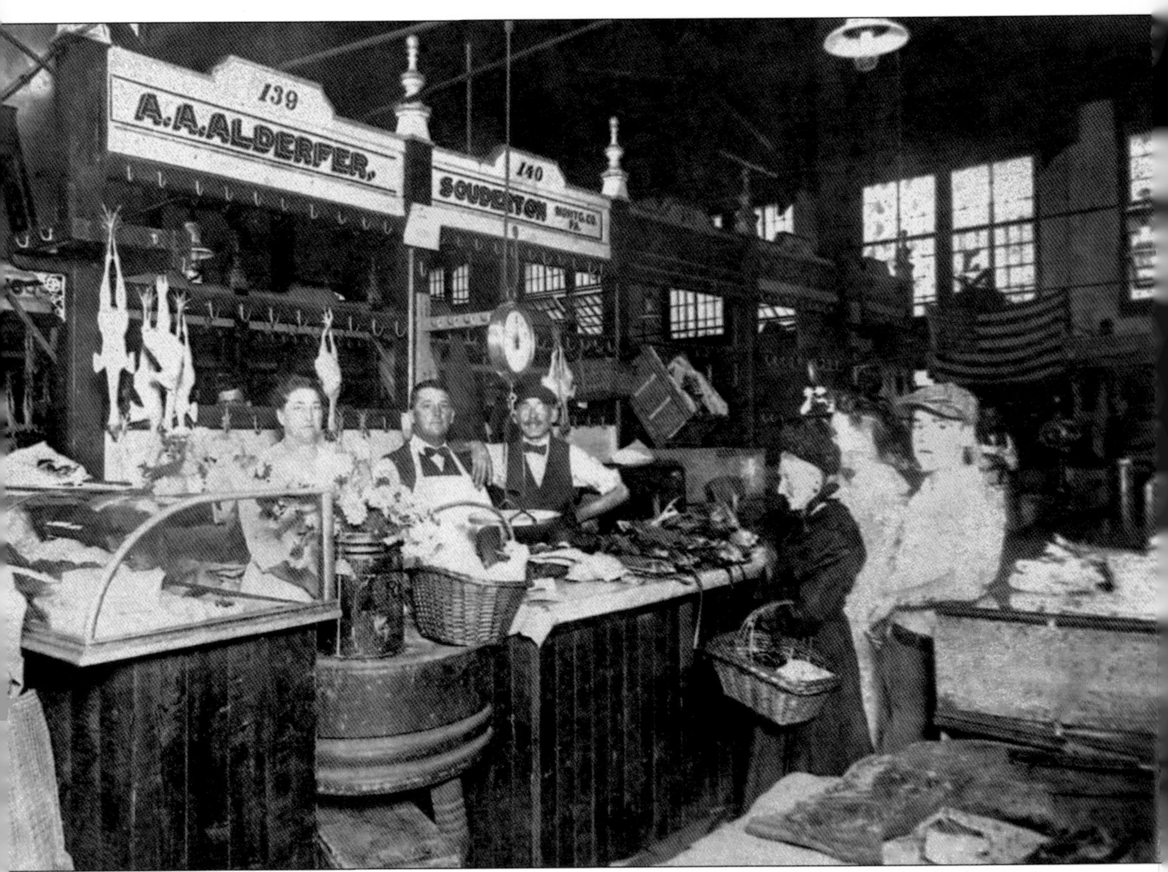

Local farm produce was always in great demand in Philadelphia. Allen A. Alderfer (center) and wife, Mary, photographed around 1918, raised chickens in Souderton to sell at their farm stand in the Reading Terminal Market. Allen Alderfer's neighbors gave him their produce to sell on commission. Market sellers, like Alderfer, often returned with oysters, an area favorite, to sell to Souderton restaurant owners. (Courtesy of Phil Ruth.)

On the Cover: Amateur photographer Antonio "Tony" Bova, who spent 60 years collecting images of Souderton, photographed Main Street as it appeared in 1937. Bova successfully captured the essence that is still familiar today—the hill and the hollow. Taken from Chestnut Street for a 50th anniversary book, *Half Century of Progress 1887–1937*, Tony photographed a Buick (left), Chevrolet (center), and Ford (right) with a trolley in the distance. (Courtesy of John Derstine.)

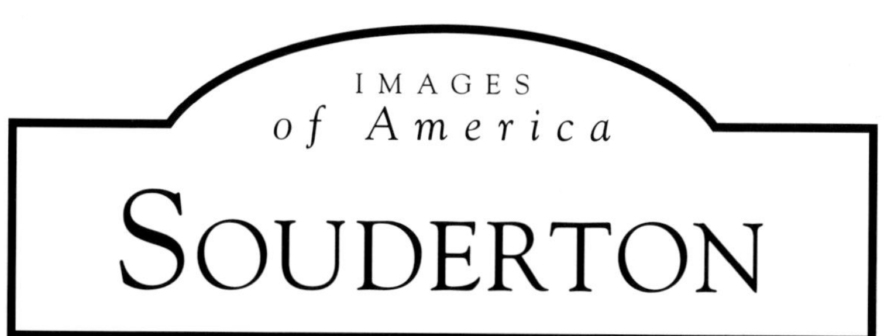

Souderton Telford Main Streets

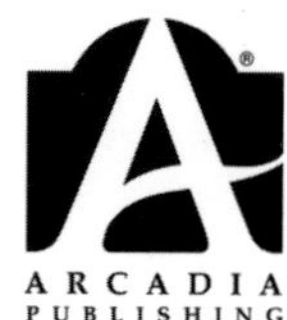

ISBN 978-0-7385-7634-3

Published by Arcadia Publishing
Charleston, South Carolina

Printed in the United States of America

Library of Congress Control Number: 2011925335

For all general information, please contact Arcadia Publishing:
Telephone 843-853-2070
Fax 843-853-0044
E-mail sales@arcadiapublishing.com
For customer service and orders:
Toll-Free 1-888-313-2665

Visit us on the Internet at www.arcadiapublishing.com

In memory of Nancy Owen, who personified the spirit of volunteerism, generosity, and community pride shared by all Souderton and Telford Main Street volunteers.

CONTENTS

Acknowledgments

We did not know if we could unearth enough photographs to make a book, but the outpouring of photos and stories is so typical of the generous spirit found in the Indian Valley. Now, I get to thank everyone not acknowledged elsewhere in this book.

First of all, the team who has spent the past five months calling, visiting, listening, scanning, researching, arguing, and forging amazing memories needs to be recognized. Cory and Ron Alderfer handled the bulk of the work with grace and enthusiasm. Virginia "Ginger" Bernd was the writer/editor who made each caption fit the word count while bringing the stories to life. Her husband, Charles, proofread her work. Borough Councillor Jeffrey Gross had the vision for the book and provided family lore, along with D. Brad Price, John and Elaine Derstine, Brent Bernd, and Nathan Rutko, who delved into research to identify photographs and to fill in story details. Phil Ruth served as source material, contributor, and inspiration.

Next, we have the many generous people who shared their treasures. The very best photographs were used in the book and the owner acknowledged there. Some photographs were duplicated from many sources who also provided tidbits, memories, and stories. They are acknowledged below. Our thanks are extended to Joel Alderfer, Larry Anders, Linda Beck, Paul Beck, Anne Benner, Linda Bossert, Martha Child, Sandra Clemmer, Joan Cope, P. Michael Coll, "Diamond Street Gang," Dennis Easterling, Wes Freed, Karen Giannini, James Gill, Donna Goshow, Charles Grasse, Norma Grasse, Bea Kaizar, Helen Keller, Alan Keyser, Dawn Kohler, Tim Kohler, Dean Kulp, Randy Landis, Lois Langevin, Joyce Markey, Beverly Miller, Emily Morris, Nancy Moyer, Wayne Moyer, James Musselman, Kristen Nonnemacher, Lester Pittman, John Ralston, Marian Rosenberger, Mary Rubin, Rachel Schmucker, Elizabeth Sell, Elvin Souder, Shelby Weaver Splain, Janet Vincent, Norman Vincent, Robert Wellington, and Robert Wood. Mennonite Heritage Center of Harleysville, PA photos are designated as "Mennonite Heritage Center." Souderton Telford Main Streets photographs are designated as "STMS collection."

Although we have done our best to log every contributor, we apologize to anyone we inadvertently missed.

—Pam Coleman
Main Street Manager
Souderton Telford Main Streets

INTRODUCTION

In the eastern portion of what would become Franconia Township, George Cressman, a land speculator and one of Souderton's first true settlers, leased and sold parcels of farmland from his 1,000 acres. By 1775, seven parcels of this land would be sold to predominantly German immigrants, whose families would enrich the area with their lives and leave a legacy that we celebrate today. One such family was that of Henry O. Souder. Around 1852, when Henry heard reports that a railroad project might link Philadelphia and the Lehigh Valley, the enterprising owner of a lumberyard and sawmill contemplated the possibilities of having rail service to transport his lumber. His entrepreneurial spirit and subsequent negotiations with the Philadelphia, Easton & Water Gap Railroad led to a shift in the proposed route of the railroad, bringing the rails, literally, to Henry's doorstep, and with them, Souderton's destiny.

Over the next 40 years, the railroad brought change to the Indian Valley, allowing the next generations the opportunity to create new businesses and meet the needs of their expanding community. As the town took shape, a dusty dirt road that ran parallel to the railroad track became Souderton's Main Street. From the southern hilltop, where it intersected Broad Street, Main Street followed the rolling landscape into the hollow and up the northern end to the village of Reliance. Here is where the community worshipped and worked, where neighbors congregated, where lives mingled, and where stories were shared.

The collective memory of a town lies in its heart—its Main Street—and in the hearts of those who have lived, worked, and played there. Souderton's Main Street is the town's most identifiable landmark, known to all as the hill and the hollow. In an essay, *Main Street Memories*, Ron Frantz, an Oklahoma architect and Main Street preservationist for 35 years, characterized "main street" as a town's "three-dimensional memory, built by our ancestors, maintained by us, and passed on to our heirs." The chapters in this Arcadia book clearly reflect that three-fold perspective.

The children, grandchildren, and great-grandchildren of Souderton's many first families proudly shared their photographs and, equally as important, their stories. Octogenarian Jean Leopold, a lifelong resident of Diamond Street, Souderton, writing for a local essay contest more than a decade ago, fondly recalled her own Main Street memories. "Everything happened on Main Street. I went to church at Zwingli, had my first dental visit, got my vaccination, and had my hair cut, to the tip of the ear and shingled up the back at Herb Shearer's barbershop. On Friday evenings, with a nickel or dime allowance clenched tightly in my fist, I entered Kline's Variety store to make a purchase of a game of jacks, a book of paper dolls, or a rubber ball," recalled Jean. She described the pump "in front of Barney Rubin's junkyard with its tin cup on which reposed the community's germs" and could still picture her father "walking down Main Street on his way home from work, pausing to watch the Liberty Bell Limited, plying its way north and south on its Main Street tracks." In the 1930s and 1940s, "life's pleasures were simple, yet so endearingly memorable," she wrote.

Philip Ruth, author of *Seeing Souderton*, the pictorial history produced for the town's centennial celebration in 1987, had also been impressed by the generosity of spirit he found here. "One needn't be born and raised in Souderton to appreciate the Borough's special qualities. My inexperience with local history projects, and the fact that I hadn't lived a day in Souderton, might have made for a rocky attempt to tell 'the Borough's Story in Photographs,' as was my assignment back in 1986-87," he writes. "But Souderton's boosters, many of whom were Main Street businessmen, weren't about to let that happen. They quickly took me under wing, gave me access to piles of archival material, and made sure I had the benefit of extensive community connections. The deep love that folks such as Floyd 'Jake' Frederick, Tony Bova, and Ted Boyer expressed for their hometown was infectious and inspiring. I had such a positive experience in preparing *Seeing Souderton* that I went on to build a career in historical research and writing. I soon learned not to expect from other communities the fulsome blend of hometown pride and memory stewardship that I encountered during my first project in Souderton. It is not common, and it should be treasured. Judging from the enthusiasm and generosity of contributors to this 125th anniversary retrospective, I'd say that—while many of the 'old-timers' who helped me a quarter-century ago are no longer with us—the Soudertonian spirit is alive and well," declared Philip.

With this book, Souderton celebrates its 125th anniversary as a borough. The Souderton Telford Main Street's volunteer committee of local history enthusiasts focused on what really created Souderton—its people, for they had been the risk-takers, the problem-solvers, the dreamers, not just at its beginning, but in every succeeding decade. Today, this volunteer-driven organization advocates the revitalization and sustainability of Souderton and neighboring Telford to advance the quality of life for the people who live and work here. They promote the unique assets of each borough, foster the growth of business and residential neighborhoods, and guide aesthetic development to enrich our communities. To promote the significance of the local history and architecture, they instigated the recognition of the Souderton Historic District and supported the local volunteer historians in producing this book.

Inside is a photographic journey that begins with Cressman's thousand acres and ends with a vision of the revitalization efforts now in the capable hands of Souderton Telford Main Streets. As Frantz wrote, "The old buildings . . . and the streets . . . beckon us to come back, to restore, to reclaim, to remember, and to respect. And though the train may no longer stop here, it seems the tracks still run home." Soudertonians agree. The tracks run home to where the heart is—to the hill and the hollow—to Main Street.

One

Cressman's Thousand Acres

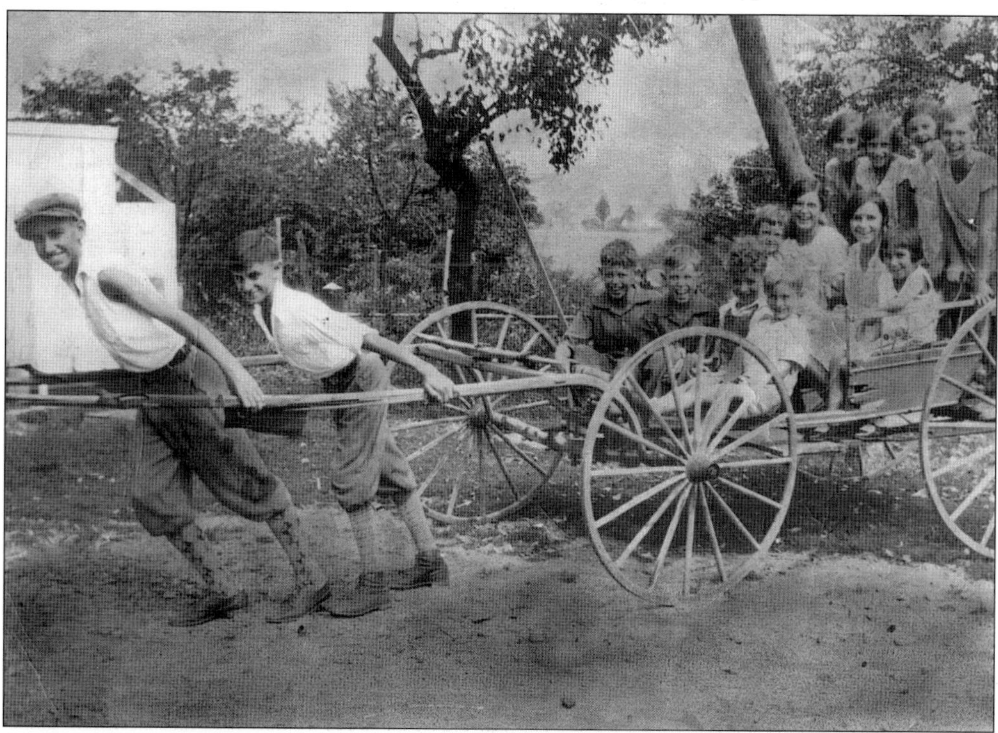

On land first settled by Lenape Native Americans in the Indian Valley of Franconia Township, early Welshtown was home to Welsh and then German immigrants. With no major roads and plenty of fertile soil, the religious farming community offered an idyllic but demanding life. Here, the Krupp, Derstine, and Detwiler children have fun at a family reunion. (Courtesy of John Derstine.)

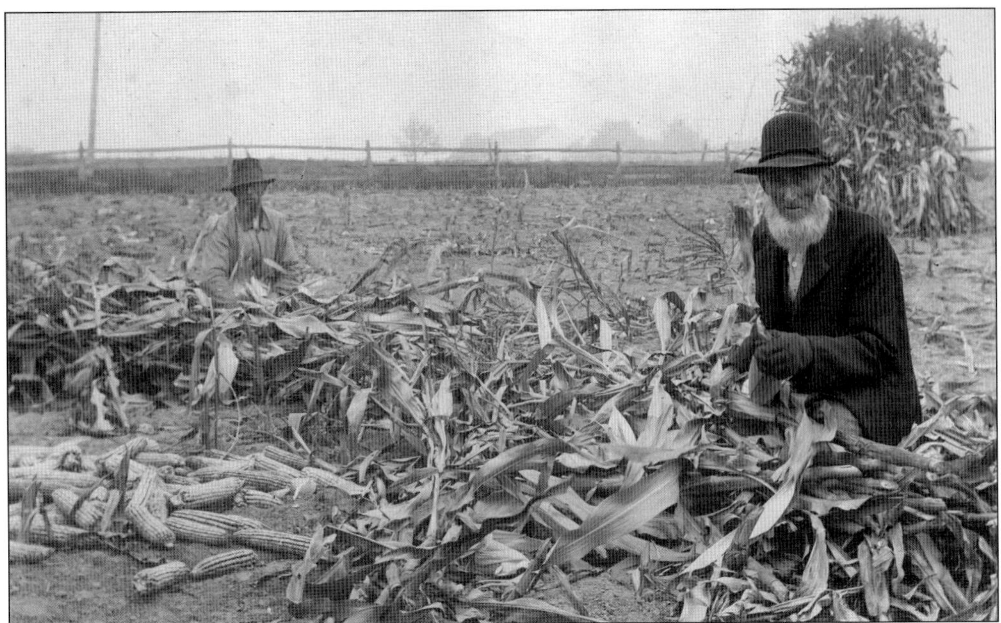

These European settlers built log homes along the Skippack Creek on land first owned by William Penn. Early farming was done by hand. Here John B. Shisler and his son John K. husk corn together on their Franconia farm. (Courtesy of Mennonite Heritage Center.)

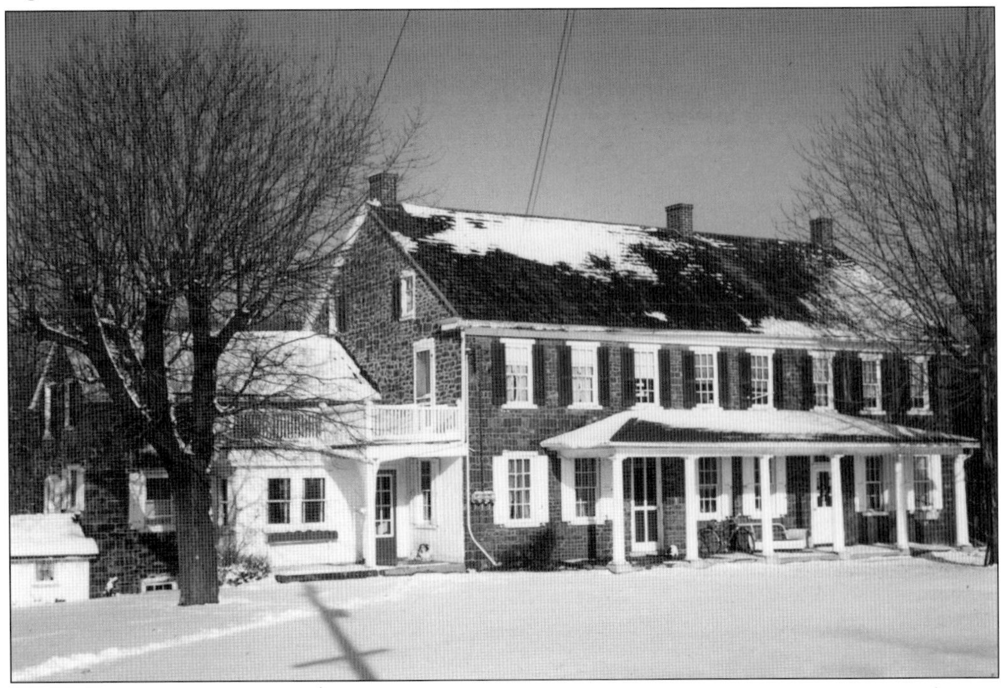

By 1683, German, Swiss, and Dutch immigrants began arriving in Pennsylvania, seeking religious freedom and a chance to own land. In 1733, over 100 acres were leased to Lutheran Ludwig Hangey. Like his Welsh predecessors, Ludwig first built a log house. Field stones cleared from the land were later used to build this more substantial home on present-day West Broad Street. (Courtesy of John Freed.)

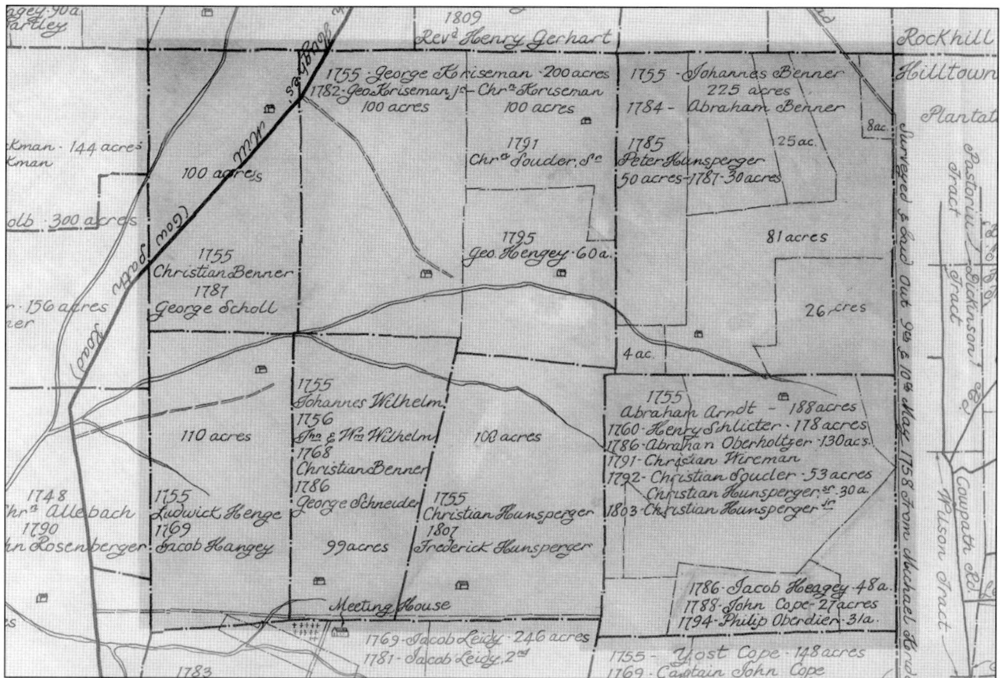

In 1734, Lutheran carpenter George Cressman leased 1,000 acres, including Ludwig Hangey's parcel, encompassing most of what is now Souderton. The large parcel was roughly bounded by what are now Reliance Road, County Line Road, Cherry Lane, and Cowpath Road. By 1775, Cressman had paid for his land in full and split it into seven plots, retaining one for himself. Hangey also bought his land. (Courtesy of Mennonite Heritage Center.)

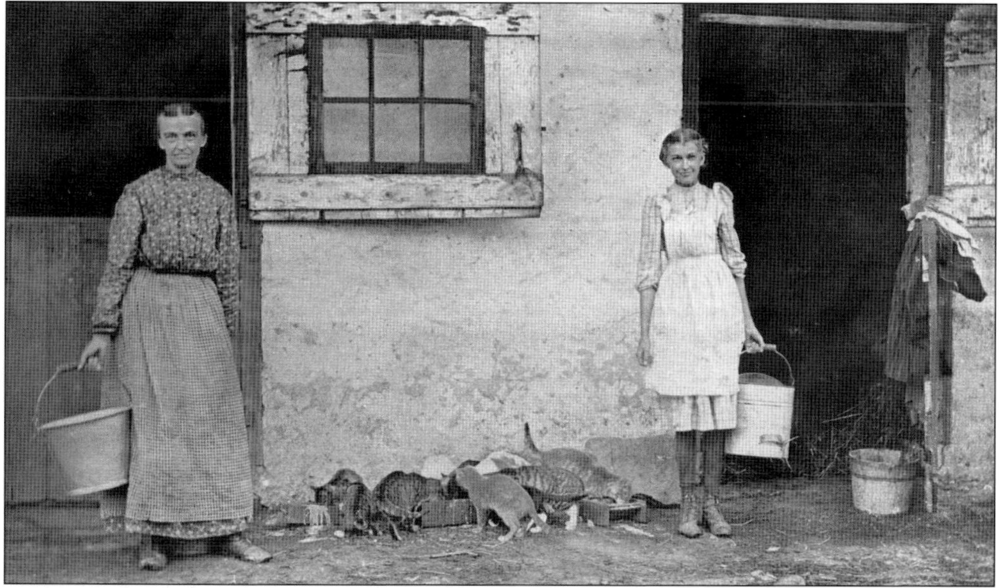

German immigrants were meticulous, hard-working people. Their farms demanded their full attention. Often barns were built before houses, and living space was shared with the animals, which were essential to the agrarian life. Every family member was needed to grow the food for the family and care for the livestock. (Courtesy of Mennonite Heritage Center.)

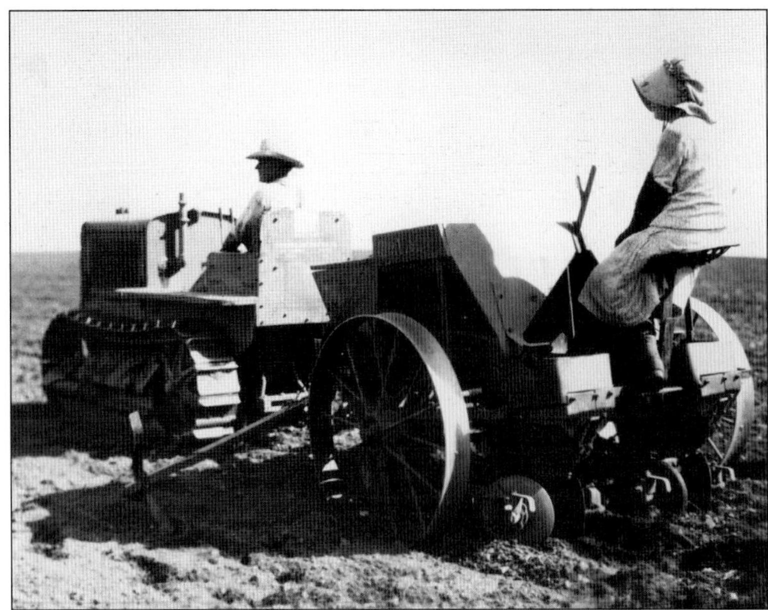

To survive, a husband, wife, and their children were needed to complete the many farming chores. In this photograph, husband and wife Jacob and Eve Wile work together to plow their fields. Wide-brimmed hats and bonnets protected untanned skin from the sun. (Courtesy of John Freed.)

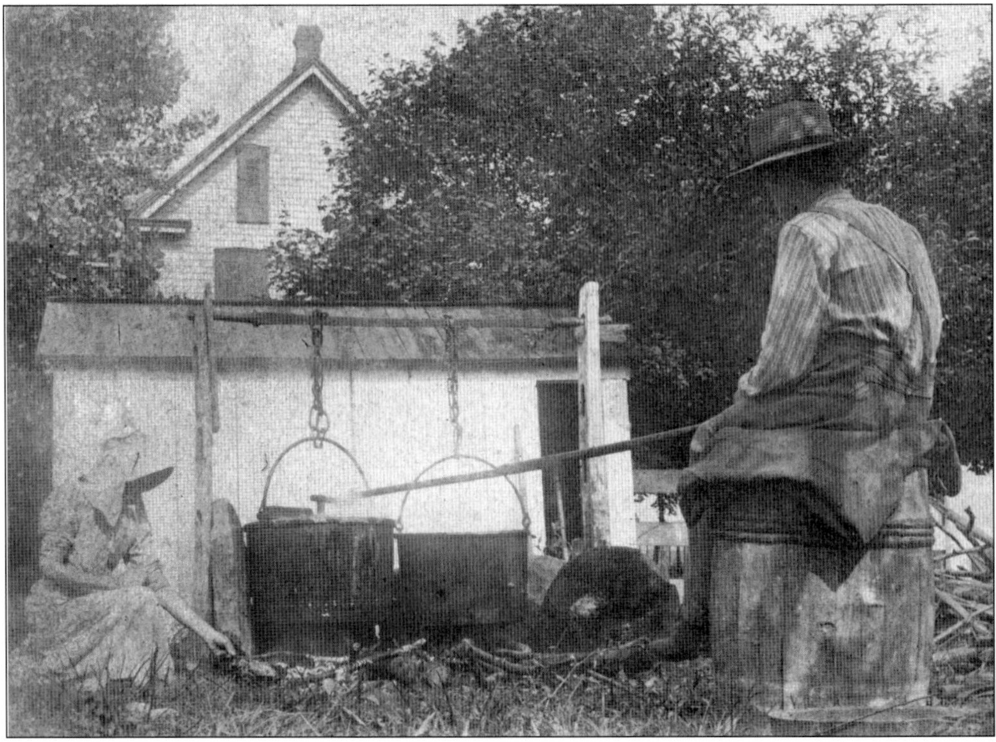

German immigrants planted plenty of cabbage to make sauerkraut. Children and adults alike enjoyed "schnitz," or dried apples, and homemade apple butter from the family's orchard. Photographed at the Gehman farm, family members tend the kettles of simmering apple butter, an activity that brought families and friends together to socialize, as did harvests, quilting parties, and barn raisings. (Courtesy of Mennonite Heritage Center.)

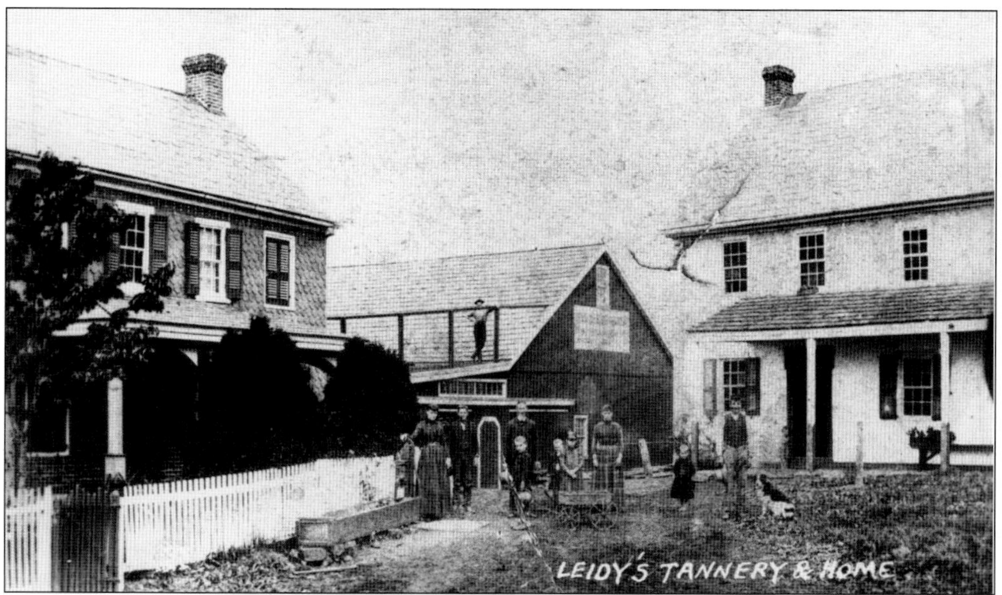

South of the Cressman properties, Jacob Leidy opened a store in 1785, and in 1788 a tannery (middle building), rebuilt after 1828. Encased within the building on the right is Leidy's original stone home. By 1753, the Leidy family established "Old Leidy's Graveyard." In 1795, that burial lot was purchased by an interfaith association of Christians, who also erected a building to use for funerals, schooling, and worship services. (Courtesy of Phil Ruth.)

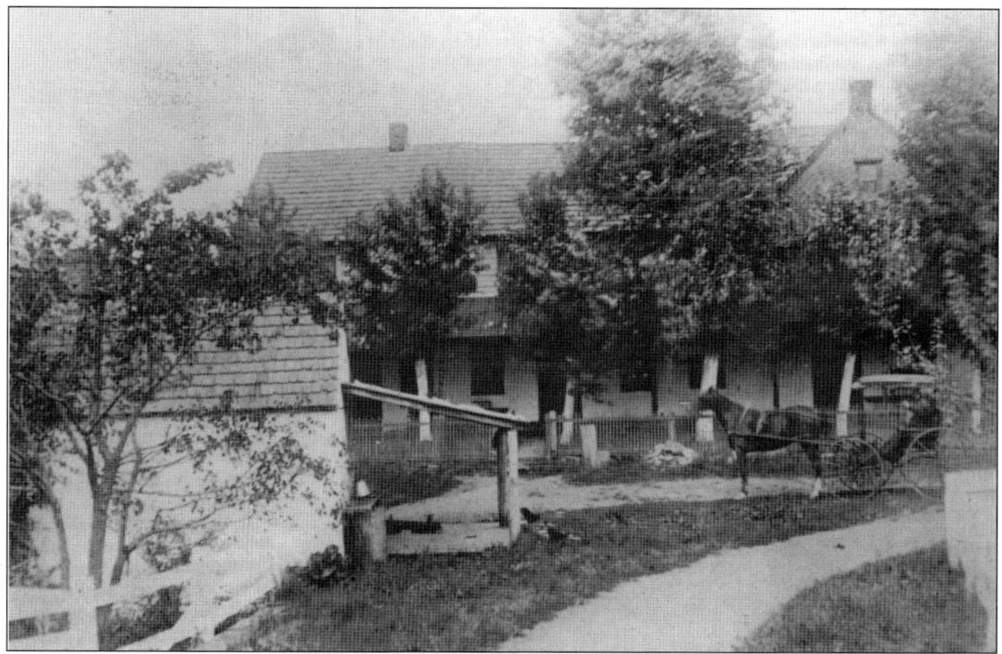

In a farmhouse adjacent to the Leidy farm lived Jacob's sister Magdelena and her husband, Maj. Jacob Reed. During the Revolutionary War, the Reeds served a hastily prepared meal to Gen. George Washington as he pursued the British from Valley Forge to Trenton, New Jersey, in June 1778. Lieutenant Colonel Reed is buried in Leidy's Cemetery. (Courtesy of Hatfield Museum and History Society.)

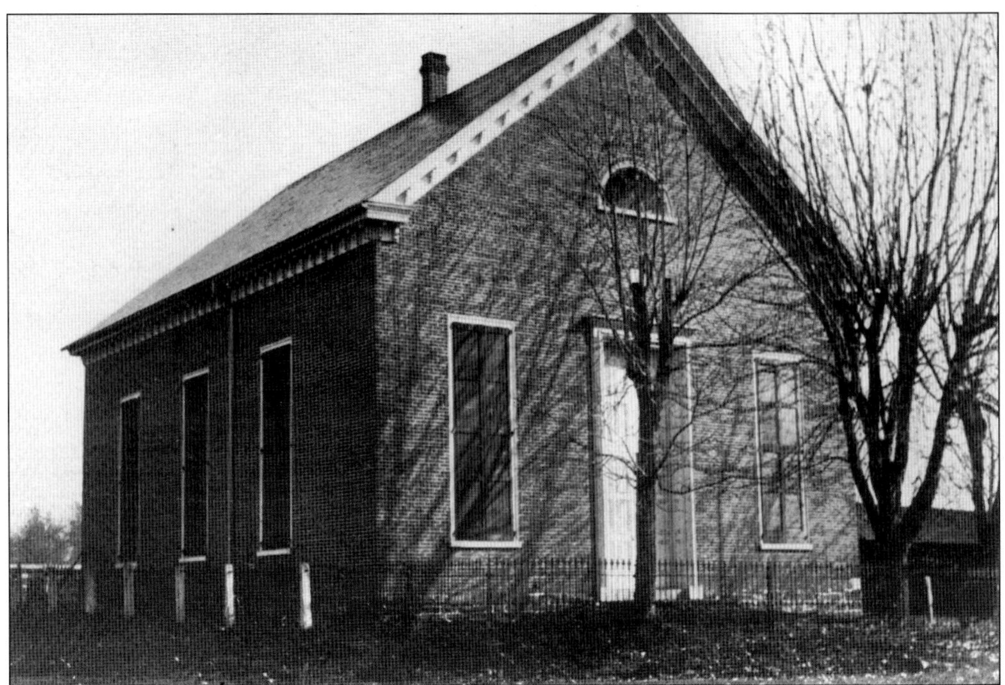

A Sunday school was established in 1854 and was held in the cemetery building. With a demand for more religious services, Thomas Leidy donated land adjoining the cemetery for the construction of this combined Lutheran and Reformed church, which was dedicated in 1859. This photograph of Immanual Leidy's or Leidy's Church was taken in 1901. Both congregations used the church until a Lutheran church was established in town. (Courtesy of Judith Leidy.)

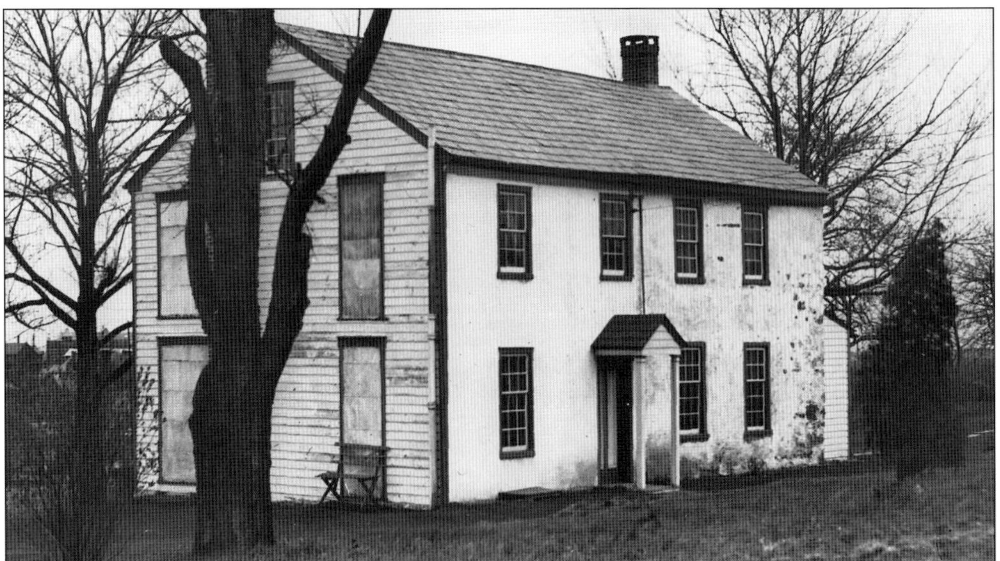

In 1755, George Cressman sold a 225-acre parcel of land to Mennonite Johannes Benner. Benner had been leasing the land that was bordered by what are today's Reliance Road, Chestnut Street, Main Street, and County Line Road. His son Abraham built this stone home in 1785. John H. Frederick, a shoemaker by trade, married Abraham's granddaughter Hannah. Around 1839, John opened a shop at his residence. (Courtesy of Phil Ruth.)

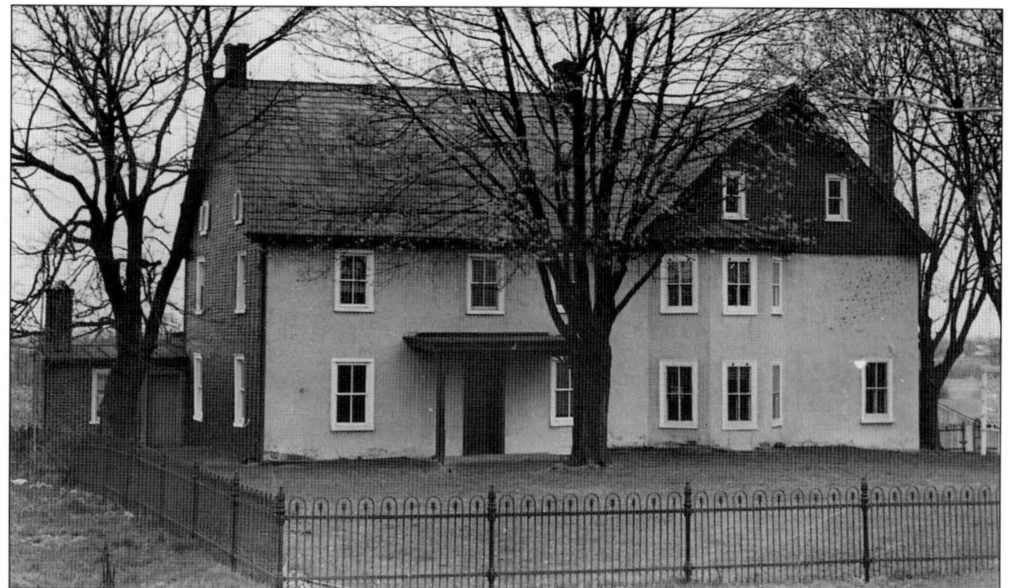

Also in 1755, another parcel, measuring 100 acres, was conveyed to Mennonite tailor Christian Hunsberger. His land lay between present-day Cherry Lane, Front Street, West Broad Street, and Mifflin Avenue. Son Frederick Hunsberger was raised in this house on what is today Lawn Avenue. Frederick was one of the first trustees of the Leidy School. He later acquired the farm. His daughter Hannah became the wife of Henry O. Souder. (Courtesy of Phil Ruth.)

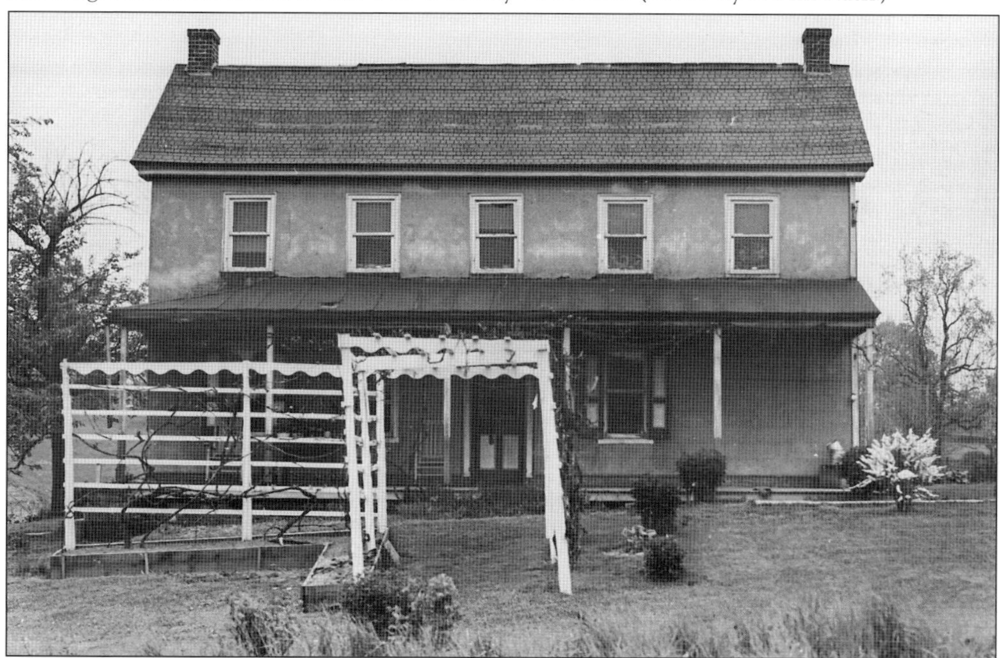

Abraham Arndt married Catherine Reed, sister of Lt. Col. Jacob Reed, and acquired 188 acres. The property is today bordered by East Chestnut Street, County Line Road, Cherry Lane, and Front Street. In 1792, the homestead, which included 53 acres, was sold to Mennonite tailor Christian Souder, who eventually acquired 150 acres of present-day Souderton. It was sold to his son Christian O. Souder in 1822. (Courtesy of Phil Ruth.)

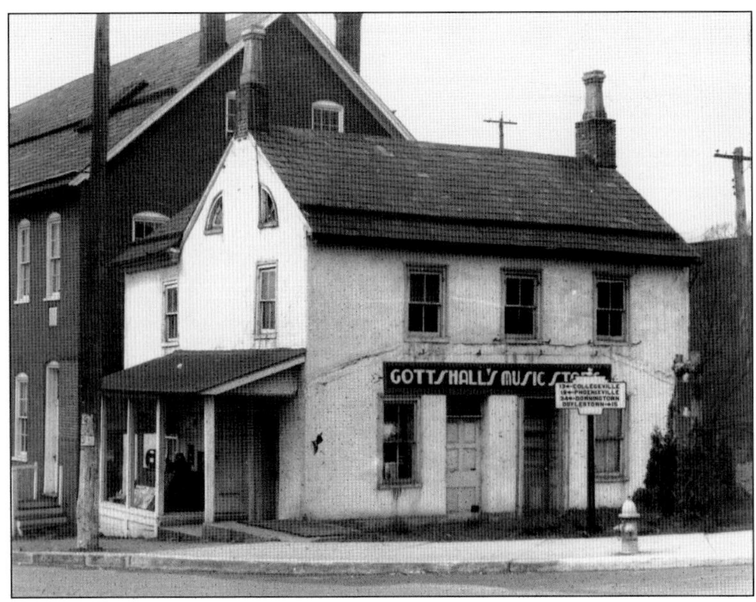

Henry O. Souder (1807–1897) married neighbor and fellow Rockhill Mennonite Hannah Hunsberger in 1834. He built this modest farmhouse with outbuildings on eight acres of land he bought from his father, Christian O. Souder. It is situated at the corner of Main Street (Possum Lane) and East Chestnut Street (Water Street). (Courtesy of Gloria Scheip.)

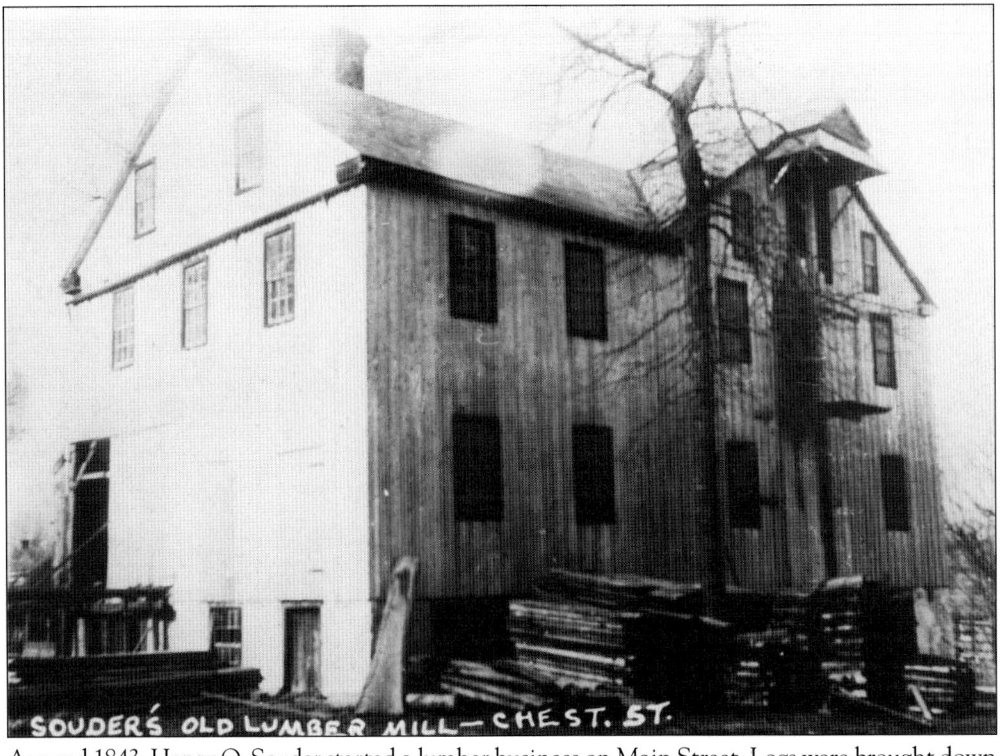

Around 1843, Henry O. Souder started a lumber business on Main Street. Logs were brought down the Delaware Canal to Point Pleasant. From there, Henry hauled the load by team 20 miles over rutted dirt roads to his sawmill. His son William purchased the lumberyard in 1868 and moved the business to West Chestnut Street, where he built this sawmill in 1872. A spoke-and-wheel factory operated there until 1910. (Courtesy of Gary Albright.)

Two

Tracking Destiny

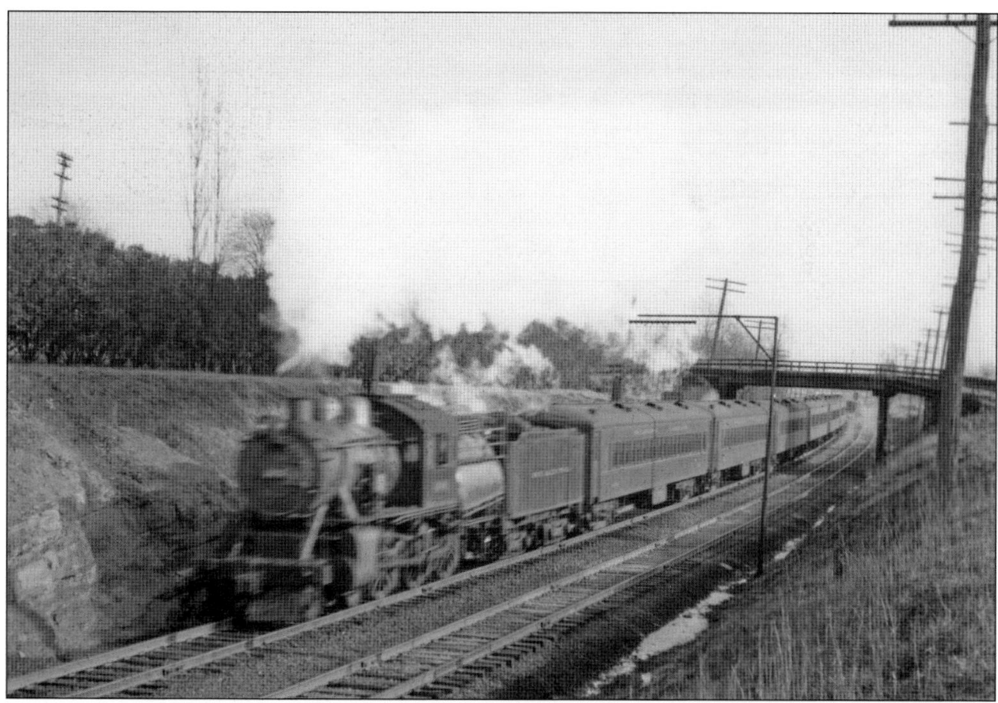

In 1852, Henry O. Souder, wishing to expand his lumber business, offered the free use of his land to the Philadelphia, Easton & Water Gap Railroad, shifting the route of the proposed railway further west into his corner of Franconia Township. In 1857, this section of the railroad opened. Photographed in 1946, this "Camelback" was heading north after crossing under the Cherry Lane Bridge toward Souderton. (Courtesy of Dale Woodland.)

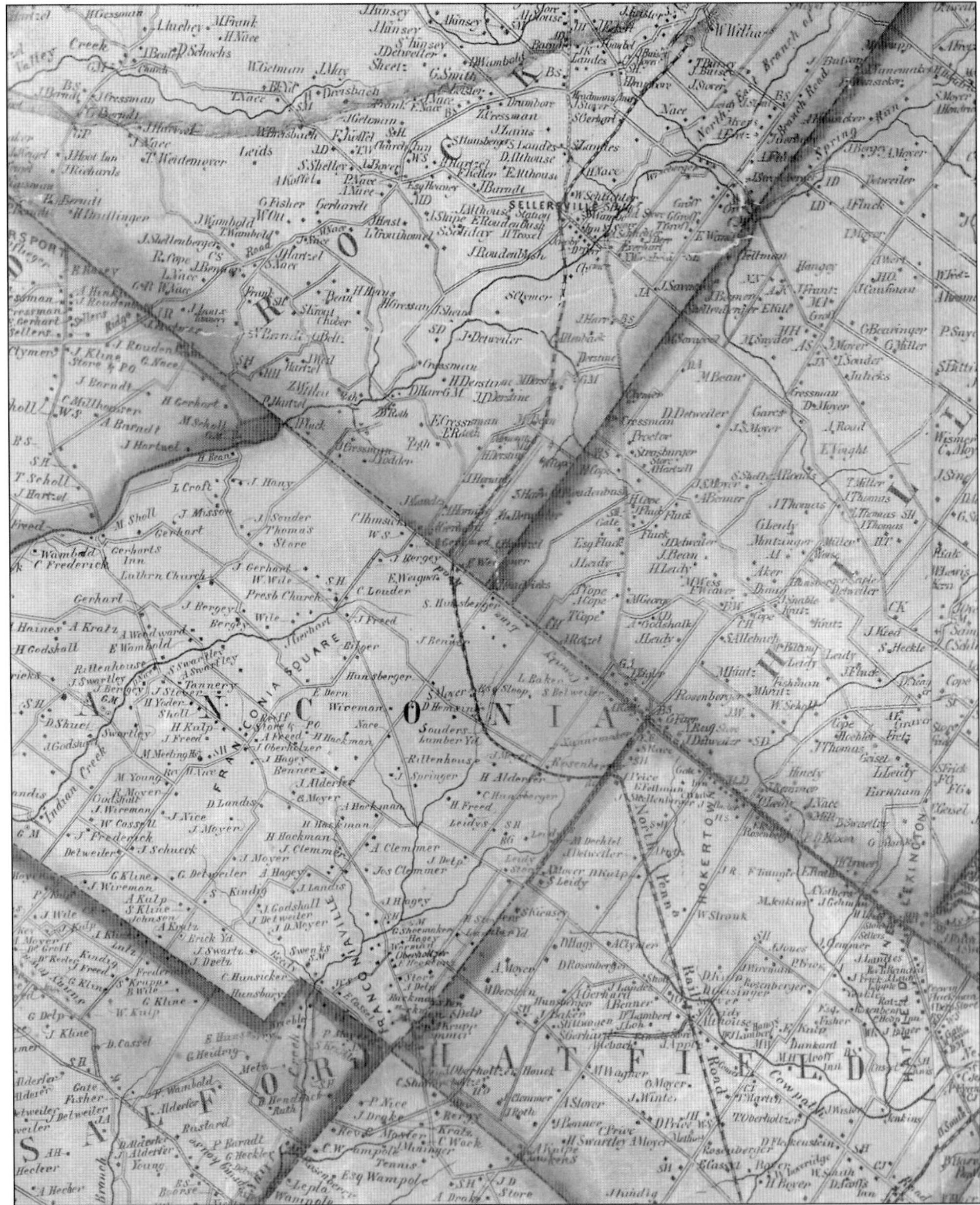

This 1857 atlas map of Franconia Township shows the villages of Franconiaville and Franconia Square along the main road from Philadelphia to Allentown. The map hints at the intended path of the railroad (the North Pennsylvania Railroad since 1853) and its sharp shift to the west. Souder's Lumberyard is seen along this curve on the map. (Courtesy of STMS collection.)

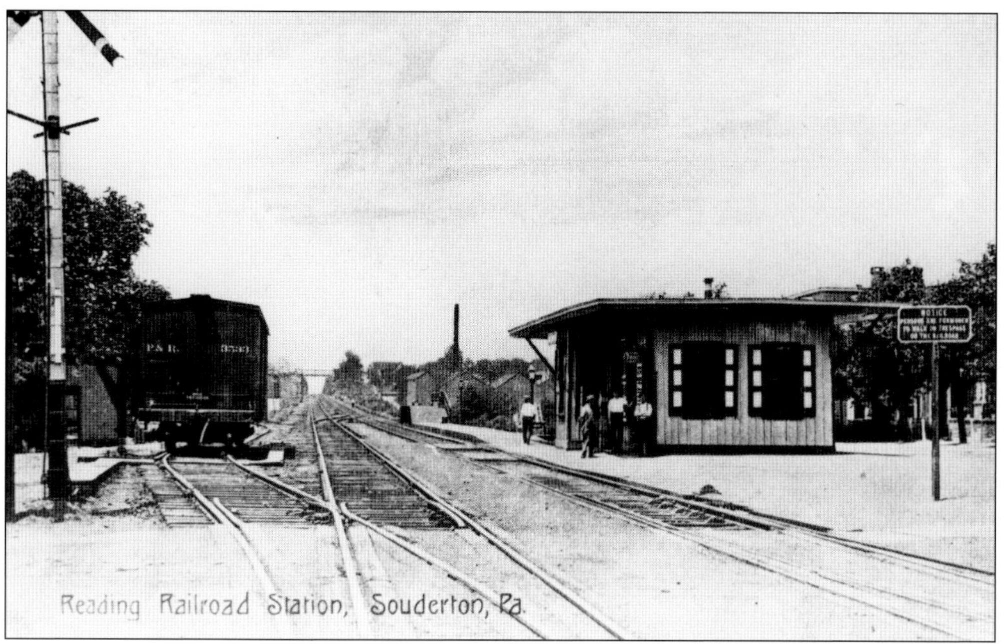

Initially, the Franconia rail stop had no station. The first railroad agent, William H. Souder, handled the railroad business from the family's lumber office. By 1860, the stop was known as Souders, and by 1863, Souderton. The first depot was built in 1865 on the east side of the tracks. Jacob C. Landes was the first stationmaster. (Courtesy of Gary Albright.)

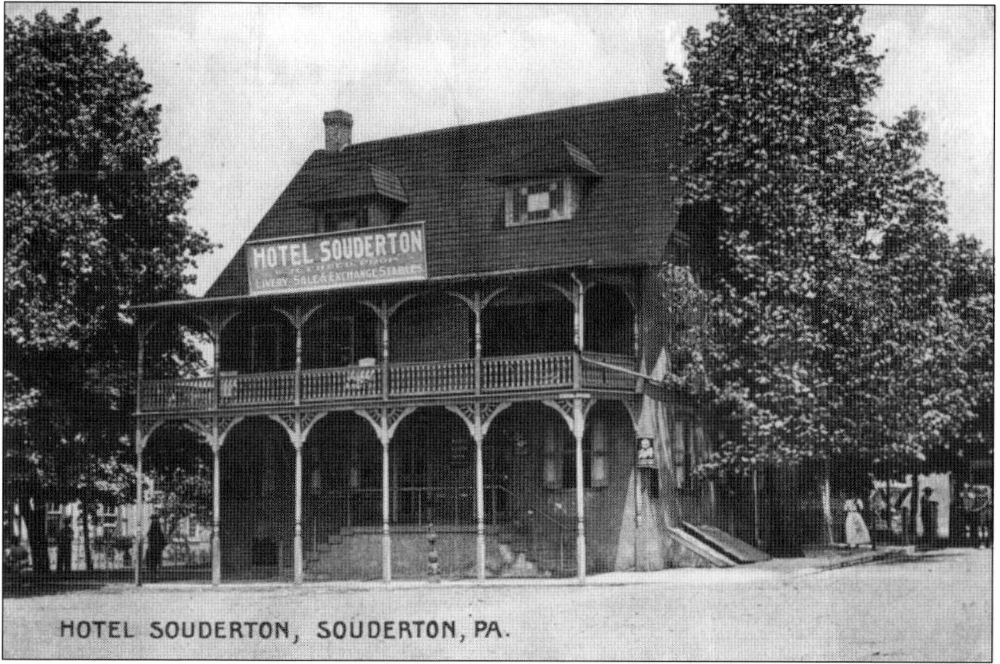

In 1858, during a depression and one year after the first steam locomotive chugged through Franconia, Jonathan Hunsberger, first cousin to Henry O. Souder's wife, Hannah, built a restaurant on the corner of East Broad Street and North Front Street. By 1860, the restaurant's proprietor, Frank Zepp, was granted a license for the Hotel Souderton, shown here. (Courtesy of James Shelly.)

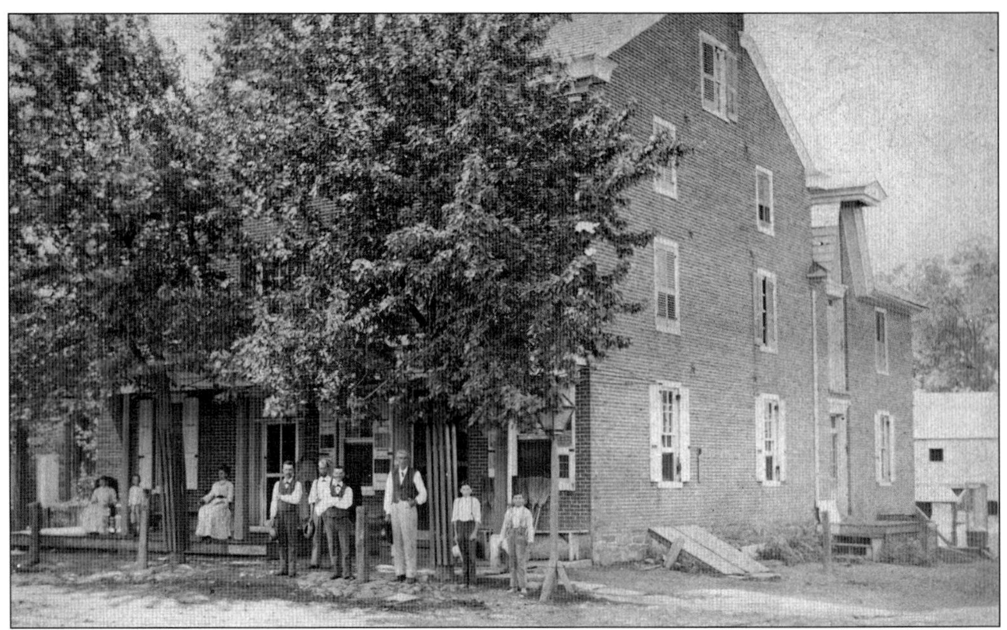

In 1860, Henry O. Souder, the tall man at center, and young Michael B. Bergey (1838–1905) opened a general store, Souder and Bergey, on Main Street in the right side of this building. The store passed to Henry's son Henry H., then to son-in-law William B. Slifer, and finally, in 1882, to son Ellis H. Souder, partnering with Jonas M. Landis. Landis and his family resided in the left half of the building. (Courtesy of Harold Yocum.)

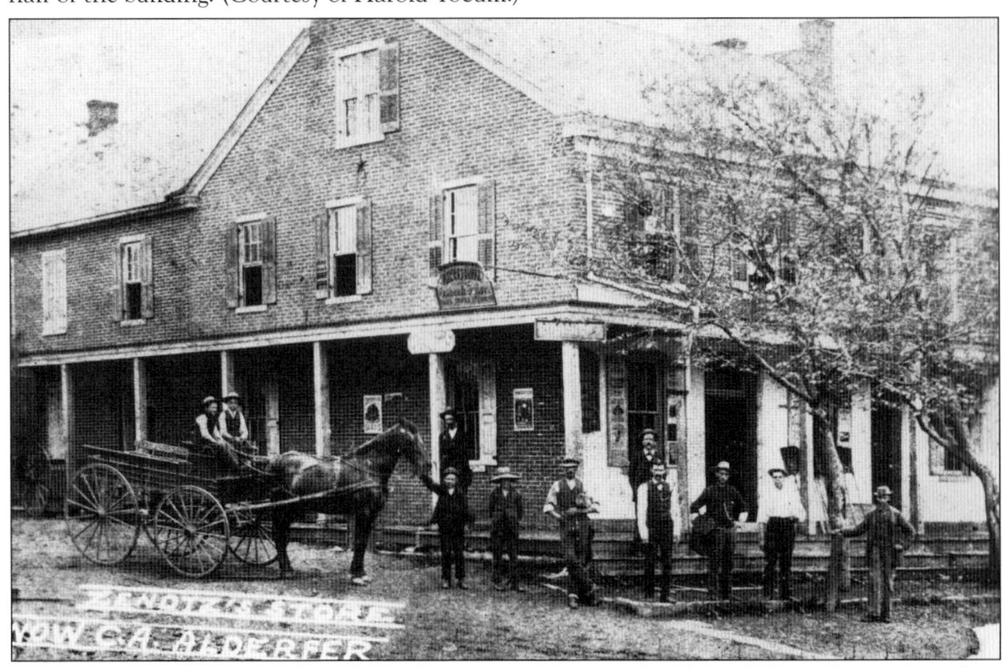

Also in 1860, within sight of Souder and Bergey, at East Broad and South Front Street, Jonathan Hunsberger's son William built a general store, creating a friendly business rivalry. Operating as S.D. Hunsberger and Brother, William and his brother Samuel were proprietors. This building was later known as the C.A. Alderfer Building. (Courtesy of Gloria Brandis.)

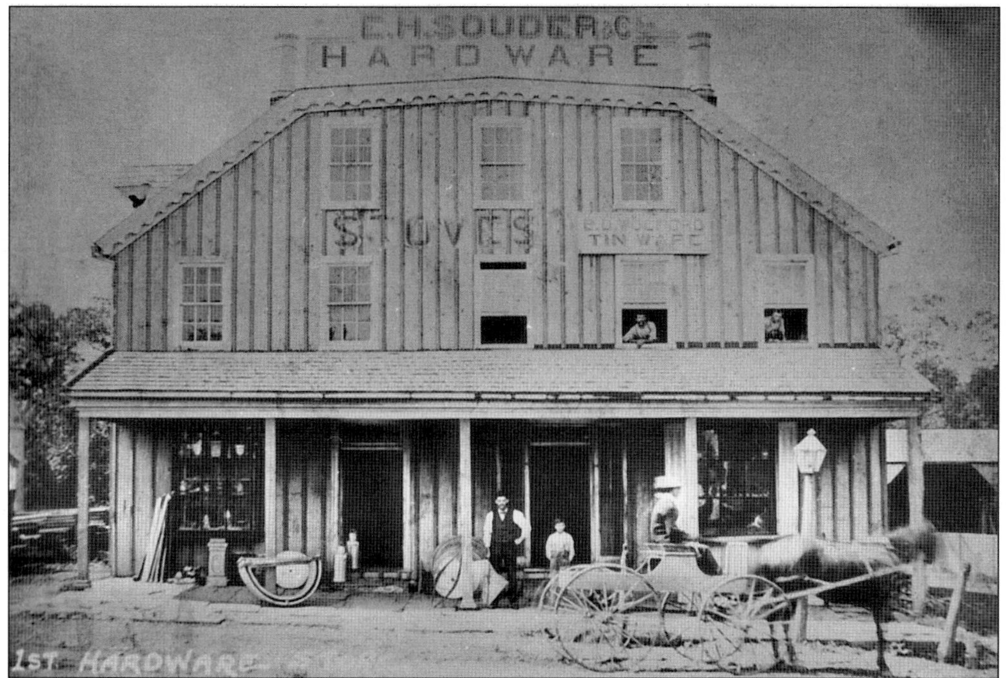

In 1861, Henry O. Souder built this frame hardware store on Main Street. Operating as Souder and Landes, the store was then sold to his second son, Edmund H. Souder, in 1864. Before 1884, tinsmith Benjamin D. Wolford's establishment was on the second floor. Lamplighter Harry Fluck would have maintained the outside oil lamp. (Courtesy of STMS collection.)

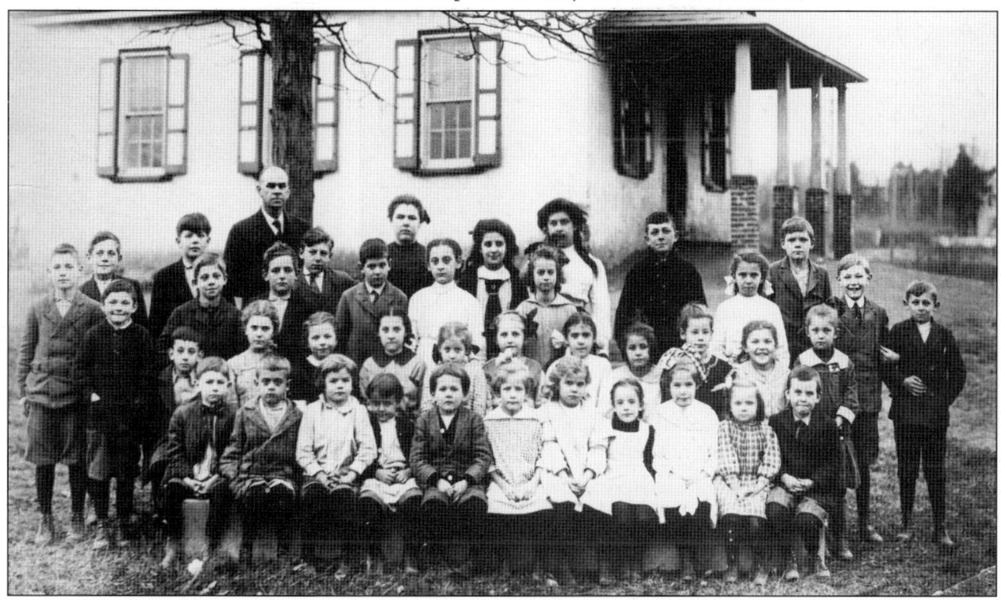

Franconia Township established the Rosenberger School around 1861 on Cherry Lane. Fondly known as Rosenberger's Academy, this photograph shows the school as rebuilt in 1885. Among the identifiable students shown are Linford, Norman, and Paul Clemmer, grouped on the left, and Allen Freed, on the far right. The children from Souders walked less than a mile to attend. (Courtesy of Vernon Clemmer.)

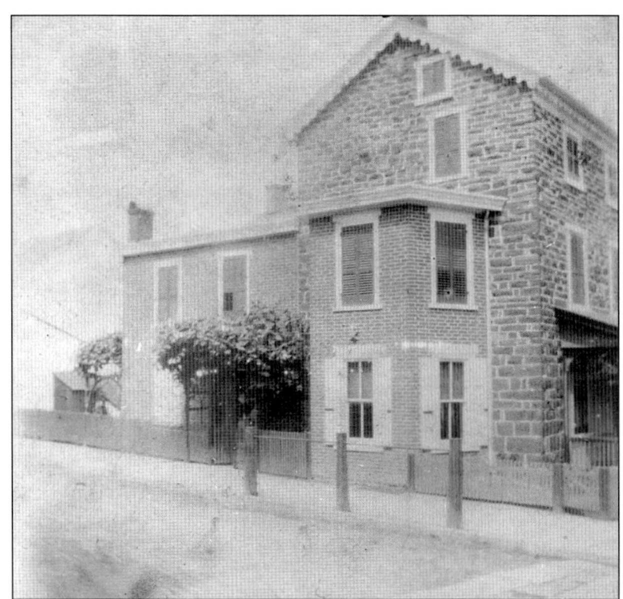

Herman K. Godshall's house, built in 1860 with excess crushed boulders from the railroad embankment, was erected across from Henry O. Souder's first home on Main Street. Godshall, who later built a feed mill on Main Street, was instrumental in the development of the Souderton Mennonite Meetinghouse and Sunday school. This civic-minded businessman served on the school board, borough council, and the board of directors of the Union National Bank. (Courtesy of Gerald Hartzell.)

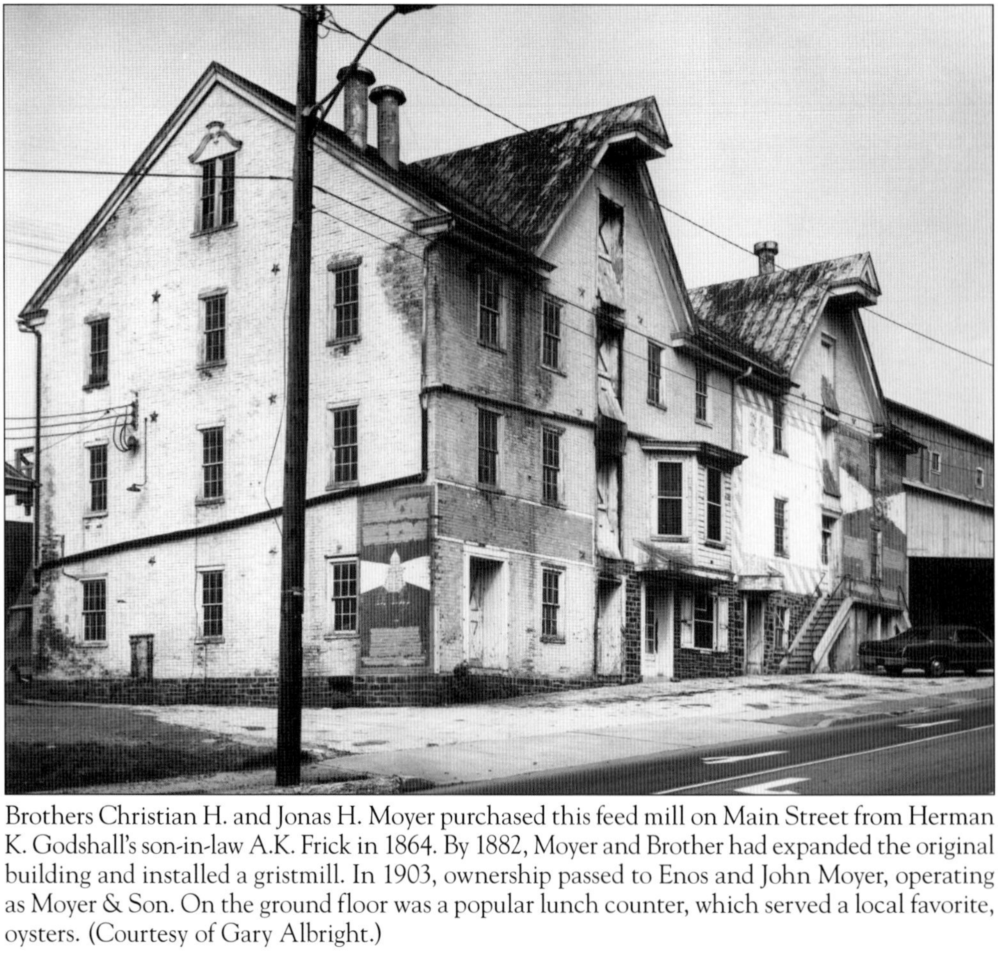

Brothers Christian H. and Jonas H. Moyer purchased this feed mill on Main Street from Herman K. Godshall's son-in-law A.K. Frick in 1864. By 1882, Moyer and Brother had expanded the original building and installed a gristmill. In 1903, ownership passed to Enos and John Moyer, operating as Moyer & Son. On the ground floor was a popular lunch counter, which served a local favorite, oysters. (Courtesy of Gary Albright.)

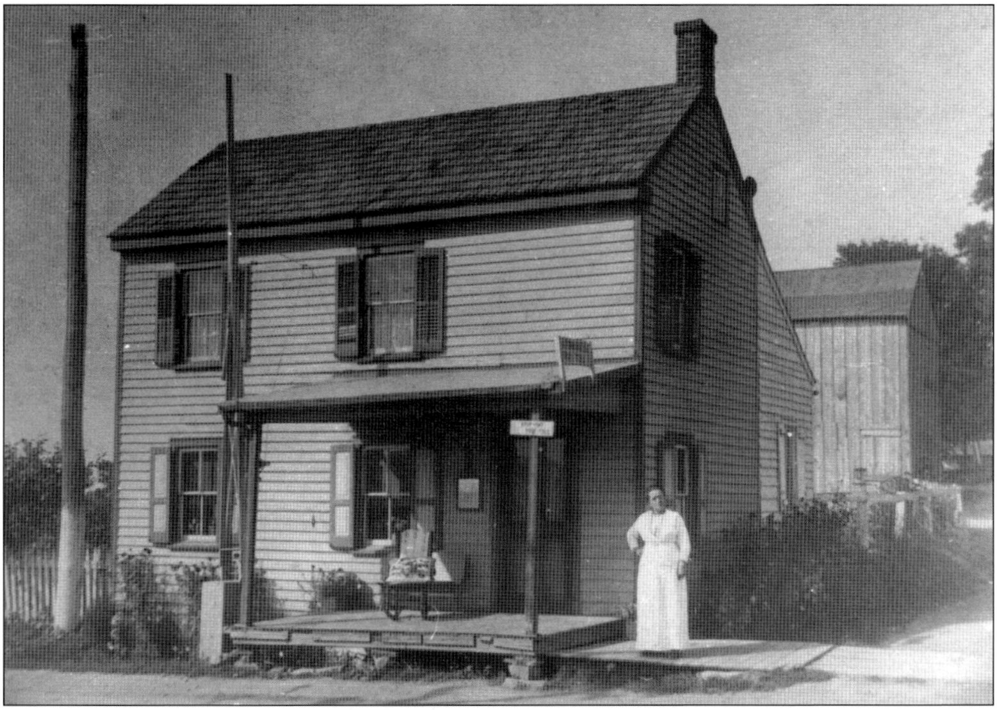

In 1866, this frame tollhouse was erected in the hollow on Main Street next to the Skippack Creek. Opened by the Harleysville and Souder's Turnpike Road Company, this graveled road made passage easier, quicker, and safer. Jesse Kline, an early toll collector, retired in 1886. Michael Delp was employed when the road became public in 1890. By extending a long-handled dipper, the collectors could gather tolls from their porch. (Courtesy of STMS collection.)

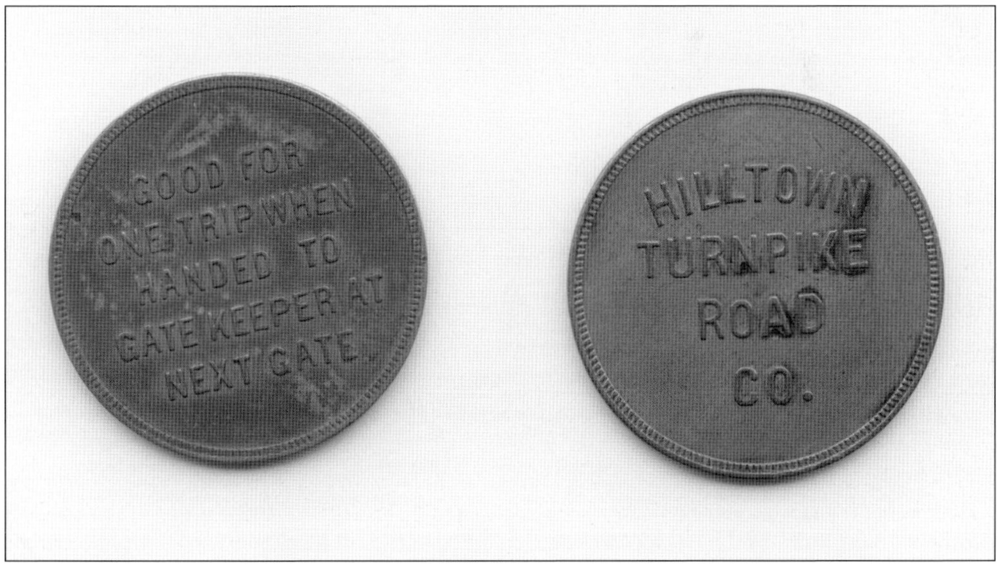

In 1885, the Dublin and Souderton Turnpike Road Company was chartered. The pike, beginning at East Broad Street in Souderton and ending in Dublin, was improved using gravel from Gehman's quarry. These Hilltown Turnpike tokens were typical of those used for area toll roads. (Courtesy of John Urich.)

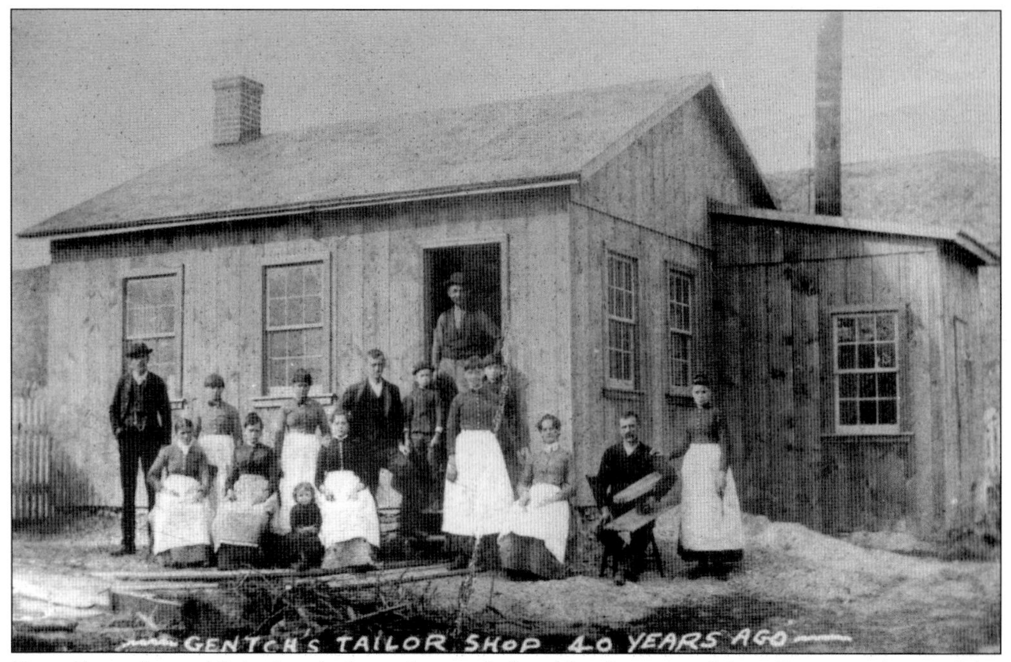

Otto Gentsch established a clothing factory behind his home on Main Street in front of the railroad embankment. He introduced steam power in 1887 and produced one-size-only men's wear. As the number of businesses increased, space became a valued commodity. In 1884, Michael B. Bergey and Company started a hosiery mill, sharing space in Gentsch's building. Later, Bergey and Company moved to Green Street. (Courtesy of STMS collection.)

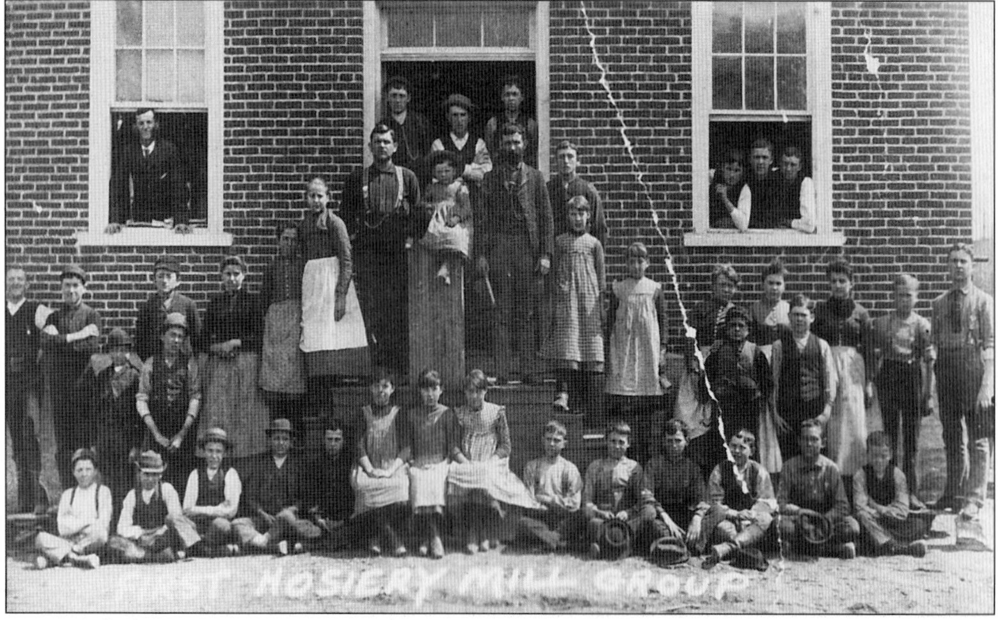

By 1885, the hosiery factory of Michael B. Bergey and Company was now located on Green Street. Michael retired in 1889, but the company still operated under the same name, expanding several times. The workforce increased with each addition to the factory. This silk hose manufacturing company proved to be a desirable place of employment. (Courtesy of Harold Yocum.)

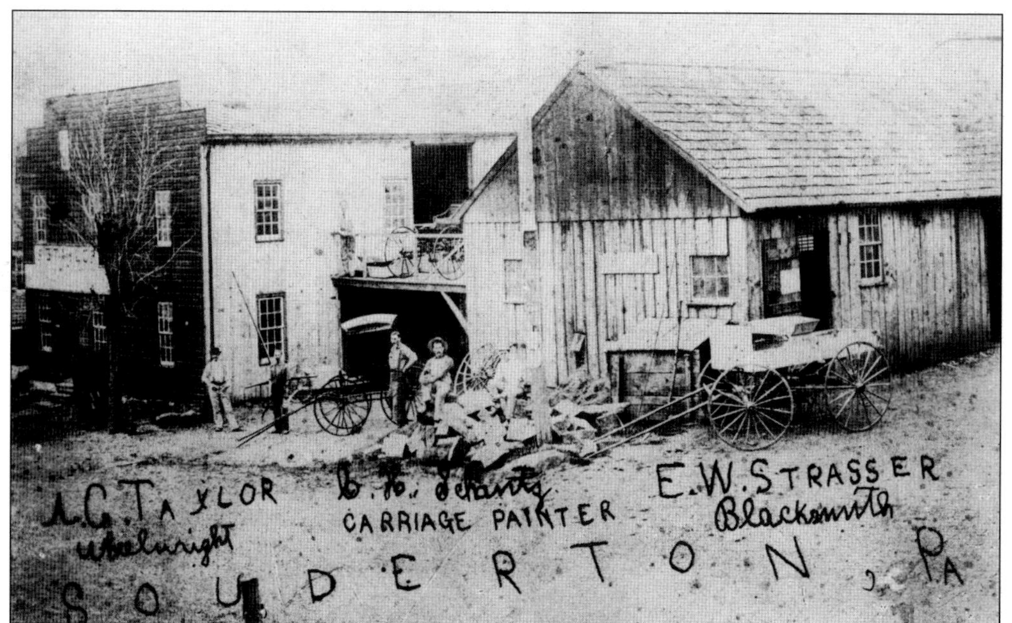

Pictured here in 1890 are the shops of A.G. Taylor, wheelwright, on the left; G.H. Shantz, carriage painter, middle; and E.W. Strasser, blacksmith, on the right. These two frame buildings were erected between the railroad house, which was Henry O. Souder's original home, and the feed mill of Moyer and Brother. The railroad's path through town had cut off the intersection of Water and Main Streets where these buildings stood. (Courtesy of Gary Albright.)

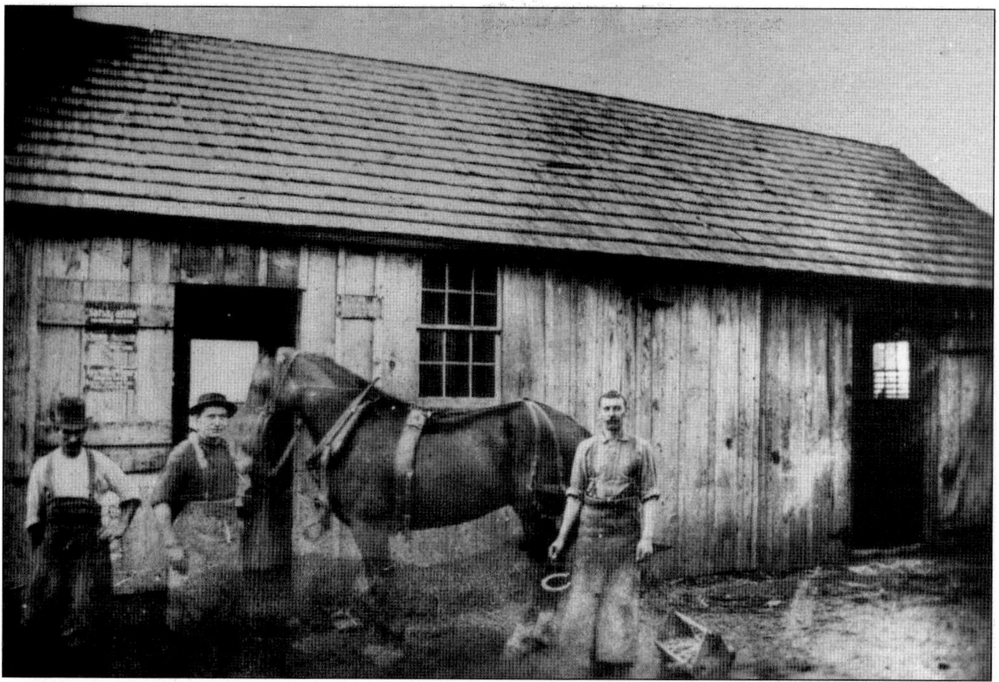

The blacksmiths at E.W. Strassers are preparing to shoe a horse. Horses were shod with different shoes depending on where they trod and the time of year. In the winter, the shoes had more traction. The building seen here was destroyed by fire in 1892. (Courtesy of STMS collection.)

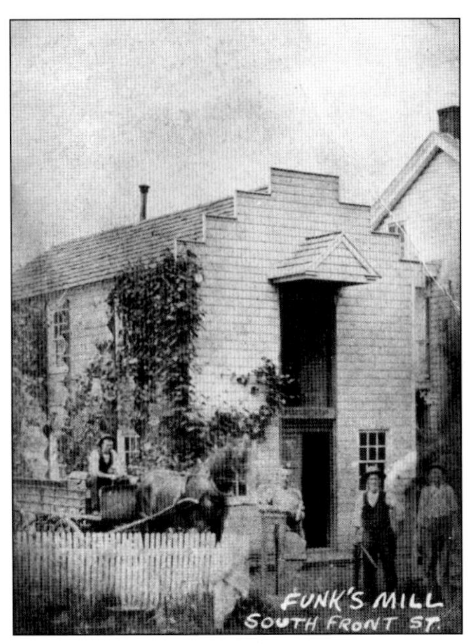

As generations of fathers divided their land among their sons, farms became smaller, making it necessary for many young people to seek other means of employment. Frame buildings, such as Herman Funk's cabinet making shop and mill on South Front Street, shown here, were quickly erected. The increased demand for lumber and hardware for the construction of new businesses kept the community thriving. (Courtesy of Phil Ruth.)

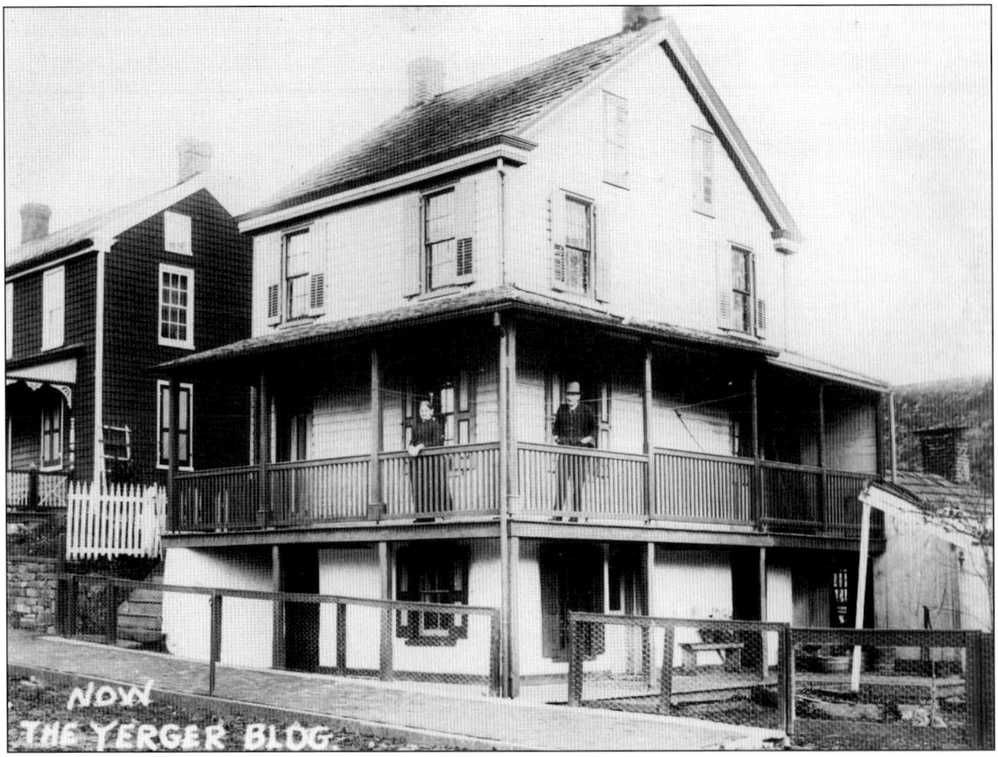

This frame house, near Gentsch's clothing factory on Main Street, was built in 1864. Just as floor space for manufacturing was in great demand, housing for employees and their families was also in short supply. Frame buildings were quickly erected and later modified, as this one eventually was, or replaced with masonry buildings. Occasionally, buildings were put on rollers and moved to other locations or disassembled and reassembled elsewhere. Often, workers lived with their employers. (Courtesy of Gary Albright.)

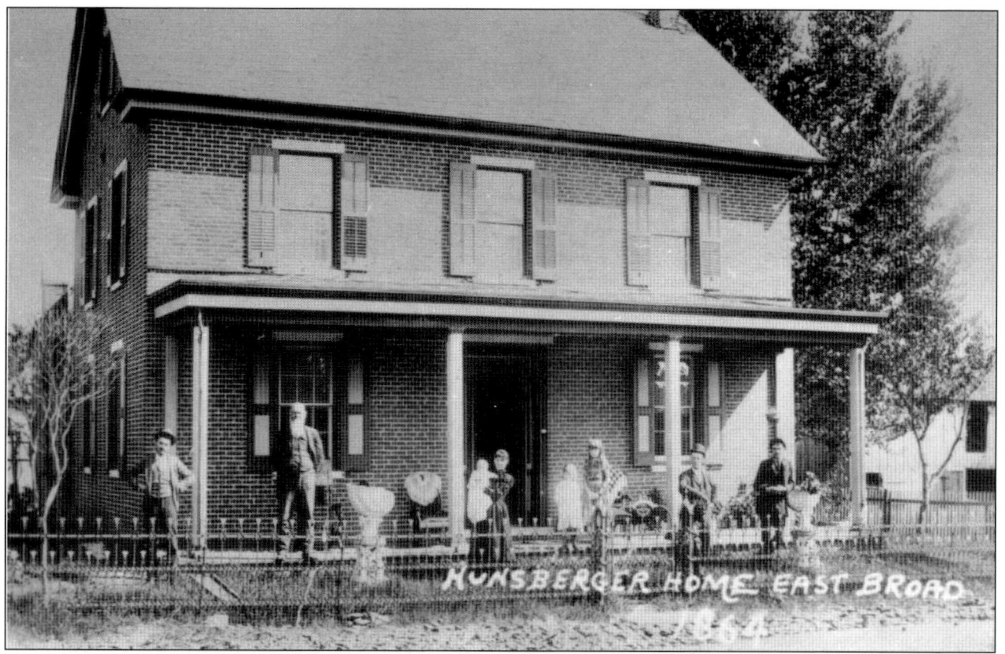

A successful entrepreneur, William D. Hunsberger (1838–1891) built this substantial home on East Broad Street around 1869. William bought Hotel Souderton in 1879, later adding a brick stable with a public hall, Liberty Hall, on the second floor. In the mid-1880s, William started a cigar factory, a lumberyard, and a hardware store and served as the first burgess (mayor.) The elderly Hunsberger poses on the front porch with his family. (Courtesy of STMS collection.)

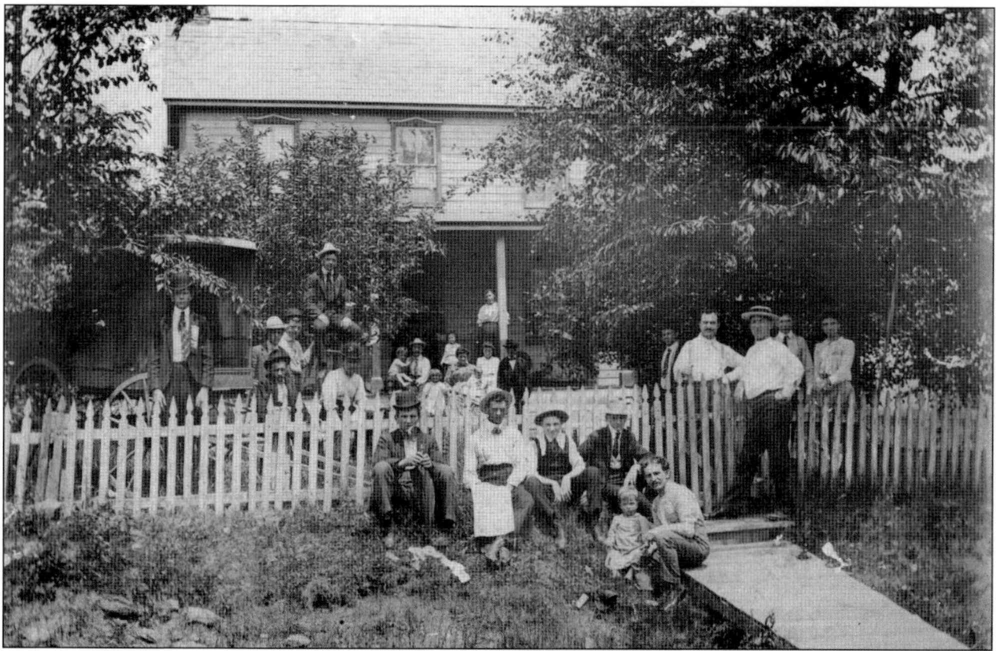

Here, the Souder family gathers at a family residence for a reunion. Although business rivals, the Hunsbergers and the Souders were neighbors and related through marriages. The importance of family and family values dominated the community. (Courtesy of Mennonite Heritage Center.)

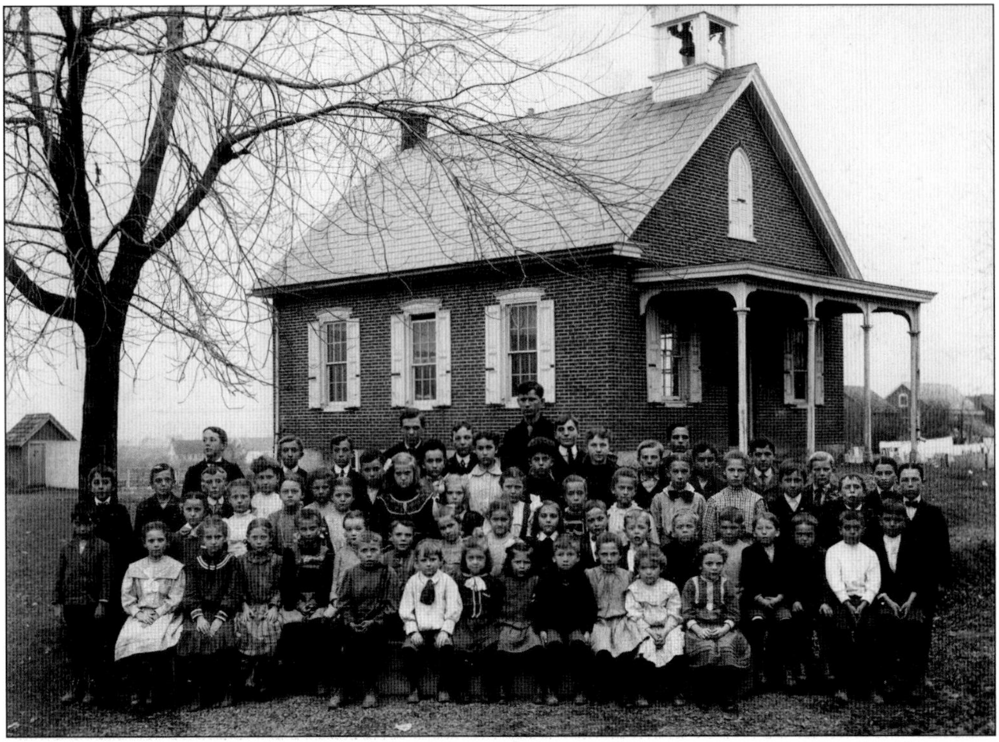

In 1870, Franconia Township established the one-room Reliance or Five Points Schoolhouse at the intersection of Main Street and Reliance Road. Souderton students were now able to attend the closer of two schools. In this photograph, the teacher and students pose in front of a second, larger school that replaced the first Reliance School in 1886. (Courtesy of Gary Albright.)

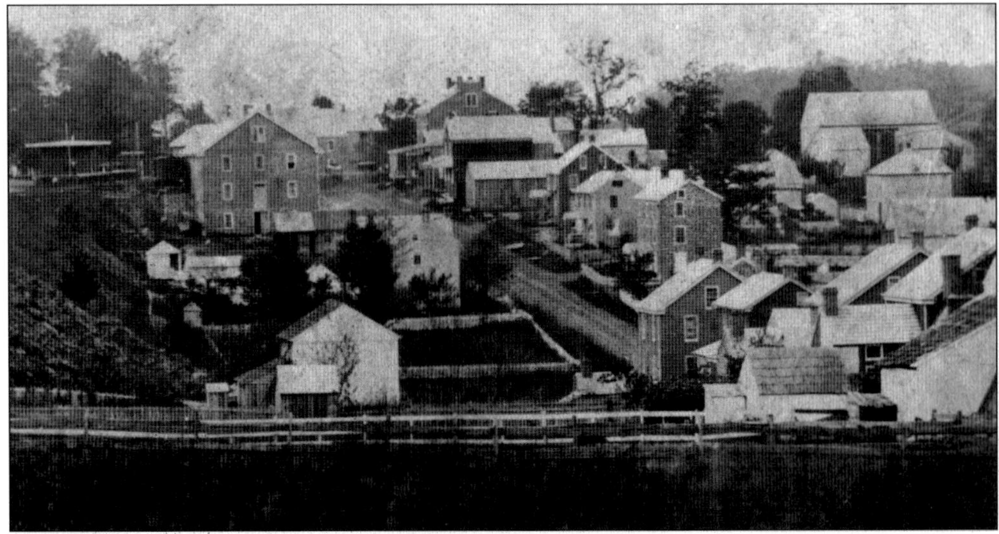

This c. 1870 streetscape of Main Street was taken from the vantage point of present-day Central Avenue. Only 13 years before, a snapshot would have captured a railroad, a small stone house, a lumberyard, and sawmill—all on a narrow dirt road. Instead, this sprawling community, a testament to Henry O. Souder's vision of what could be, reflects the thriving center of commerce it had become. (Courtesy of Susan Long.)

Three

The Changing Landscape

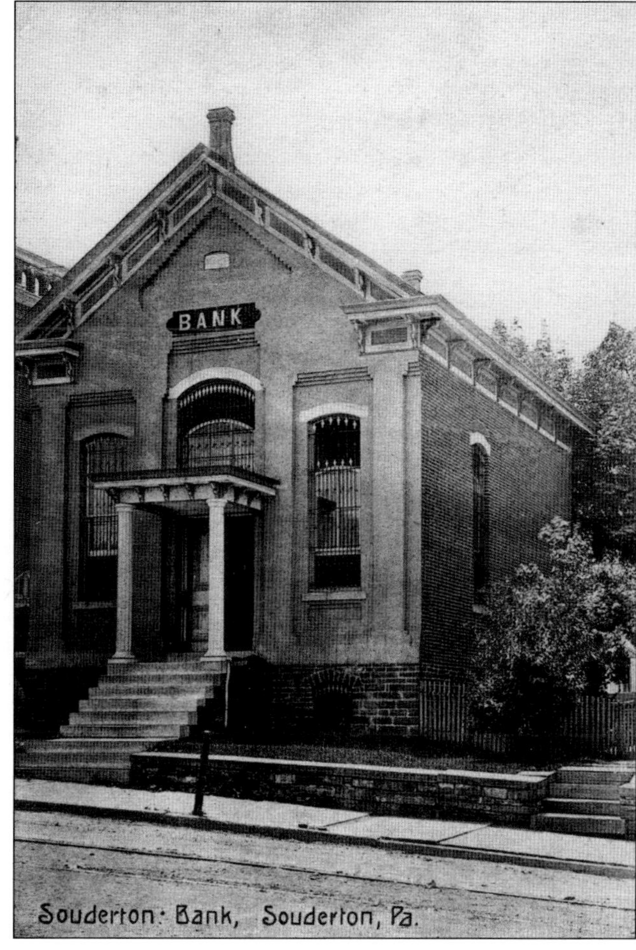

The Union National Bank, Souderton's first bank, was chartered in 1876 with Issac G. Gerhart as president. Initially, business was conducted from Henry O. Souder's home on Main and West Broad Streets. Debates over the bank's new location continued. In 1877, when it was erected on the Souder side of the tracks on Main Street, 106 subscribers who had preferred the Hunsberger side withdrew in protest. (Courtesy of Gloria Brandis.)

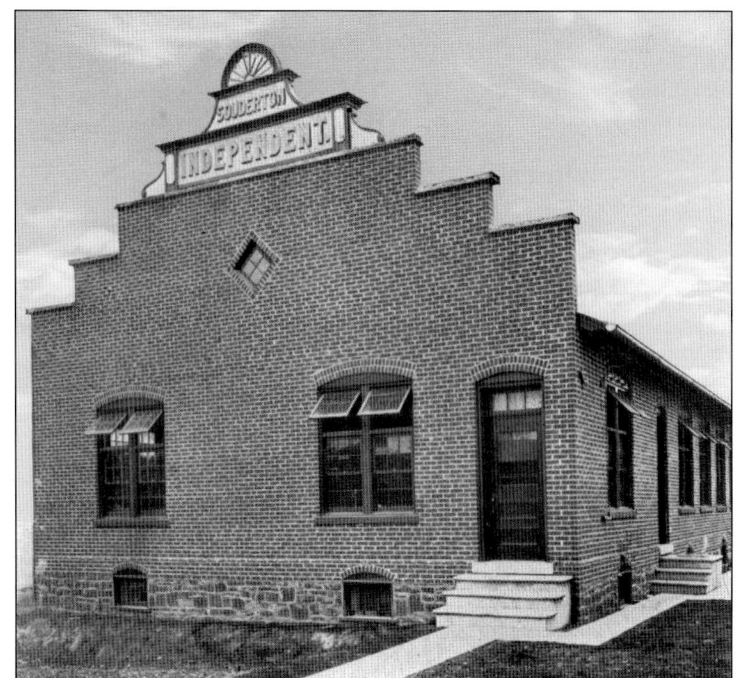

William F. Goettler and Charles L. Peale first published the *Germania Gazette* newspaper in German in 1878, but by 1879, Goettler was the sole owner. When the name changed to *Souderton Independent* in 1881, the newspaper switched to English. In 1907, after several moves, this building on South Front Street became its home. (Courtesy of STMS collection.)

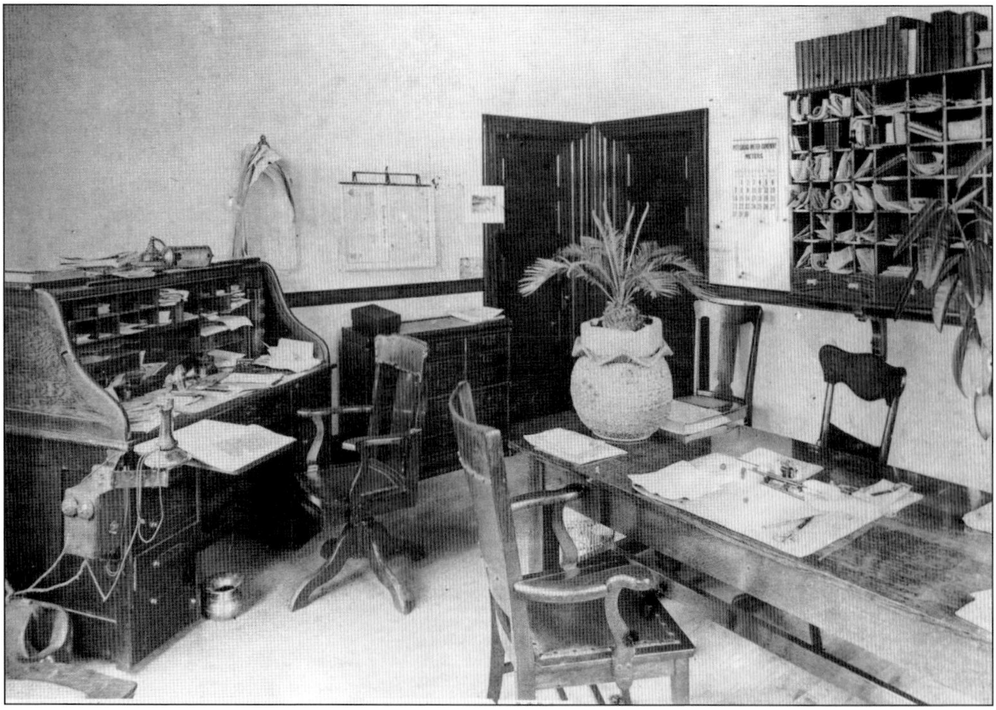

From this office, Goettler reported the local and world news. He became the voice of the nearby small villages of Bean, Derstine, and Garis and reported the goings-on in Telford and Souderton. Goettler was known to report on unkempt properties, pass along anecdotes, and gently tease the opposite sex. In 1898, the Keystone Telephone Company opened with seven telephones in town. Not surprisingly, Goettler had one of them. (Courtesy of Gary Albright.)

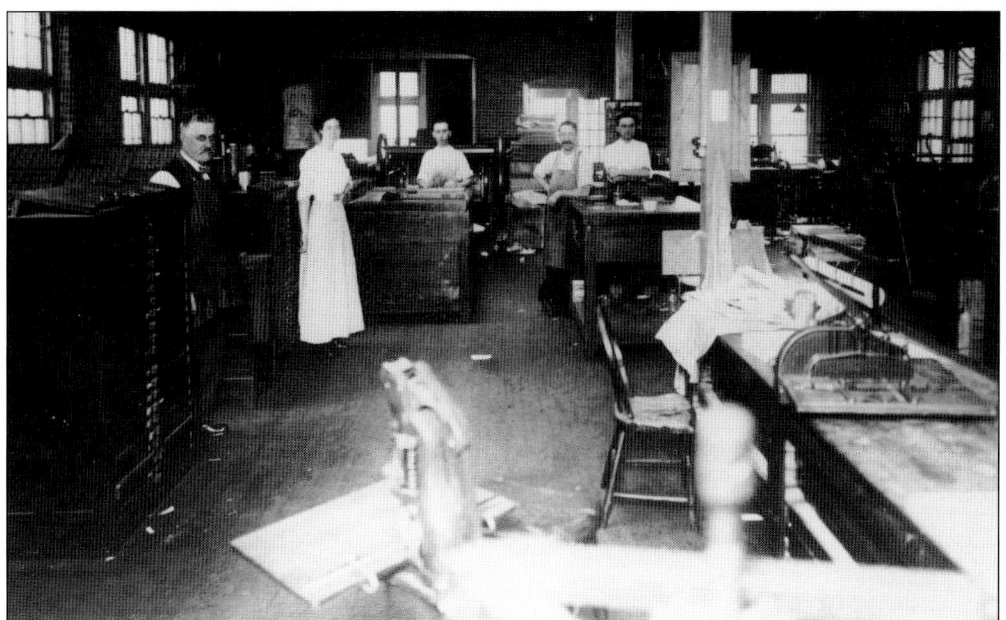

Here, the *Souderton Independent* employees pause from the task of printing the weekly newspaper, which was billed as a "journal for the home circle, the business, and the laboring man." By the early 1900s, a one-year subscription cost $1, and business was growing steadily. (Courtesy of Gary Albright.)

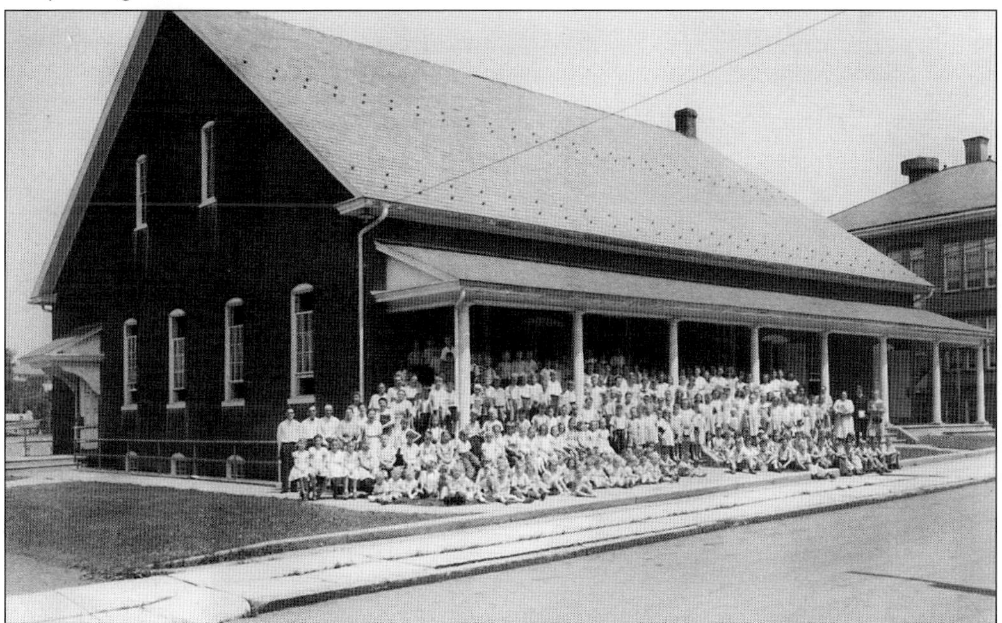

Religion continued to play a major role in the community. Residents attended established Mennonite, Reformed, and Lutheran churches. In 1879, the dream of erecting a church within the town was realized with the Christmas Day dedication of the Souderton Mennonite Meetinghouse at Chestnut Street and Wile Avenue. Initially, services were held here every third Sunday. Vacation Bible Schoolers, decades later, gather in front of a newer, larger building that replaced the original structure in 1915. (Courtesy of Kurt Scherzberg.)

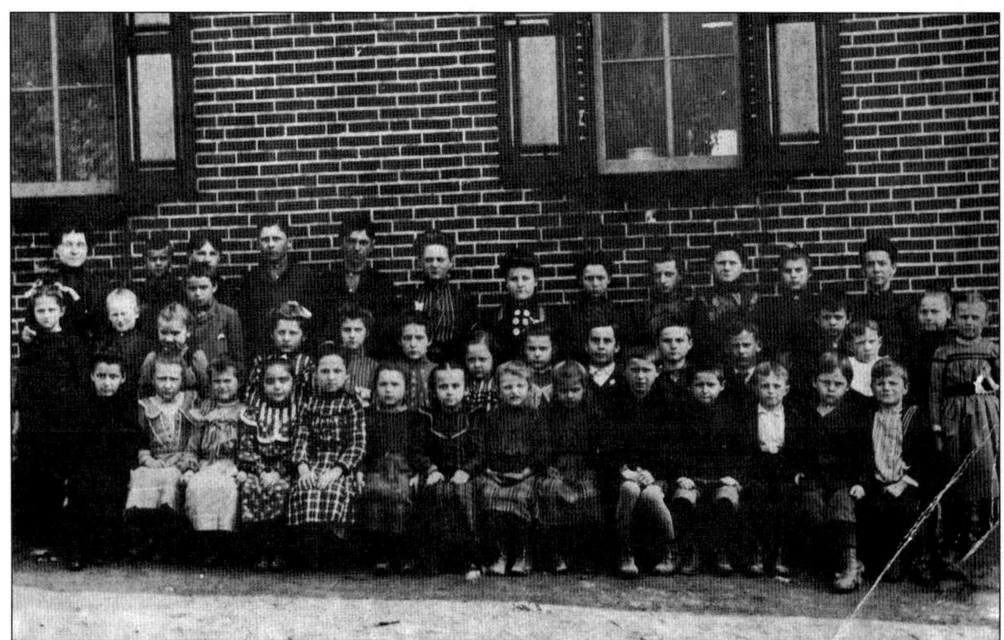

In 1875, as the population of Souderton continued to increase, Franconia Township added a one-room school (above) on a corner of Chestnut Street and Wile Avenue. Only five years later, in 1880, the first Chestnut Street School was razed and replaced by this two-story building (below), much to the consternation of some community members who had raised money for the first school. Frustrated by not having representation on the more conservative local school board in Franconia Township, Souderton residents petitioned to become a borough in 1887. (Both, courtesy of Susan Long.)

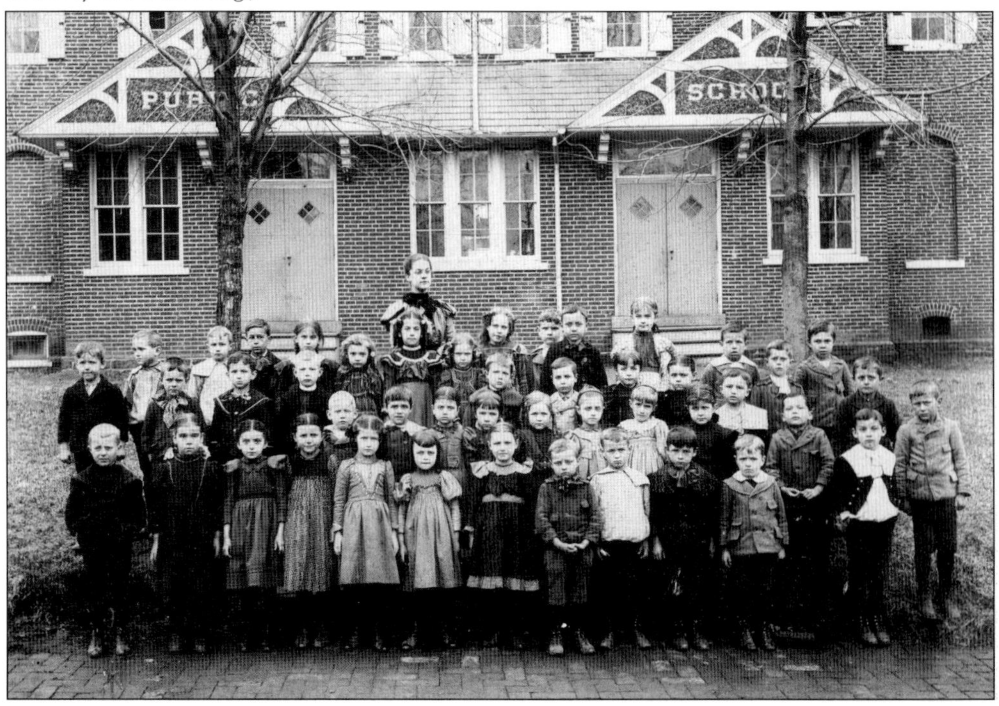

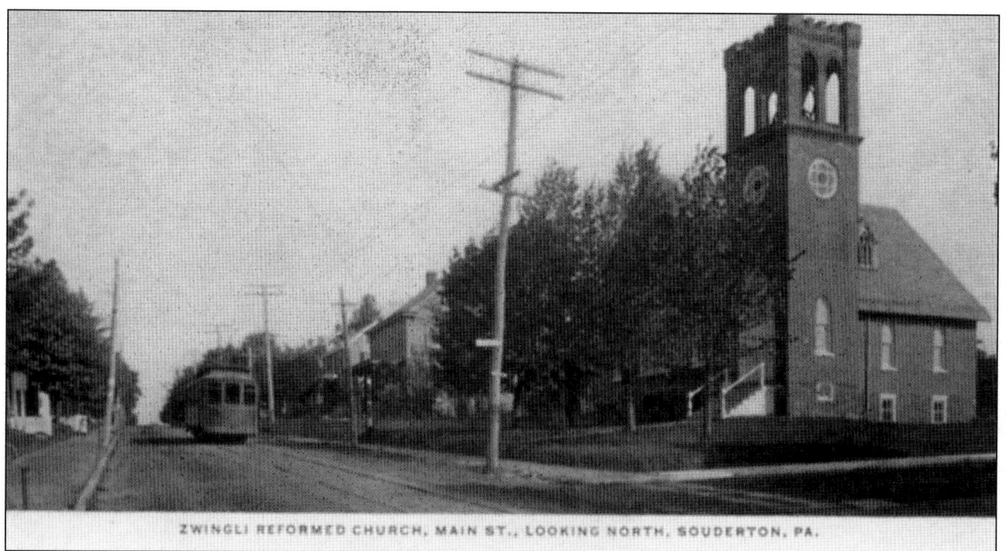

The Rev. James G. Dengler of Leidy's Church, where both Reformed and Lutheran services were held, wanted a Reformed church in town. In 1887, Zwingli Reformed Church, named after the Swiss leader of the Reformation, was built on the corner of Main and Church Streets. The bell in the tower called parishioners to worship and also tolled the loss of those who died, one strike for each year of life. (Courtesy of STMS collection.)

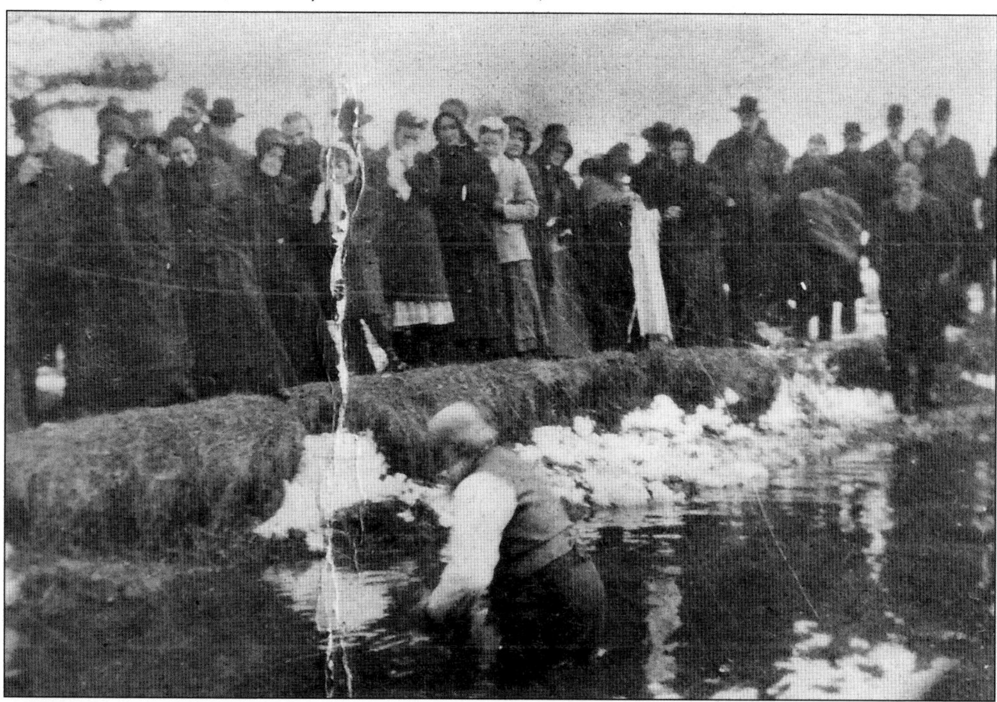

Members of the Mennonite and Brethren denominations practice adult baptism. It was not uncommon to remove ice from the creek in order to perform winter baptisms. This photograph shows Emma Kindig being baptized by Bishop Joseph B. Detwiler in 1909. The Brethren in Christ meetinghouse was built on the corner of Church Street and Railroad Avenue in 1899 and was enlarged in 1915. (Courtesy of Brethren in Christ Historical Library and Archives.)

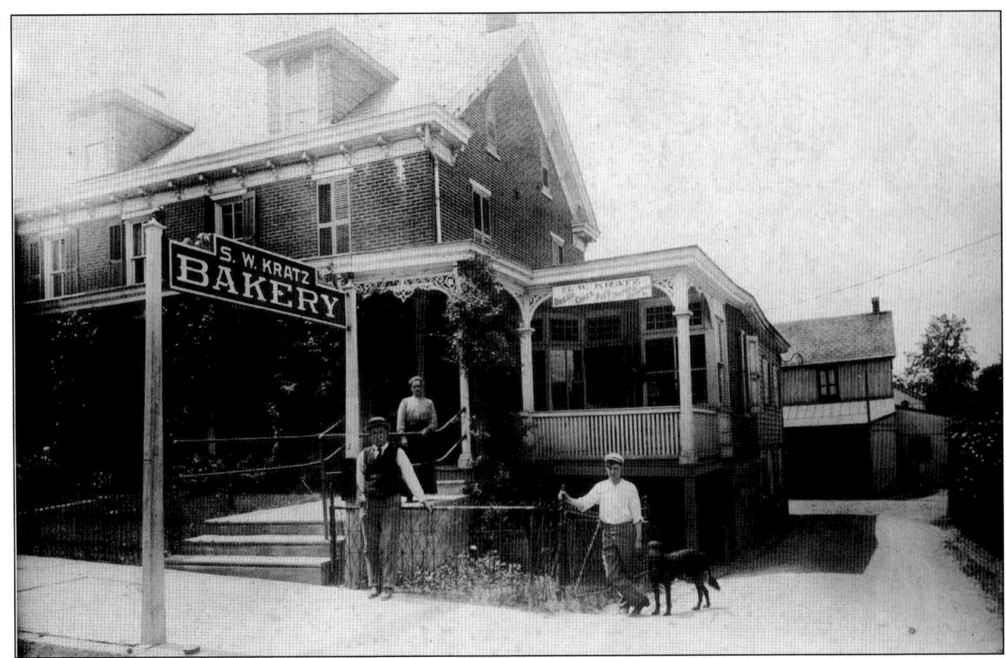

In 1874, Henry Hemsing and brother-in-law Henry H. Souder built this brick double home on Main Street (above). Hemsing and his wife, Mary, lived on the left; the Souders occupied the right. Mary and Henry H. were the children of Henry O. Souder. By 1883, Souder had sold his half to George Becker. George built an outdoor bake oven, expanded the building, and opened a bakery. By 1897, S.W. Kratz owned and operated the bakery, selling bread, cakes, pies, confections, pretzels (a Pennsylvania German favorite), and ice cream. Although local churches preached against enjoying ice cream and Coca-Cola, some Mennonite communities later accepted the concept of the ice cream social. From 1900 to 1903, Samuel S. Gehman was the owner. His customers looked forward to seeing his horse-drawn wagon pull up with fresh baked goods (below). (Both, courtesy of Karl Fox.)

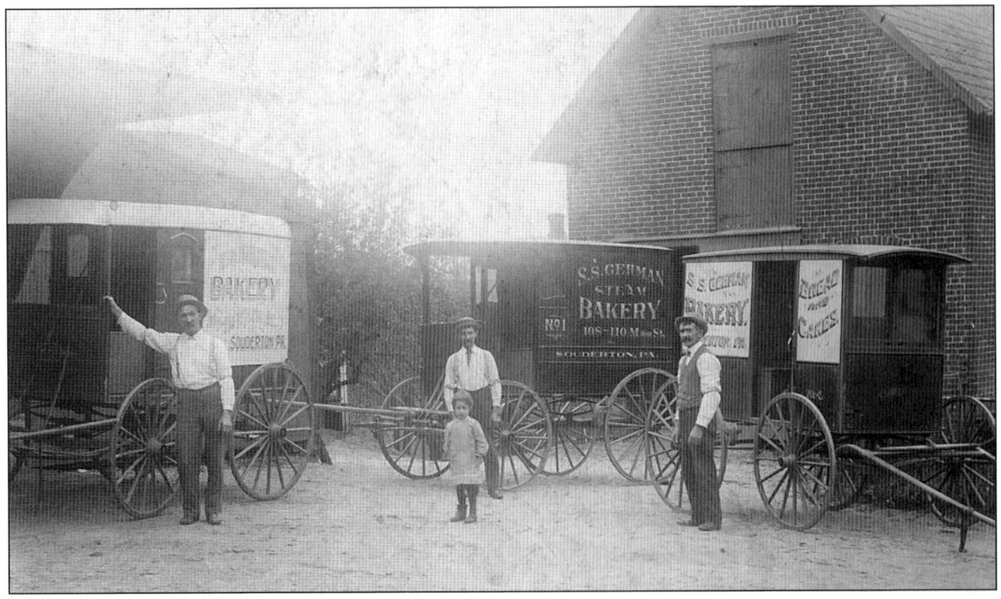

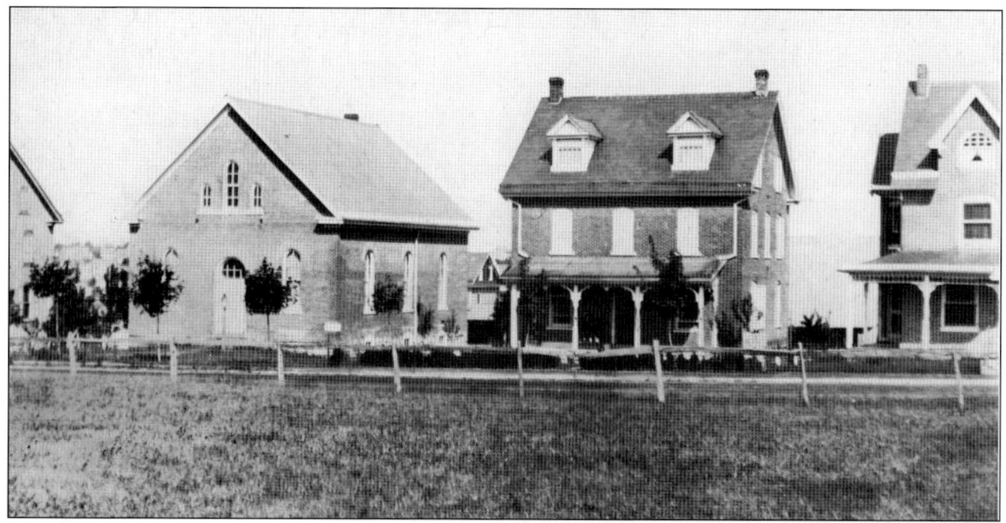

The Zion Mennonite Church on East Broad Street, on the left, with a parsonage in the center, was built in 1893. Mennonite churches in the Eastern District Conference were more liberal than their Franconia Conference brothers at this time. However, both considered Sunday a strict day of rest. Editor Goettler of the *Souderton Independent* warned that boys playing ball on Sunday could face legal action from local police. (Courtesy of Mennonite Heritage Center.)

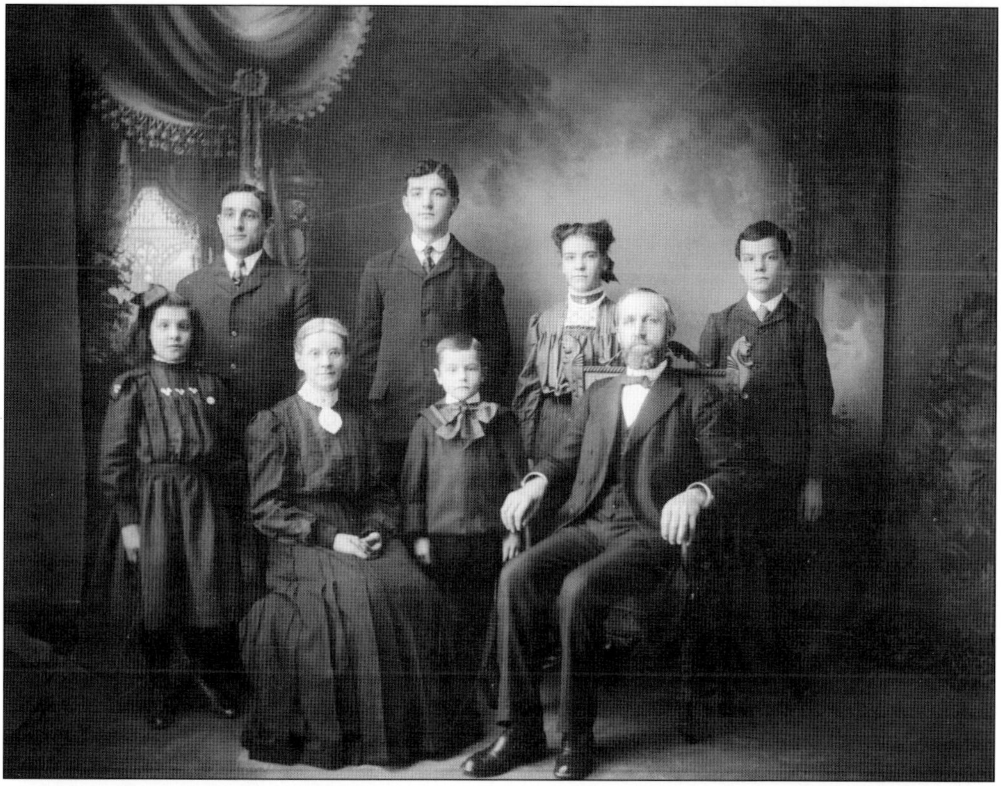

Rev. Allen M. Fretz, the first minister to serve Zion Mennonite Church, continued in this capacity for 17 years. His family is shown here from left to right: (first row) Agnes, Anna, Osmond, and Reverend Fretz; (second row) Jacob, Ely, Viola, and Allen. (Courtesy of Mennonite Heritage Center.)

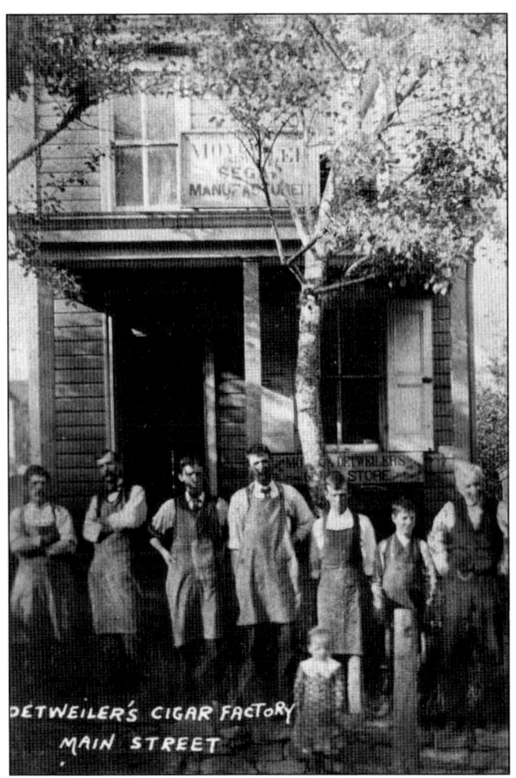

This two-story cigar factory on Main Street was operated by Joseph P. Moyer and William D. Detwiler around 1882. Between 1864 and 1925, twenty-four cigar factories and two training schools were established. For $25, one could attend the school on Highland Avenue, taught by J.H. Wisler in 1911, and after six to ten weeks of training, the advanced skills learned there would net an employee better wages. (Courtesy of Gary Albright.)

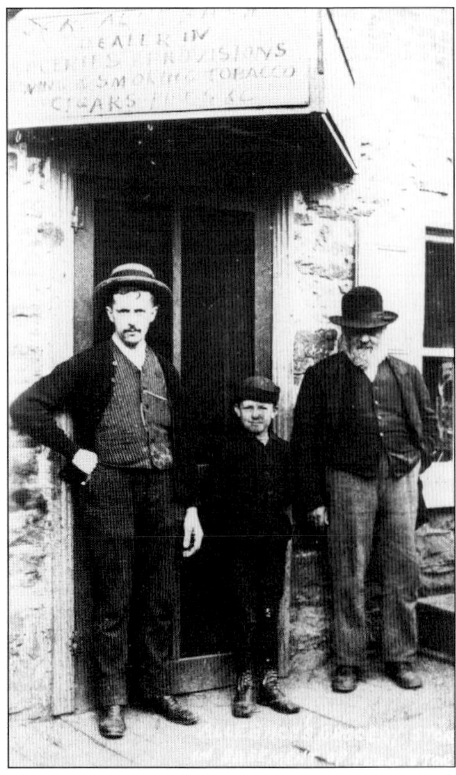

Owner Jacob K. Allebach, on the left, stands in front of his grocery and provision shop, located in the basement of Moyer & Son Feed Store, around 1883. With him are Penrose Hunsberger, center, and Sam Greaser, right. As the sign suggests, Jacob could provide a shopper with any type of tobacco product he could ever want. (Courtesy of Gary Albright.)

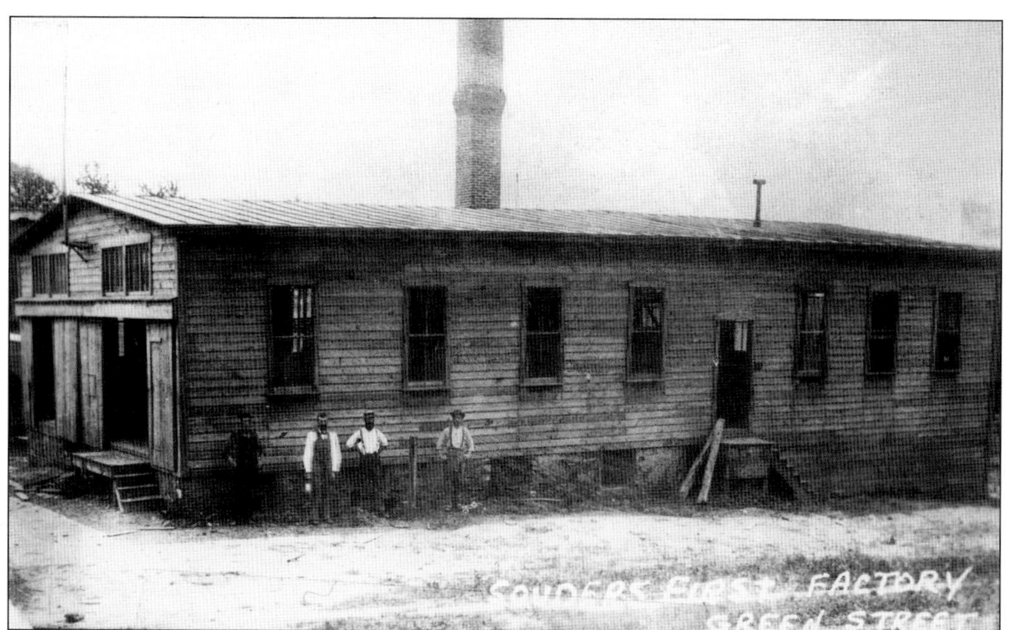

Harvey Souder, grand-nephew of Henry O. Souder, with partner John Newbold, began manufacturing wooden cigar boxes, establishing this frame factory on Green Street in 1887. Initially, Souder made the boxes by hand, and by 1891, with two additions to the original factory, this entrepreneur turned out 1,600 boxes daily. After his partnership with Newbold dissolved, Souder added steam-run sewing machines so his wife, Elizabeth, could make tailored clothing. (Courtesy of Phil Ruth.)

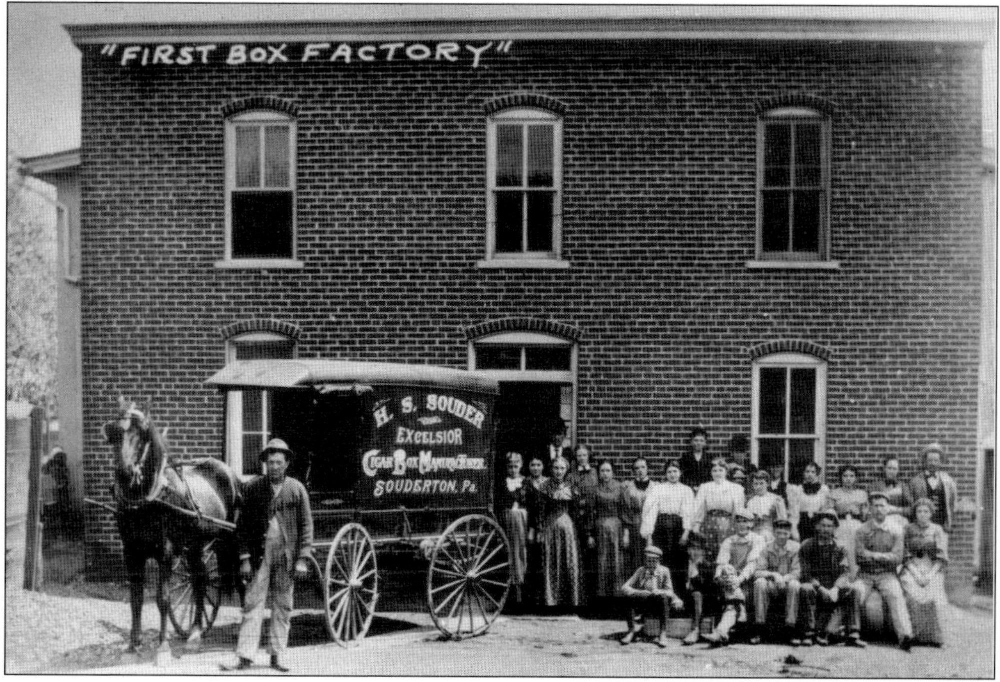

Harvey Souder poses with his employees beside his 1890 delivery wagon. This 20-by-22-foot addition was added to the Excelsior Steam Cigar Box Factory, along with a larger boiler, in 1891. (Courtesy of STMS collection.)

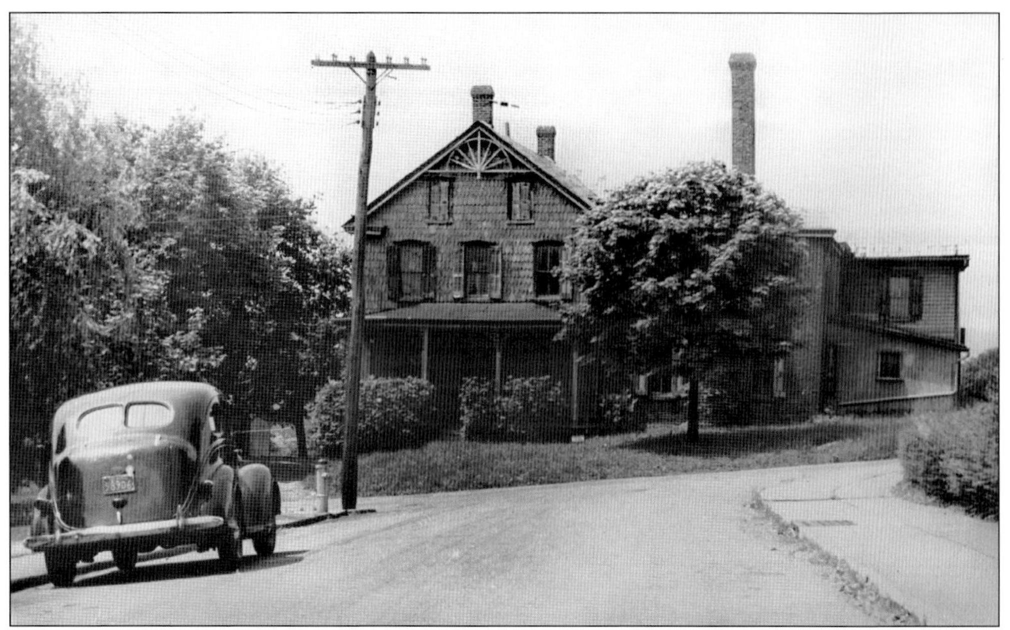

Best remembered for the smell rather than the taste, the cheese factory on Wile Avenue was opened in 1889 by Adolph Erdin and sold to the Holly brothers, Charles and Theodore, in 1892. When Theodore died in 1927, ownership passed to Charles. This photograph was taken from Diamond Street. (Courtesy of Phil Ruth.)

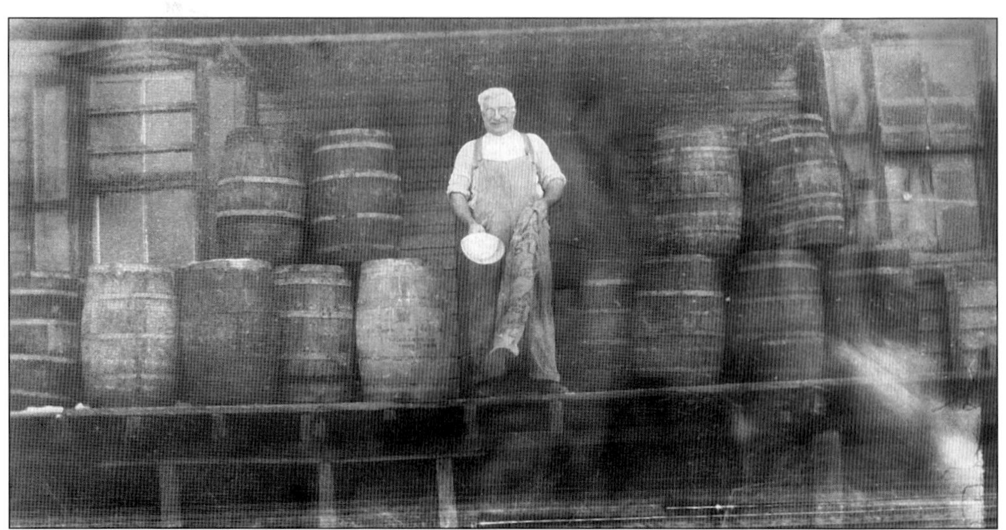

An employee stands on the loading dock of the "stinky cheese" factory, surrounded by barrels of cheese. Today, the Holly's Hill Park, named in honor of the Holly family, is located on the site of the Holly Cheese Factory and the family's Victorian home. (Courtesy of Elsenia Miller.)

In 1886, William D. Hunsberger erected a large hardware store on East Broad Street, clearly outshining his rival Edmund H. Souder's frame building on Main Street, which was operated by Benjamin C. Barndt. The artist, Kolly Rosenberger, depicted the store with the often visited tower next to the Hunsberger homestead. In front is a town water pump. (Courtesy of Jeffrey Landis.)

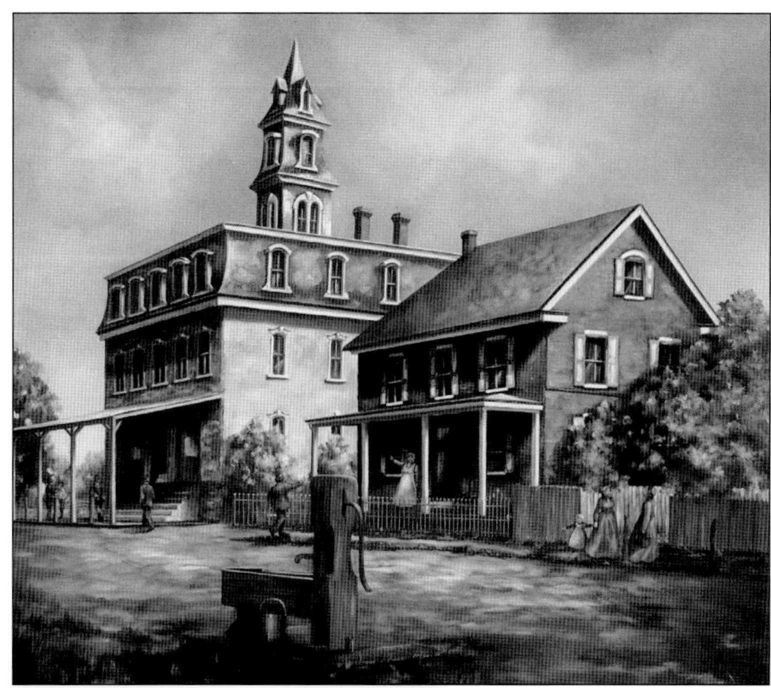

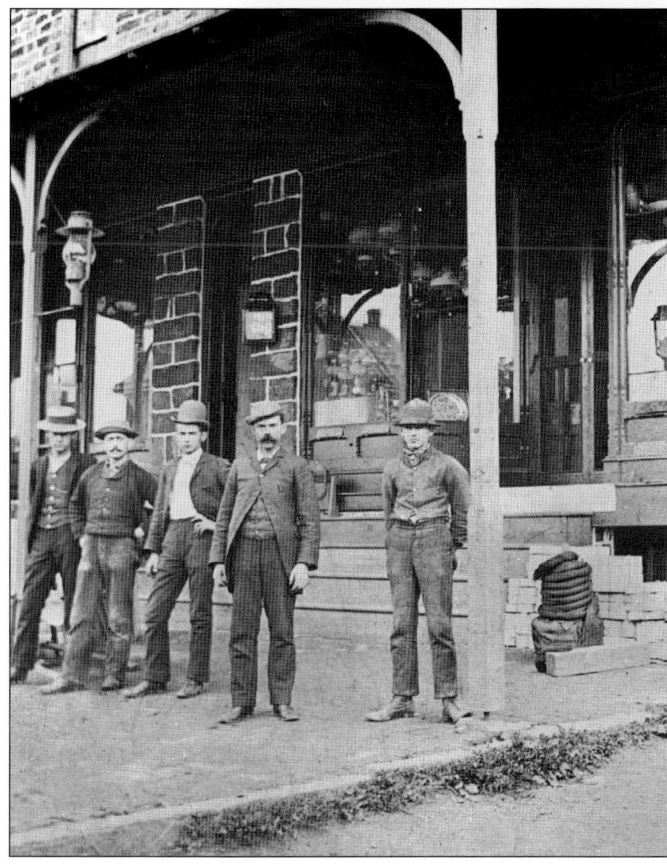

Men standing in front of Hunsberger's Hardware store must have felt pride in the growth of their vibrant community. (Courtesy of Phil Ruth.)

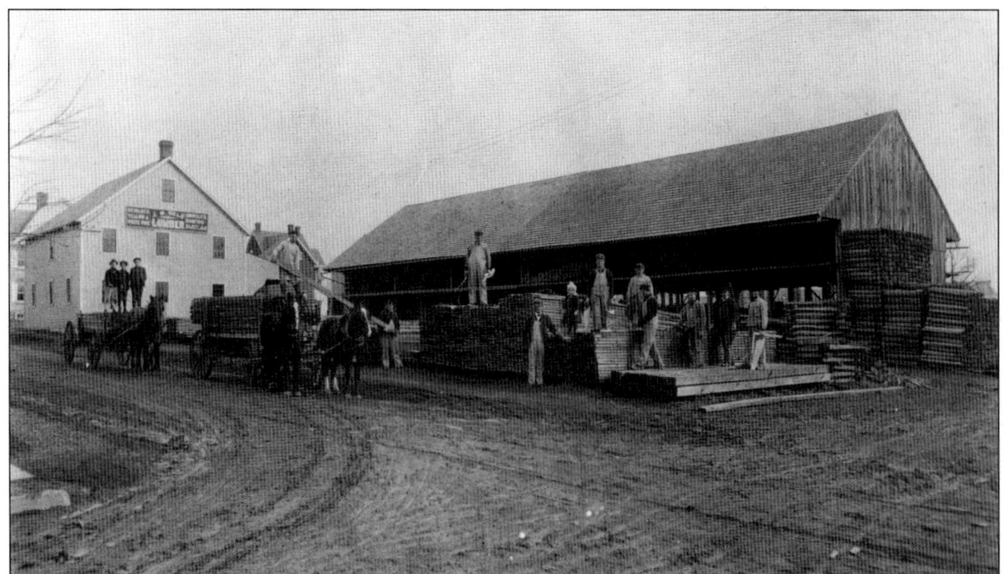

With the rapid growth of the town and the increased demand for lumber, Jacob B. Delp established this lumberyard on Highland Avenue in 1899, competing with William H. Souder on Chestnut Street. (Courtesy of Gloria Brandis.)

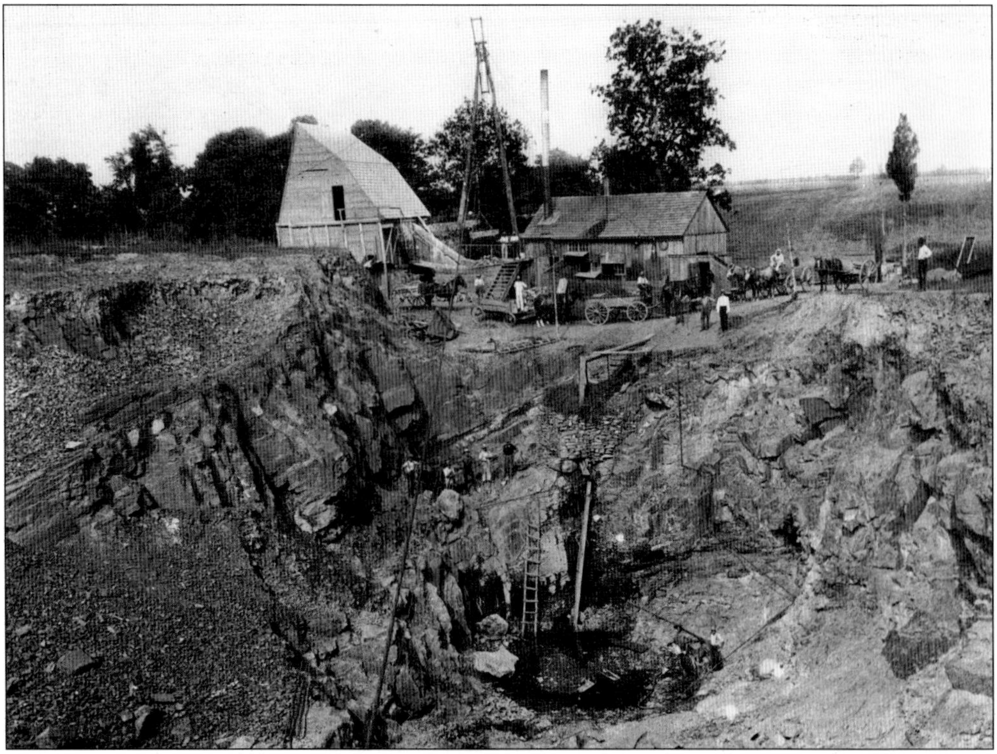

Contractor Jacob B. Delp worked for the Progressive Realty Company, constructing stylish new homes to attract potential employees to the area. The company acquired five local quarries to help in this venture. This one was located south of town along the township line. (Courtesy of Gary Albright.)

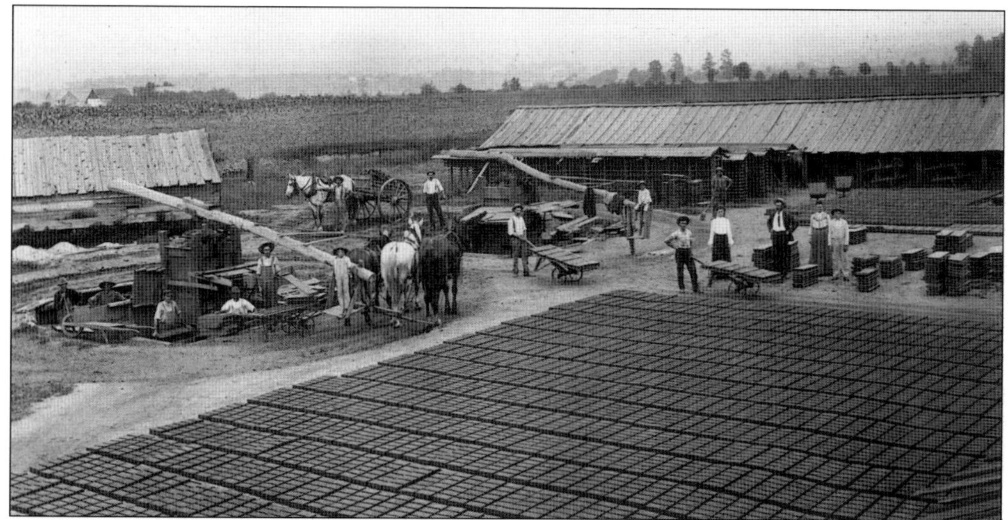

Joseph D. Stover opened the first brickyard in 1877 on North Wile Avenue. The operation of the Hilltown Township brickyard, shown here, was similar to Souderton's. The clay was first dynamited, loosely shoveled into piles, placed in pits, and watered. Horses attached to a clay press would walk, forcing the clay into molds, which would be set to dry in the sun before being fired in kilns. (Courtesy of Duane Reinford.)

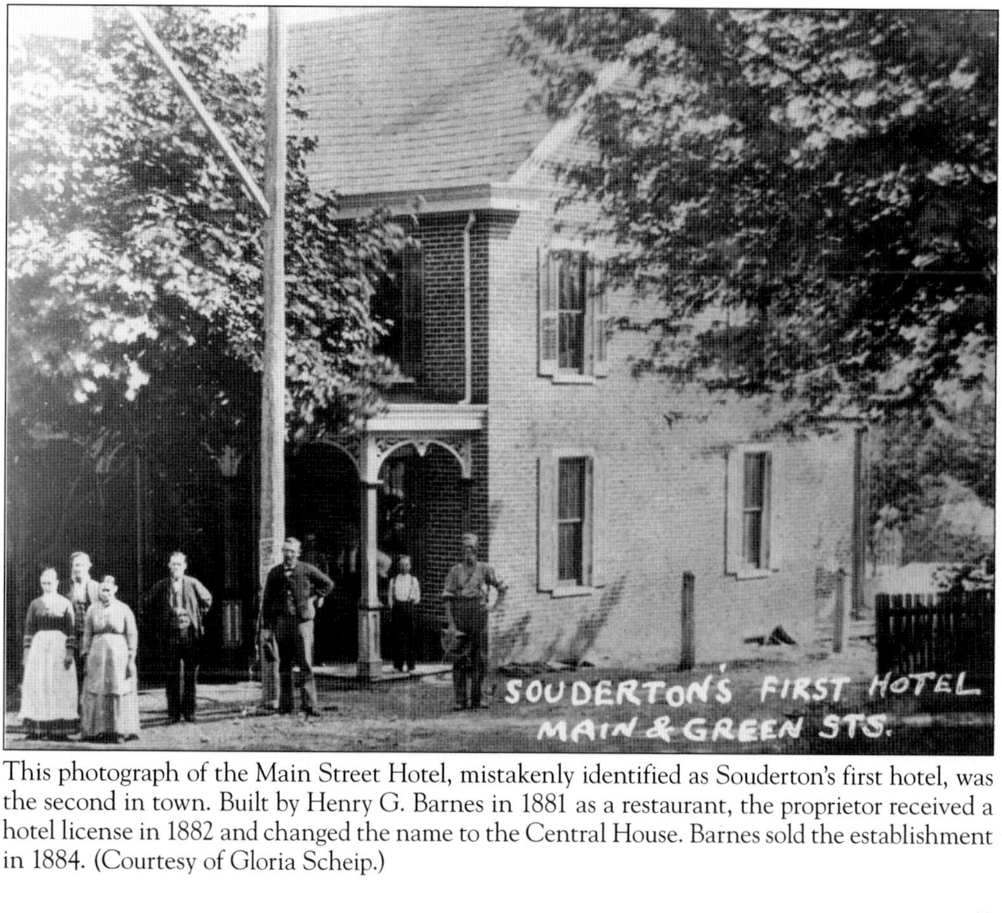

This photograph of the Main Street Hotel, mistakenly identified as Souderton's first hotel, was the second in town. Built by Henry G. Barnes in 1881 as a restaurant, the proprietor received a hotel license in 1882 and changed the name to the Central House. Barnes sold the establishment in 1884. (Courtesy of Gloria Scheip.)

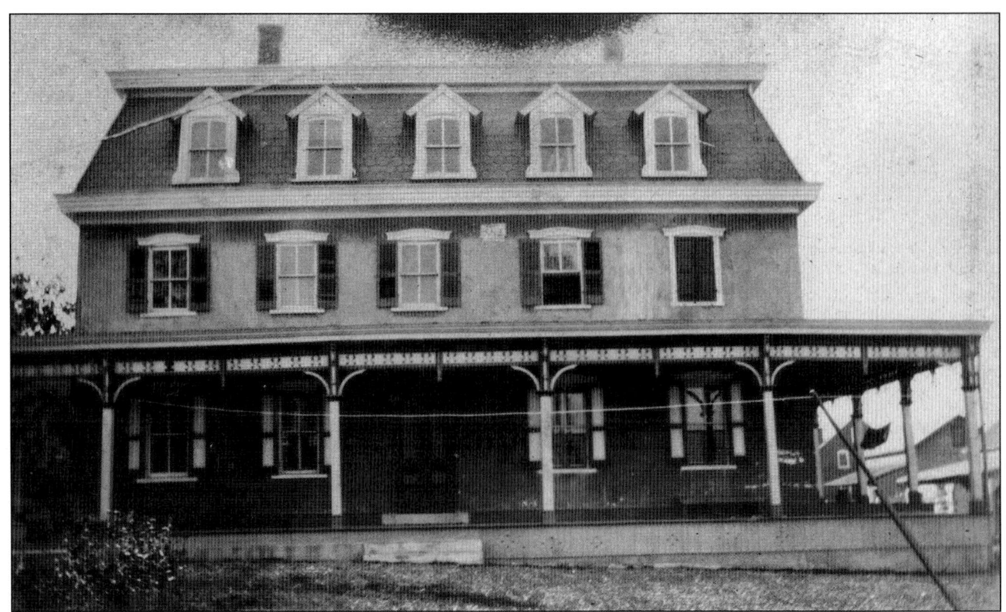

When Souderton became a borough in 1887, the village named by the railroad as Midway, but better known in the community as Reliance, was not included. Pictured here is the Reliance Hotel established in 1882 by Robert L. Preister, son-in-law to Henry O. Souder's brother Sam. The hotel, located on Reliance Road, first opened as a restaurant. (Courtesy of Fred Seitz.)

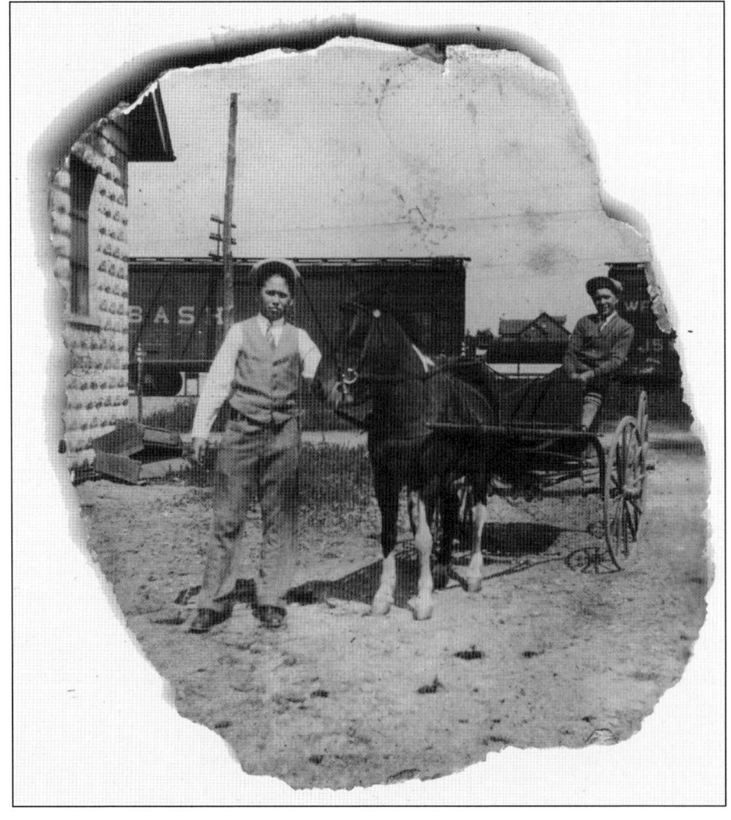

Martin R. Seitz, the 14th owner of the Reliance Hotel, purchased it in 1922. Seitz was leasing the Central House while he and his wife, Deborah, made improvements on the Reliance, which had been closed for several years. Adding a barn, cows, chickens, and pigs, the new owners served family-style meals from home-raised stock. Here, two of their younger children, John (left) and Clarence, are shown near the Midway Train Station. (Courtesy of Fred Seitz.)

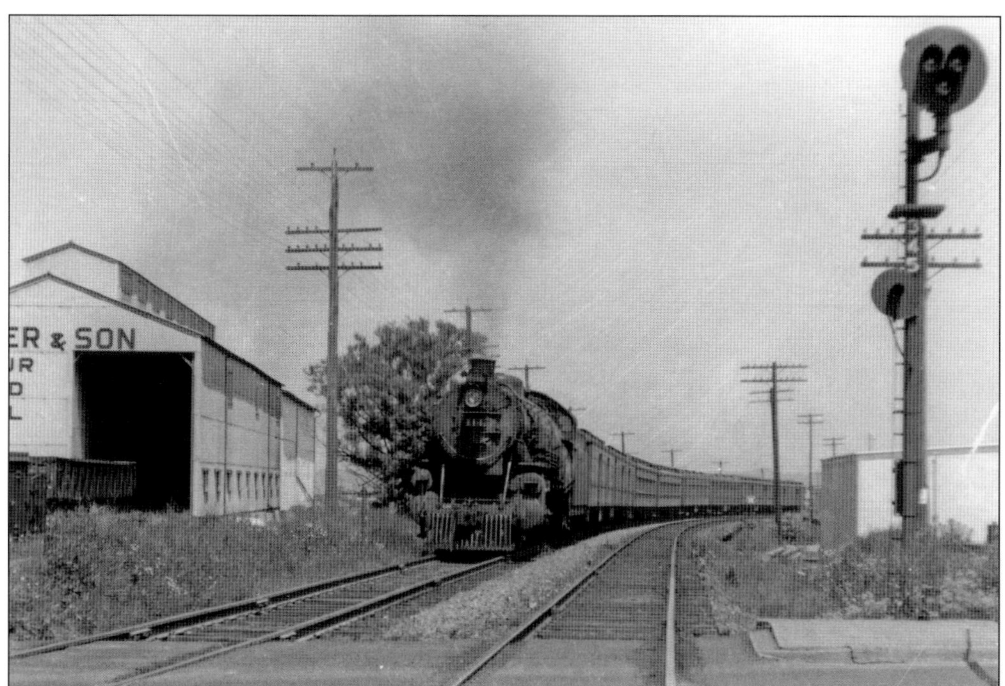

A station and waiting room were operated by the railroad (now the Philadelphia & Reading Railroad since 1879) at Midway (Reliance) from 1891 to 1927. A Reading RR G2 Pacific-style locomotive, photographed in 1946 at the Reliance Road crossing, is heading south toward Souderton. (Courtesy of Dale Woodland.)

In 1885, a brick tollhouse was erected in Reliance at the intersection of Main Street and Reliance Road. Henry Barndt was the last toll collector to lower the bar to collect tolls. Photographed in 1963, with the roof already removed, the old building was in the process of being razed for an automobile service station. (Courtesy of *Souderton Independent*.)

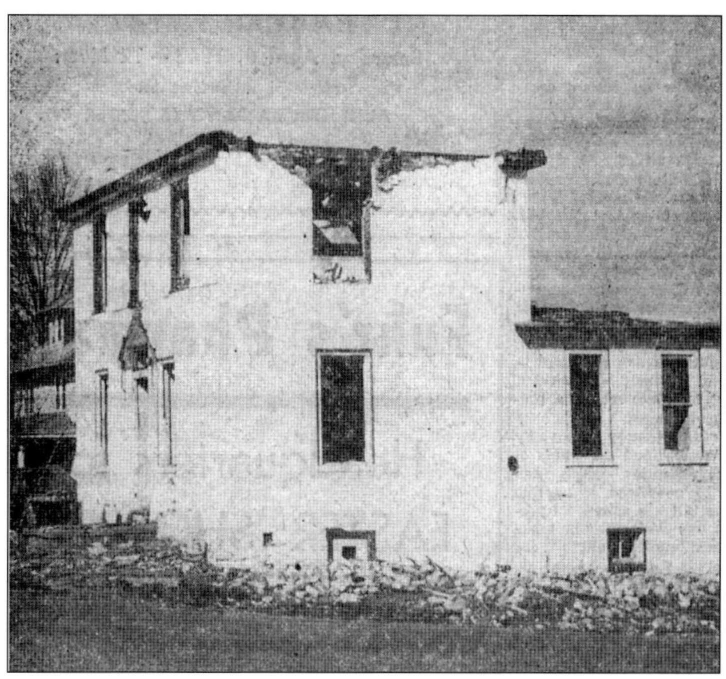

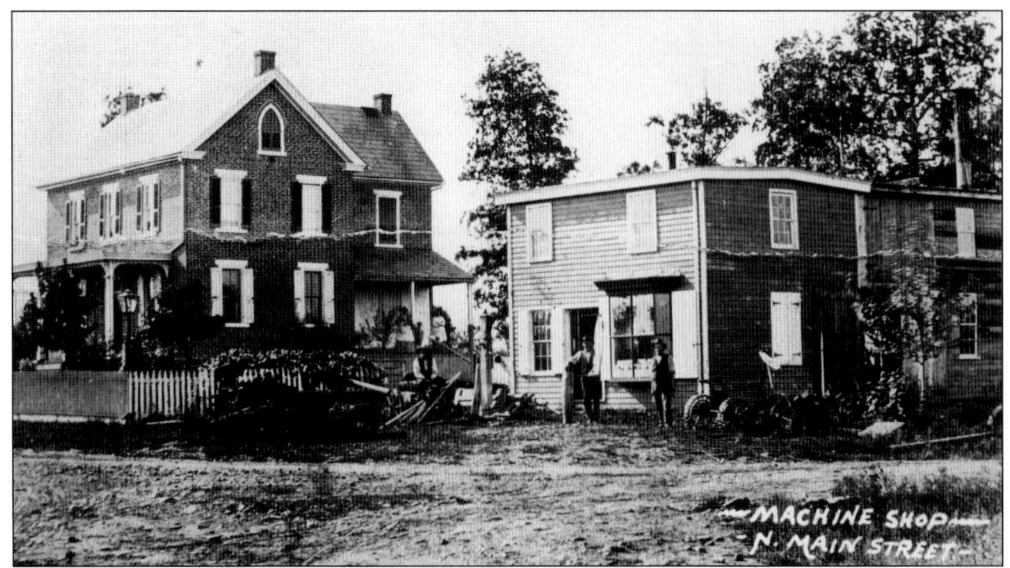

Voegtlin and Preister opened this shop in 1881, specializing in the manufacture of machine parts. Located at Main Street and Reliance Road, the shop was sold to Charles Preister in 1882, who continued its operation for several years. (Courtesy of Gary Albright.)

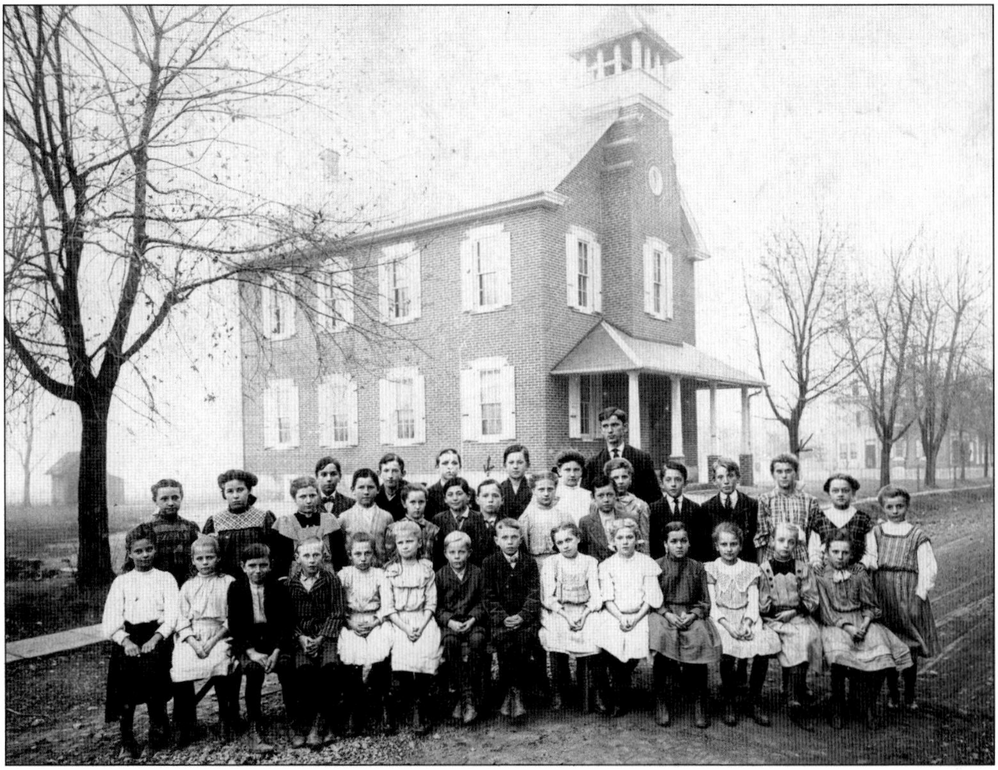

By 1908, the population of the Reliance section of Franconia Township had increased so much that the one-room Five Points Schoolhouse needed to be expanded. By adding a second floor and extending the front of the building, the contractors were able to provide more comfortable classrooms. An attractive bell tower was also added. (Courtesy of Gary Albright.)

Four

A Borough Responds

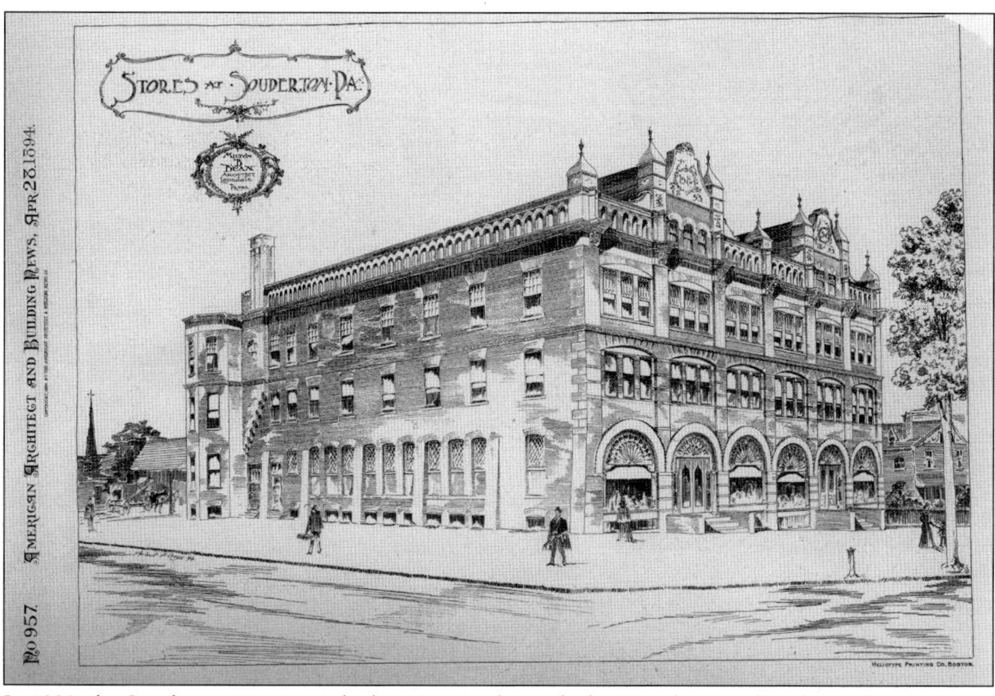

In 1893, the Souders, continuing the business rivalry with the Hunsbergers, hired Lansdale architect Milton B. Bean to design two separate buildings that would be artfully joined to appear as one large store. Contractors Hemsing and Son built the general store for J.M. Landis & Co. (left). John Frederick built the hardware store for Edmund H. Souder and his son-in-law Adam Crouthamel (right). The magnificent edifice, an architectural gem, simply commanded attention. (Courtesy of the William A. Keely Collection, Bryn Mawr College Library, Special Collections.)

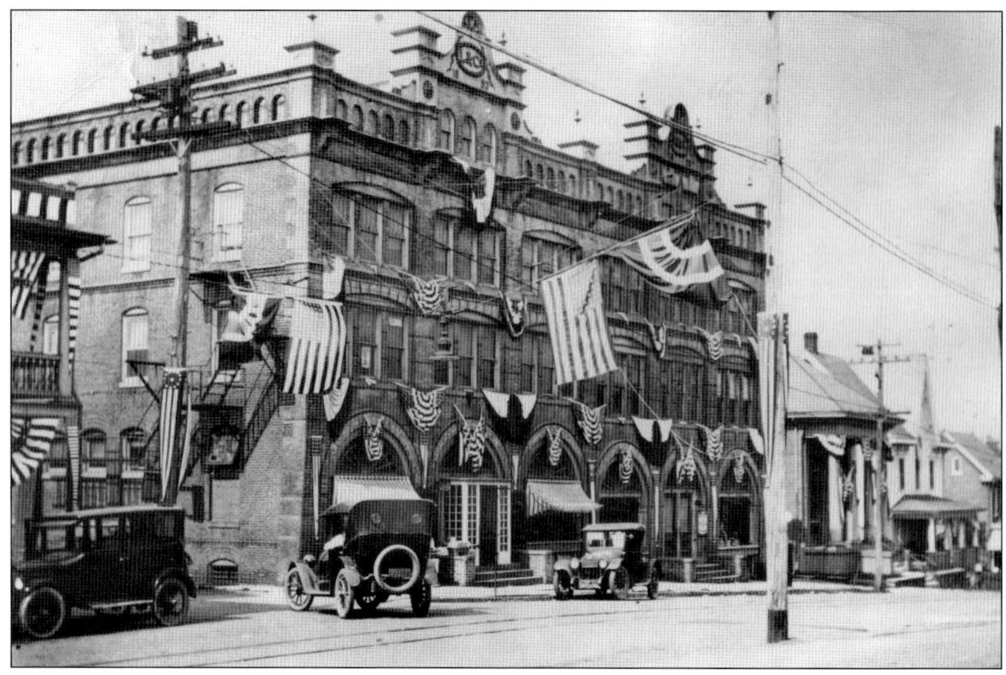

Now the largest store between Philadelphia and Allentown, J.M. Landis & Co. and Souder and Crouthamel took every opportunity to decorate their beautiful building. Whether to celebrate holidays, honor veterans, or recognize the borough's milestones, rows of bunting adorned the facade, creating a festive focal point for the special occasions. (Courtesy of STMS collection.)

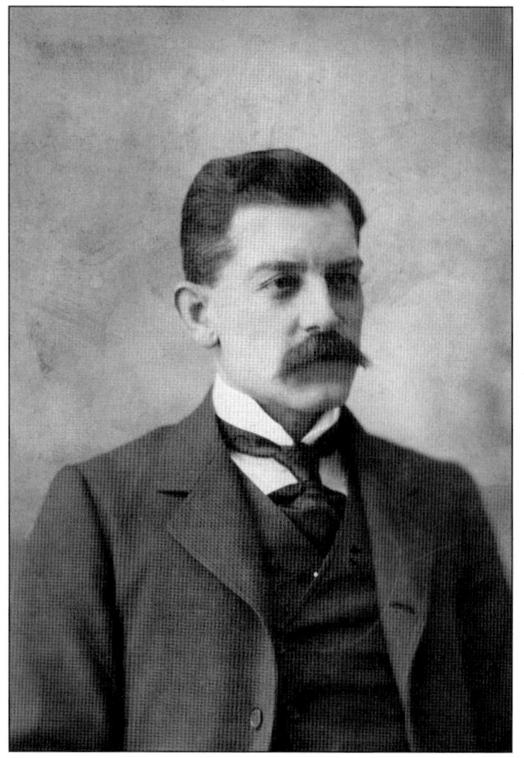

Ellis H. Souder (1858–1932), the ninth child born to Henry O. and Hannah Souder, chose to remain a silent partner in the ownership of J.M. Landis & Co. in 1882 and of Yocum, Godshalk & Co. in 1926. Civic-minded, Ellis served on borough council, on the school board, and as an elder of Zwingli Reformed Church. Around 1879, he became one of the first telegraph operators in Souderton. (Courtesy of Susan Long.)

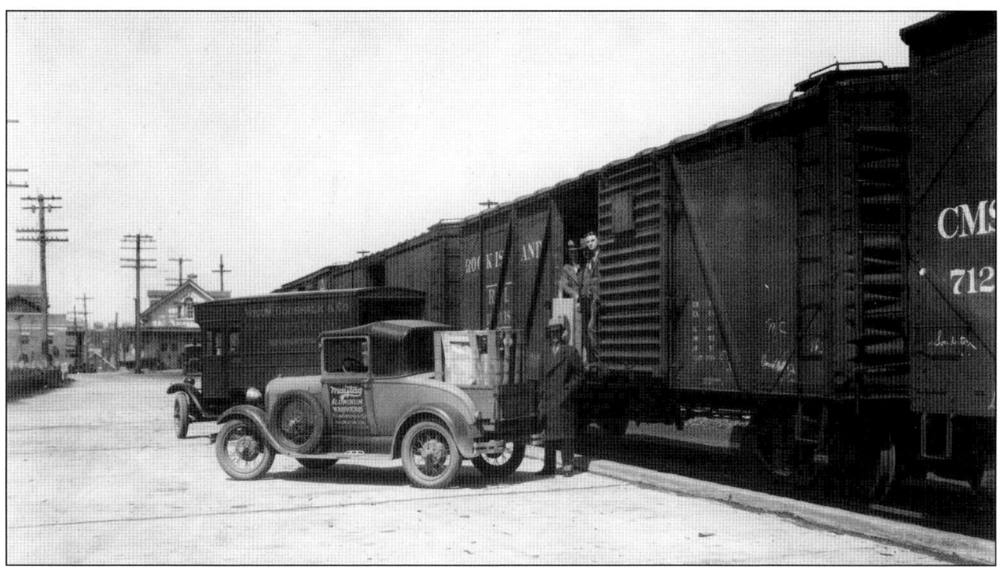

In 1926, J.M. Landis & Co. was sold to Ellis H. Souder and two sons-in-law, John G. Yocum and E. Stanley Godshalk. Pictured here at the train station, around 1928, are the Yocum, Godshalk & Co. trucks, waiting to take new Maytag wringer washing machines to their general store on Main Street. (Courtesy of Harold Yocum.)

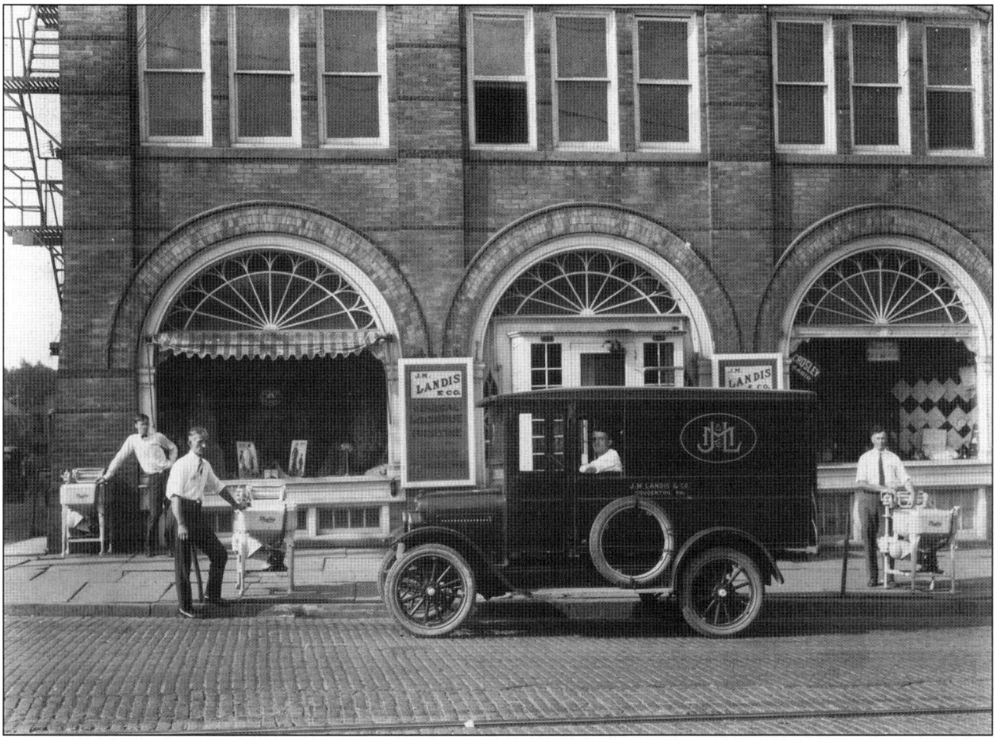

After water and electric were introduced to the borough, Yocum, Godshalk & Co. did a brisk business selling state-of-the-art wringer washing machines. Posing outside their store with their latest delivery are, from left to right, Ralph Freed and John Alderfer, Clarence Derstine (in truck), and E. Stanley Godshalk. (Courtesy of Harold Yocum.)

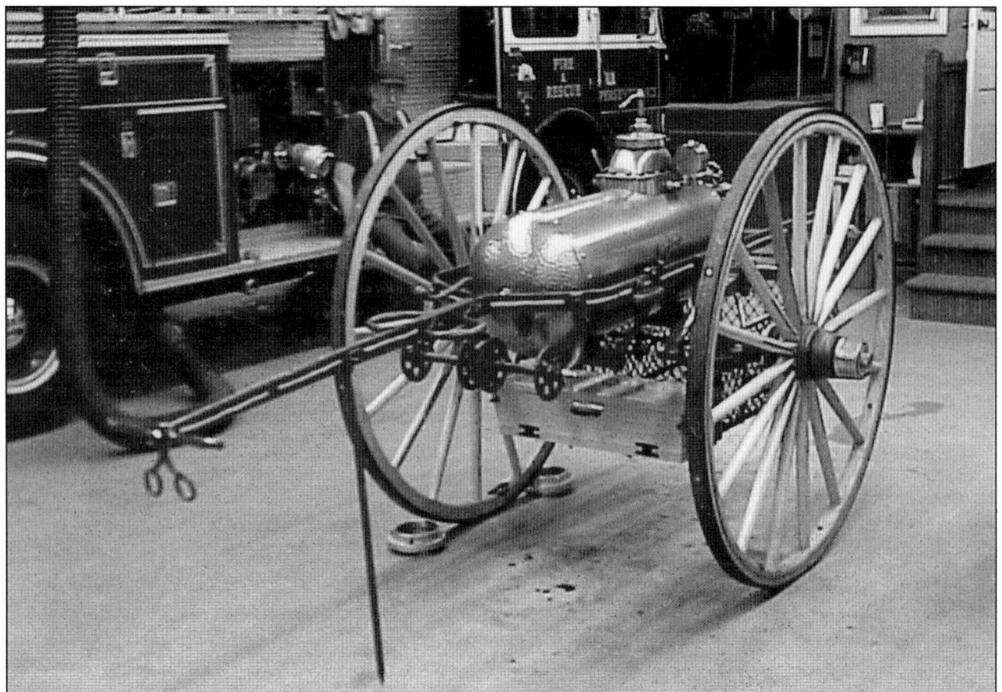

After public water was introduced in the borough in 1896, thirty-six fire hydrants were installed. The town then purchased two hand trucks, keeping them at opposite ends of the town, one in a barn on Central Avenue and the other in Freed's hotel shed. Appointed firemen were paid by the hour. Today, the restored hand trucks are displayed at the firehouse museum on Second Street. (Courtesy of Perseverance Fire Company.)

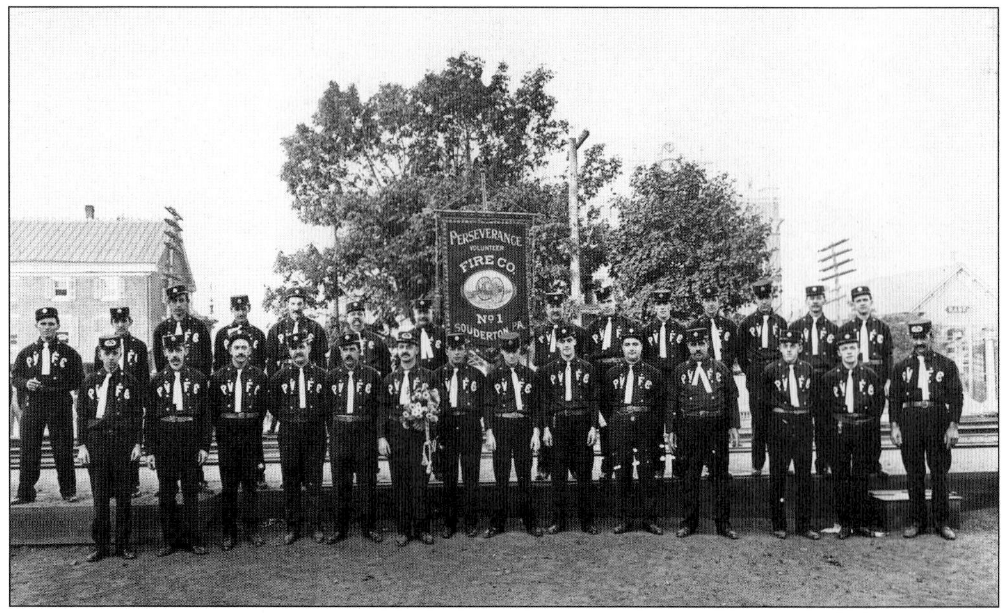

In 1901, the Perseverance Volunteer Fire Company No. 1 was organized. From 1902 until 1927, the fire company operated out of borough hall on Main Street. Here, members of the company stop in formation during a parade. (Courtesy of Mennonite Heritage Center.)

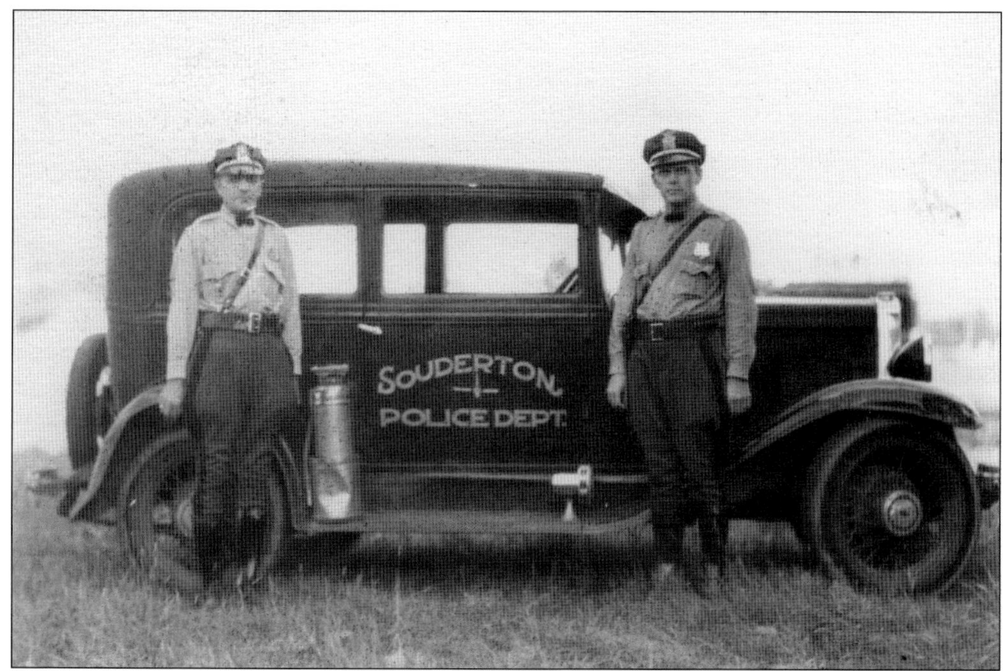

Prior to 1910, Souderton Borough relied on constables from Franconia Township to serve their needs. In 1910, the borough council appointed their first police officer. In the photograph are Chief George Kulp, left, and Officer Charles Greaser. The officers knew everyone in the community and enjoyed the respect of Souderton's citizens. (Courtesy of Gary Albright.)

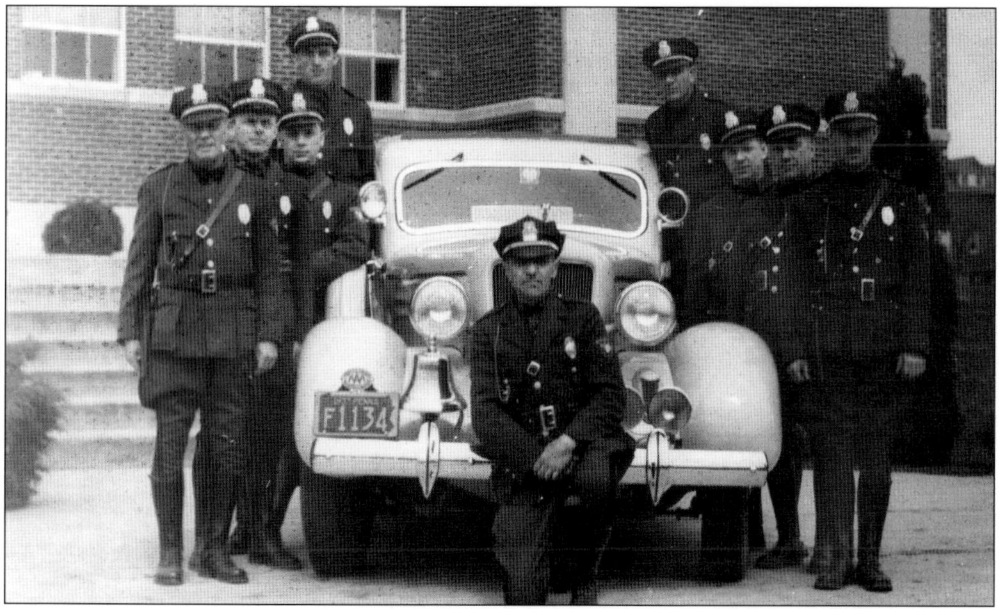

In 1924, the Souderton Fire Police organized as an appointed body of the fire company. The men were called upon to help in civil disruptions and to assist in community events. Four years after becoming an official unit, the fire police members were sworn in as policemen with full authority in 1934. Here, the men are photographed with their Dodge ambulance in 1937. In 1951, the Souderton Community Ambulance Association was formed. (Courtesy of Kurt Scherzberg.)

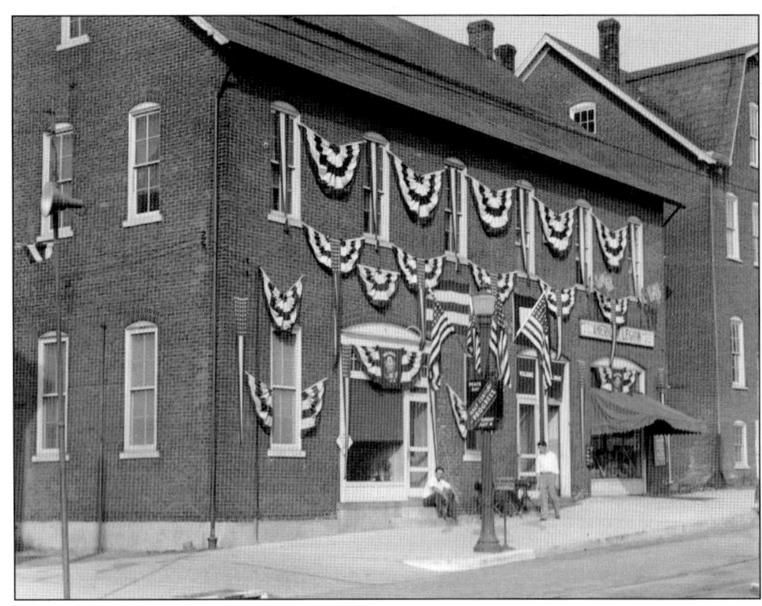

Borough hall was erected in 1899 on Main Street. In 1902, the Perseverance Fire Company opened its headquarters here. Photographed in 1937 at the 50th anniversary parade for the borough, the hall was home to gatherings of councilmen, civic organizations, and police officers. For one year, the hall even served as a school. (Courtesy of STMS collection.)

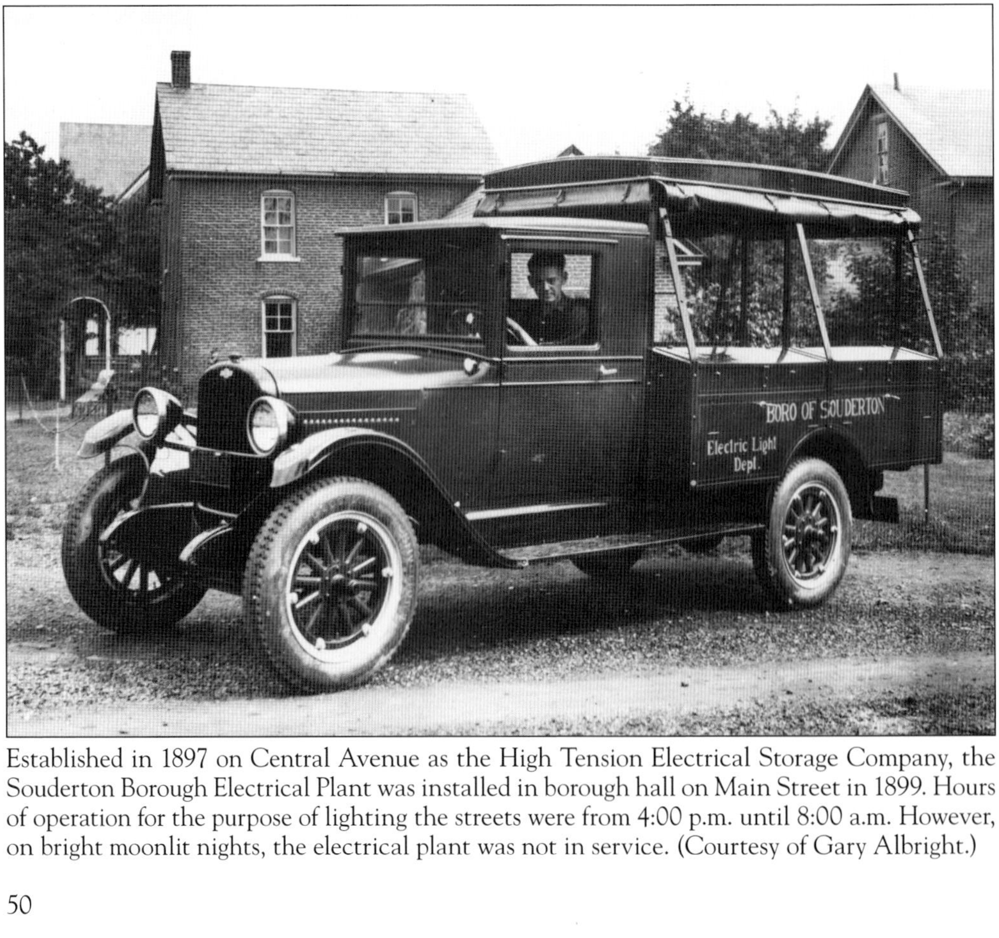

Established in 1897 on Central Avenue as the High Tension Electrical Storage Company, the Souderton Borough Electrical Plant was installed in borough hall on Main Street in 1899. Hours of operation for the purpose of lighting the streets were from 4:00 p.m. until 8:00 a.m. However, on bright moonlit nights, the electrical plant was not in service. (Courtesy of Gary Albright.)

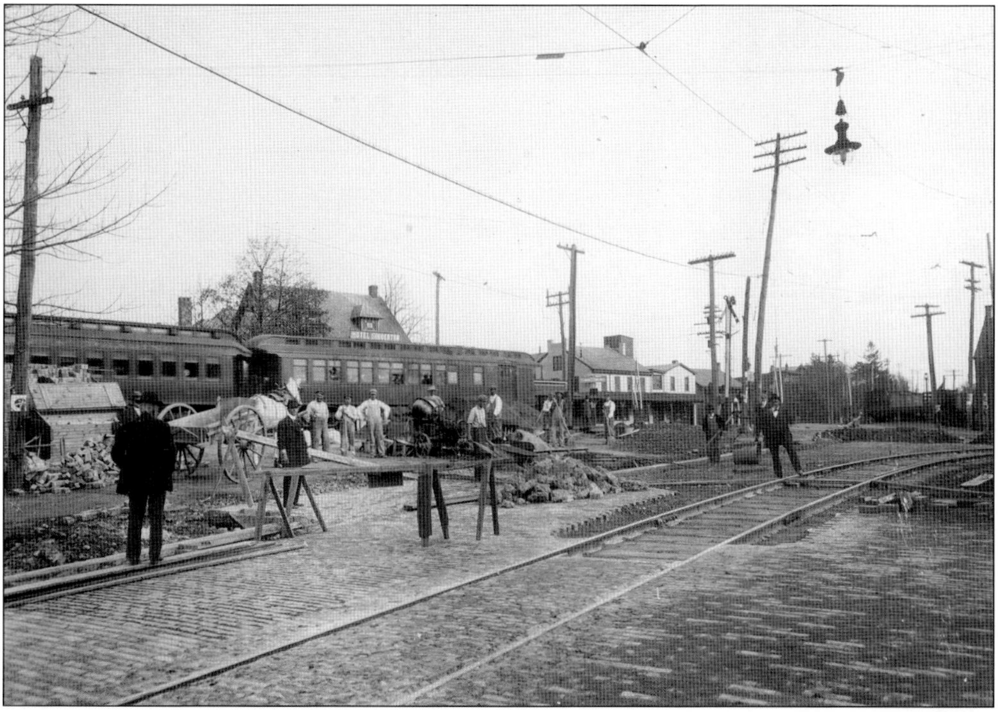

In 1911, Main Street from borough hall to Central Avenue was set with road pavers. A year later, Main Street was paved from Central Avenue to Summit Street and, as shown in this photograph, from borough hall to Broad Street and then on to Penn Avenue. The residents enjoyed not having to contend with the inevitable dust, mud, and ruts of unpaved roads. (Courtesy of Phil Ruth.)

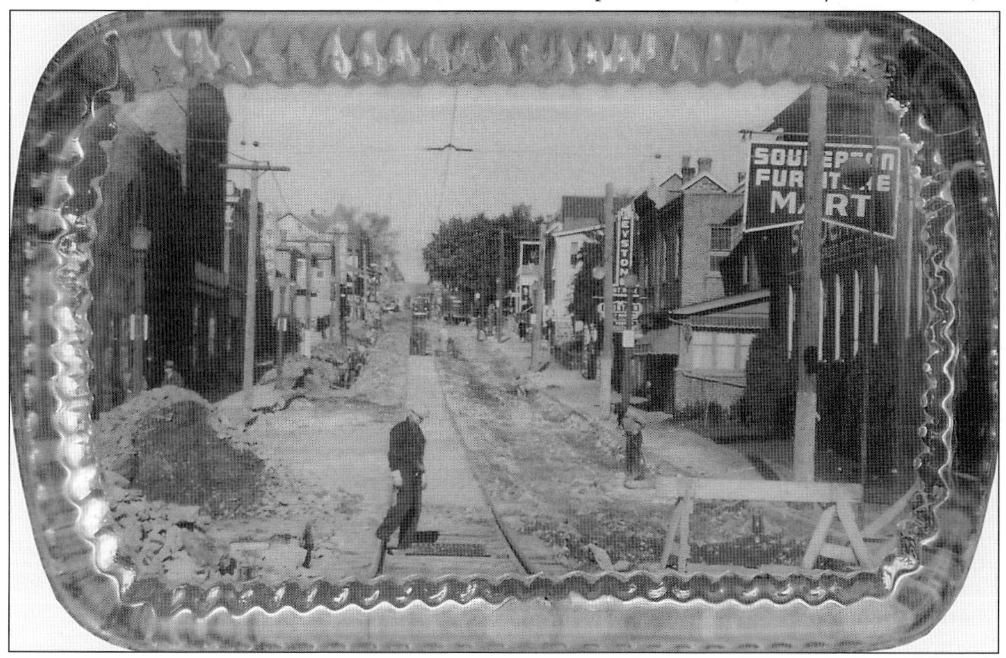

As shown in this glass paperweight, the pavers on Main Street were replaced with modern asphalt around 1940. (Courtesy of Vernon Clemmer.)

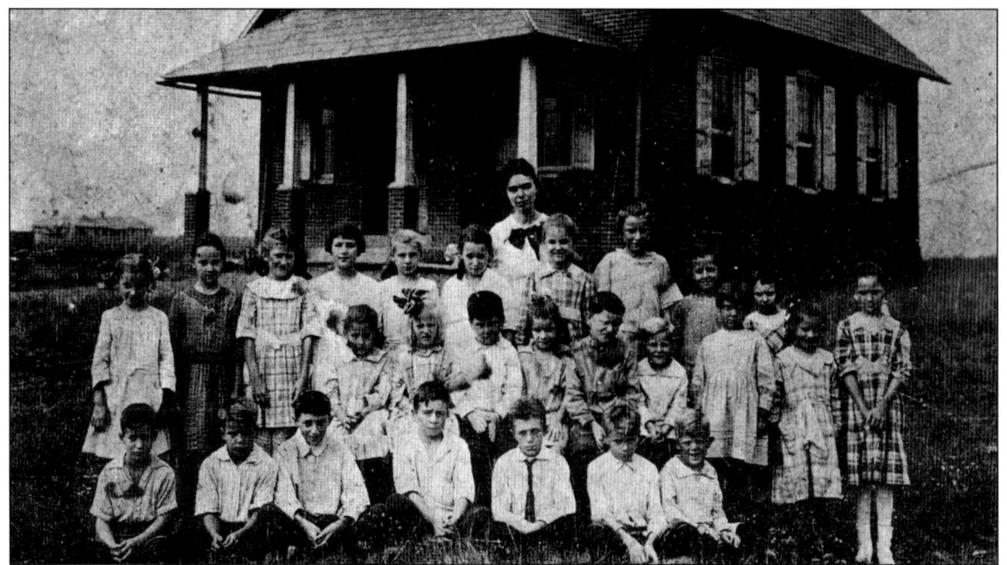

In 1904, Franconia Township added another school, the Hillside School, on the corner of Central Avenue and present-day School Lane, which served the families living along County Line Road. This vicinity was annexed to Souderton and became the jurisdiction of the Souderton Borough School Board in 1916. (Courtesy of Fred Seitz.)

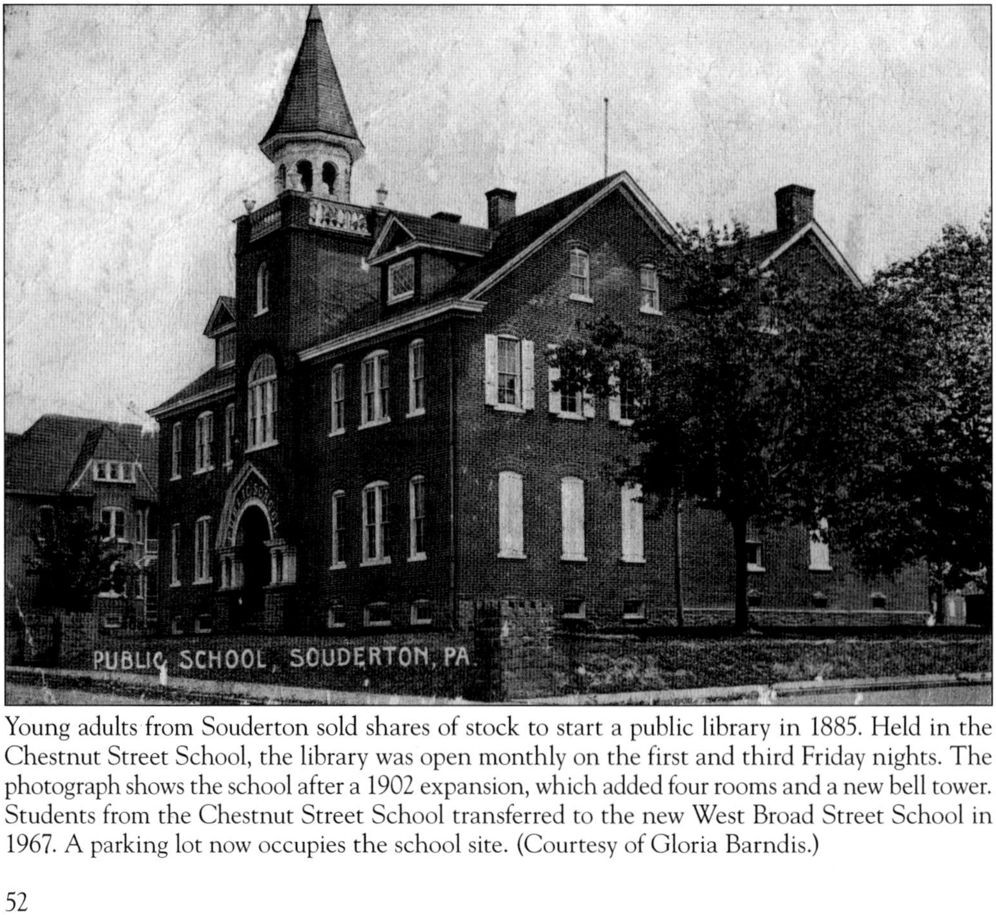

Young adults from Souderton sold shares of stock to start a public library in 1885. Held in the Chestnut Street School, the library was open monthly on the first and third Friday nights. The photograph shows the school after a 1902 expansion, which added four rooms and a new bell tower. Students from the Chestnut Street School transferred to the new West Broad Street School in 1967. A parking lot now occupies the school site. (Courtesy of Gloria Barndis.)

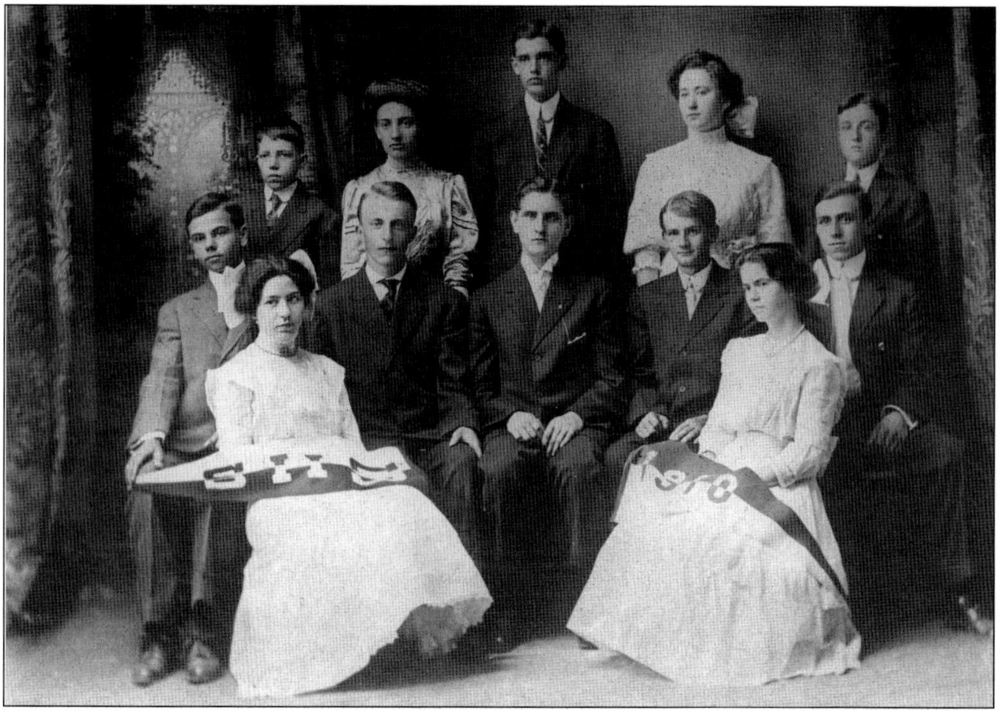

The graduating class of 1910 was the last high school class to graduate from the Chestnut Street School. Listed in alphabetical order are the following members: Joseph B. Allem, Marco G. Bean, Ada B. Gehman, W. Ralph Gehman, Russell B. Hearing. Earl Q. Hunsberger, Irwin H. Krupp, Regina E. McColgen, Ella F. Ritter, Sophia O. Schwenk, Warren K. Smith, and J. Carroll Souder. (Courtesy of Susan Long.)

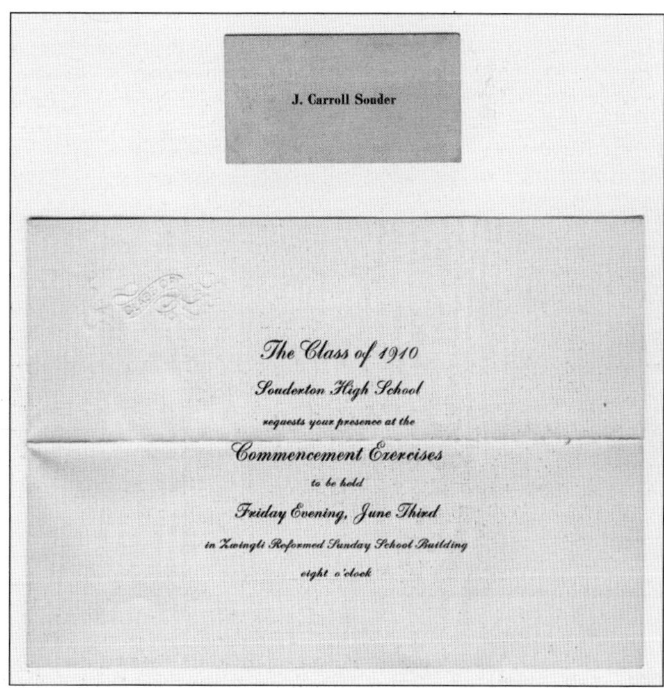

J. Carroll Souder

The Class of 1910

Souderton High School

requests your presence at the

Commencement Exercises

to be held

Friday Evening, June Third

in Zwingli Reformed Sunday School Building

eight o'clock

This is the formal invitation to the 1910 graduation ceremony. The class of 1911 held a banquet to honor the 1910 graduates preceding the ceremony. A special baccalaureate sermon was preached in Emmanuel Lutheran Church. Class day exercises were held in Freed's Hall. Congressman Irving P. Wanger delivered the address to the graduates. (Courtesy of Susan Long.)

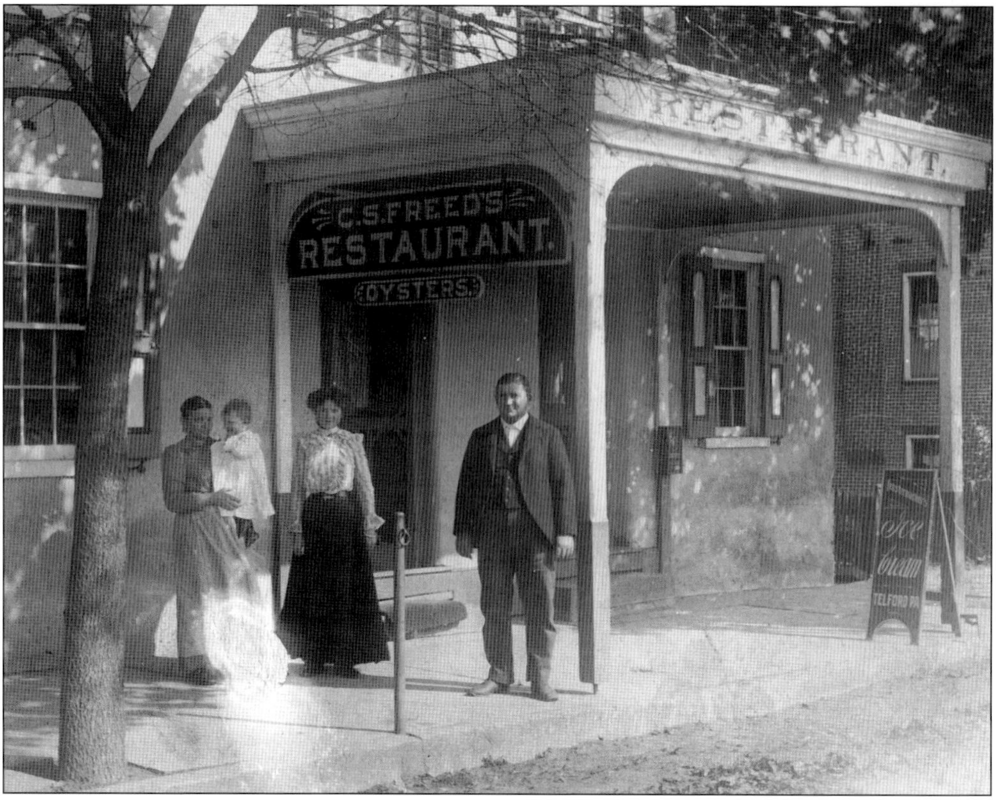

From 1897 to 1944, Christian S. Freed operated this restaurant on South Front Street. One side of the restaurant was open to families, while the other side served gentlemen only. Patrons enjoyed restaurant specialties, oyster stew, and Fenstermacher ice cream, made in neighboring Telford. Seen here are Christian Freed and his daughter Alice Freed Shelly; Christian's wife, Emma, holds their grandson Merwyn L. Shelly. (Courtesy of James Shelly.)

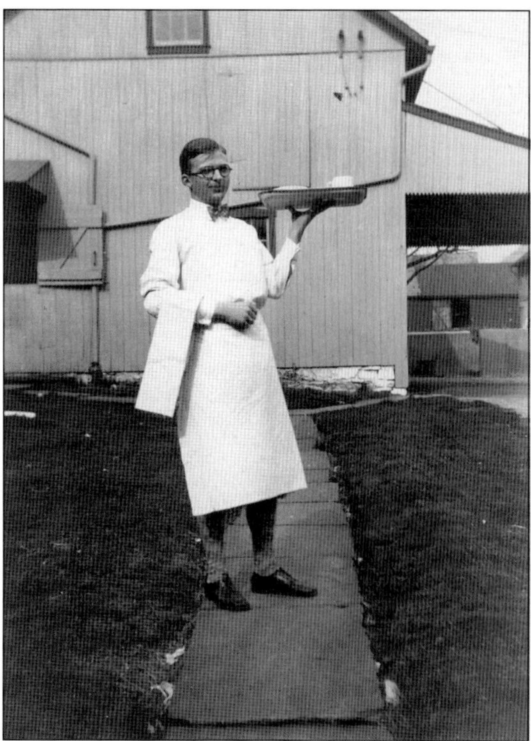

Merwyn L. Shelly, grandson of Christian S. Freed, born in 1909 in Sellersville, Pennsylvania, waited tables in the restaurant run by his grandfather. The photograph was taken in the back yard of the restaurant on South Front Street. Merwyn became an ordained Lutheran minister, serving in that capacity from 1937 to 1980. (Courtesy of James Shelly.)

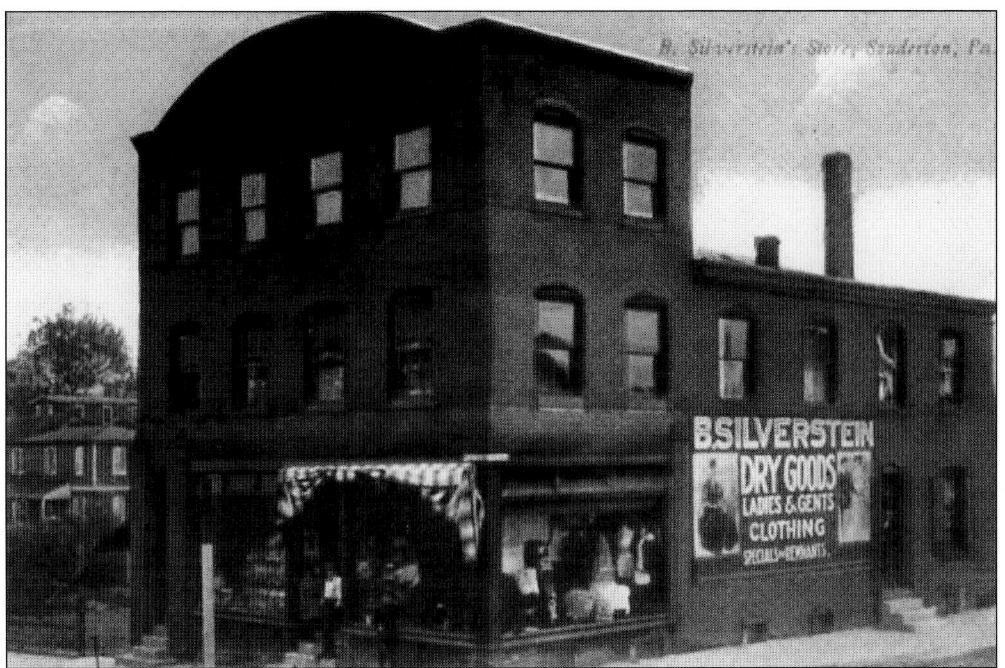

On the site of the first cigar factory, Benjamin Silverstein erected this new building on Main Street and Hillside Avenue in 1908. Here, he opened a clothing store and advertised "Ladies and Gents Clothing." In 1929, Wallace Cressman and Ray Silverstein purchased the store and operated as Cressman Company. At various times, a grocery store, a restaurant, a barbershop, and a poolroom occupied the building. (Courtesy of Robert Greenwood.)

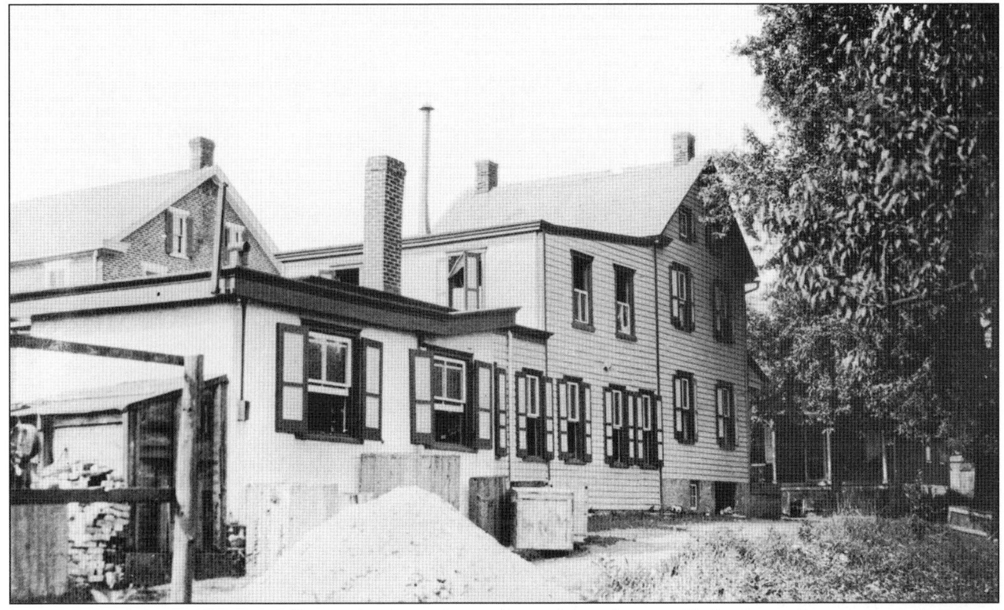

In 1886, Hilary and son William A. Crouthamel purchased a small clothing factory at Main and Walnut Streets, which is seen here after several additions were made to the building. Hilary's grandson George later joined the family business, which was then known as W.A. Crouthamel and Son, specializing in the manufacture of men's trousers. (Courtesy of Phil Ruth.)

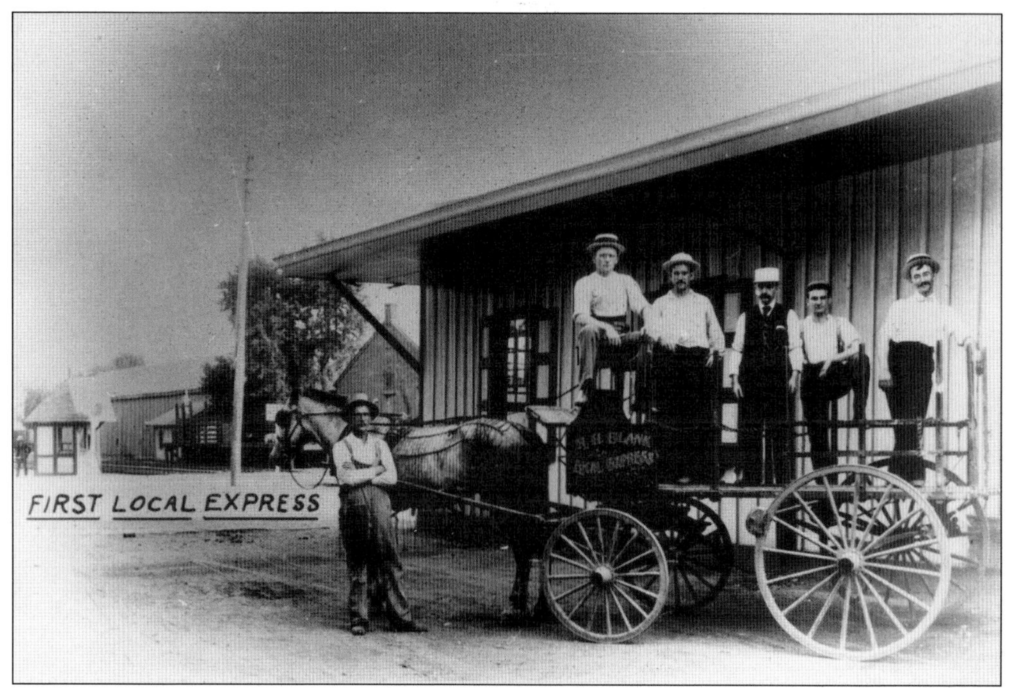

Milton S. Frederick, in the driver's seat, owned a local express and delivery service for a brief time in 1899 while proprietor of his grocery store. Purchased from Edwin Myers, Milton sold the delivery business to William Anglemoyer, standing far right. Here, the men are waiting at the train station to pick up a delivery, after which Milton turned the operation over to Anglemoyer. (Courtesy of STMS collection.)

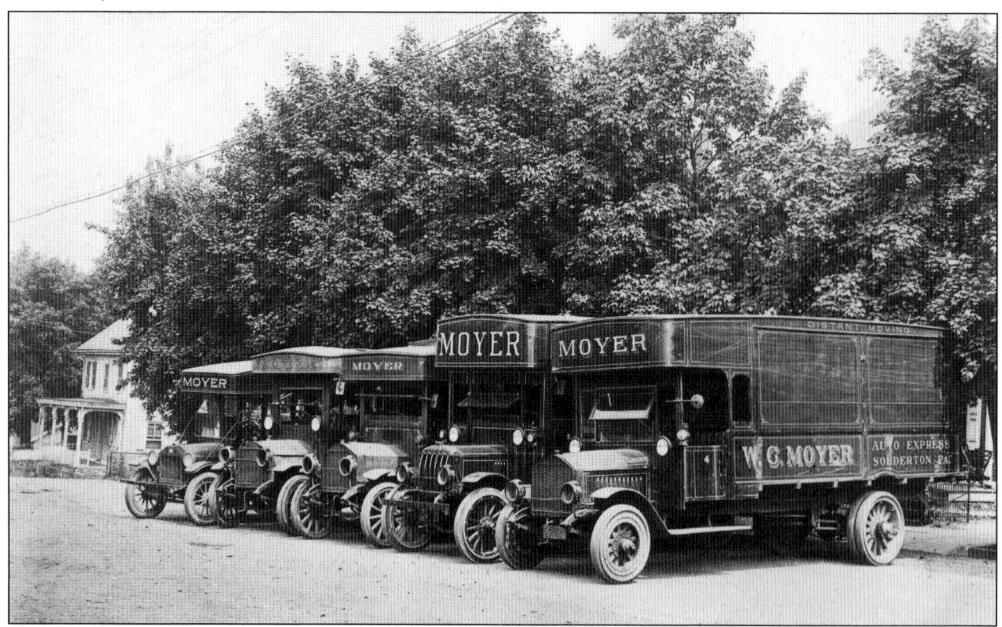

Willliam Anglemoyer sold his delivery service to Warren C. Moyer in 1912. W.C. Moyer Auto Express had an office on North Front Street. Moyer discontinued the use of horse-drawn wagons. Here, his fleet of trucks stands ready for service. (Courtesy of James Shelly.)

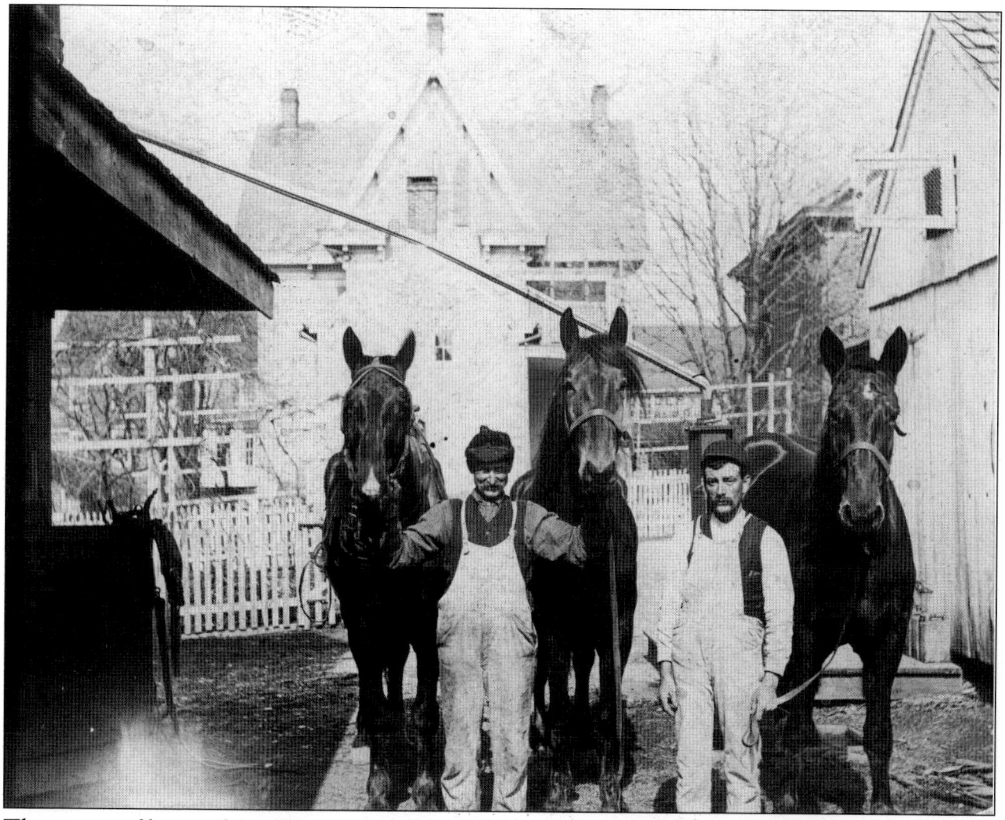

The teams of horses from Warren C. Moyer's local express and delivery service were sold to Horace Souder, on the left. Abe Freed stands on the right. Lady, a favorite horse of Horace's son J. Carroll, could find her way home without a driver. Rumor has it that Carroll took full advantage of Lady's talent when courting his future wife! (Courtesy of Susan Long.)

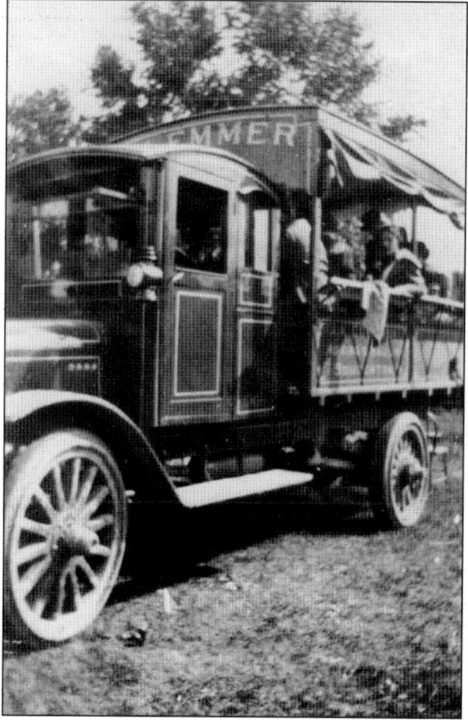

Owner and operator of a hauling business in 1904, Josiah K. Clemmer and his sons used his horse-drawn wagons to transport cheese to New York City, move furniture, and excavate basements. After replacing his horses with trucks, Clemmer earned extra money by chauffeuring people to Menlo Park in Perkasie. Josiah's son Norman took over the enterprise, conducting business first from the old Vetterlein Building and then the Eisenlohr Building. (Courtesy of Vernon Clemmer.)

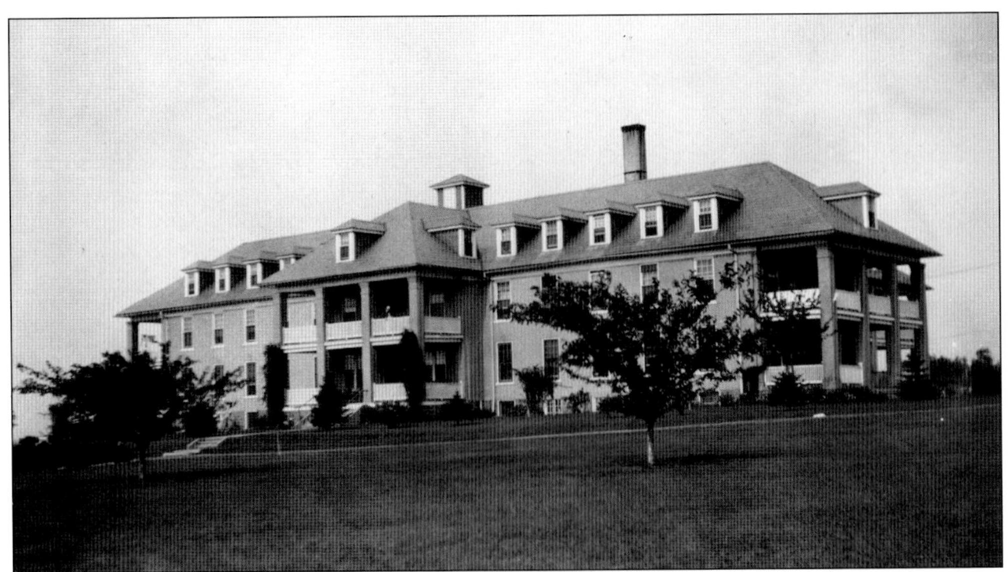

The Eastern Mennonite Home of the Franconia District, built in 1917 on Summit Street, was designed by Horace Trumbauer Architects of Philadelphia, who also designed the Philadelphia Art Museum. At first, the home generated controversy since caring for the elderly was thought to be a family's responsibility. However, the caring Mennonite community created a warm extended-family environment respected by all those whose family members resided there. (Courtesy of James Stauffer.)

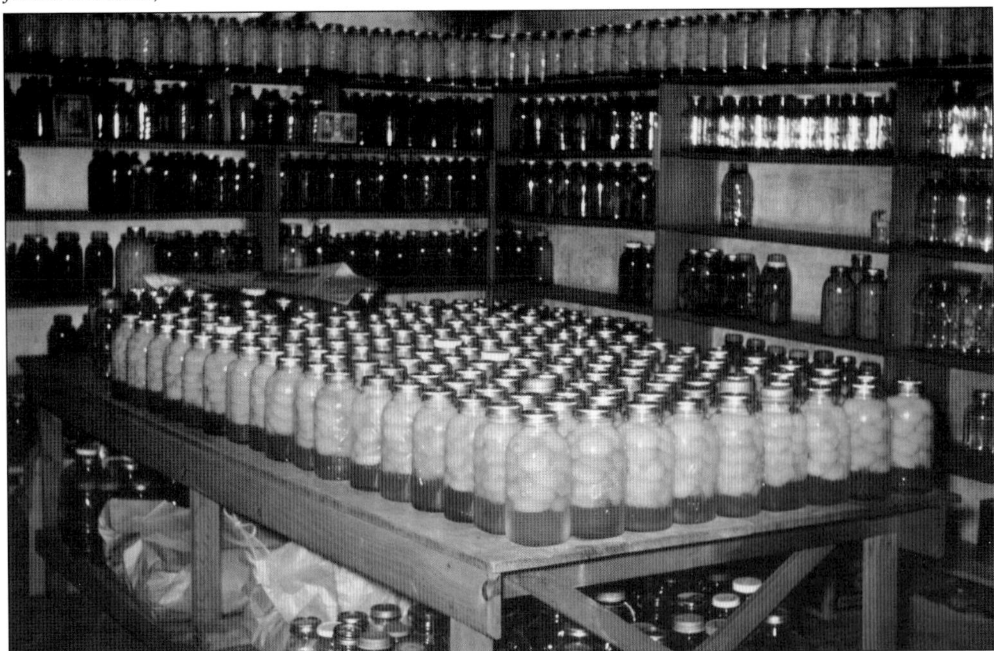

The staff of the Eastern Mennonite Home felt called to service. In the beginning, employees also lived in the home where residents and workers joined together to get chores done. Gardens and an apple orchard were planted, providing the home with much of its own food. The excess fruit and vegetables were canned and stored for the winter, photographed here. Eventually, additional housing took the place of the gardens. (Courtesy of Souderton Mennonite Homes.)

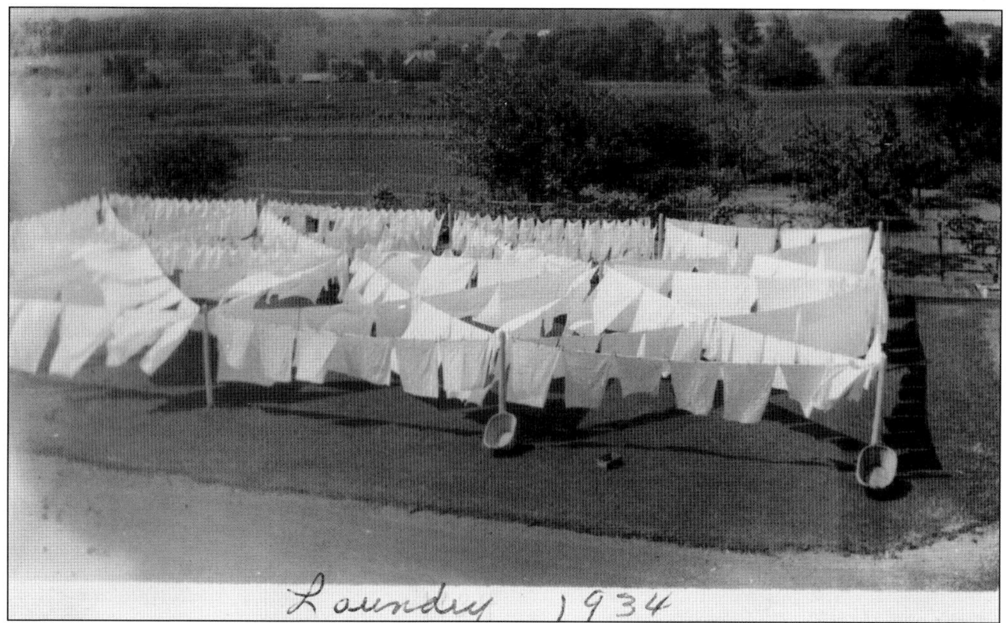

The women working in the laundry at the Eastern Mennonite Home had quite a job before the advent of clothes dryers. In the winter, their hands needed the protection of mittens as they hung many sheets to dry on lines. Clothing often laid over bushes and grass to dry. All linens and garments were ironed. (Courtesy of Souderton Mennonite Homes.)

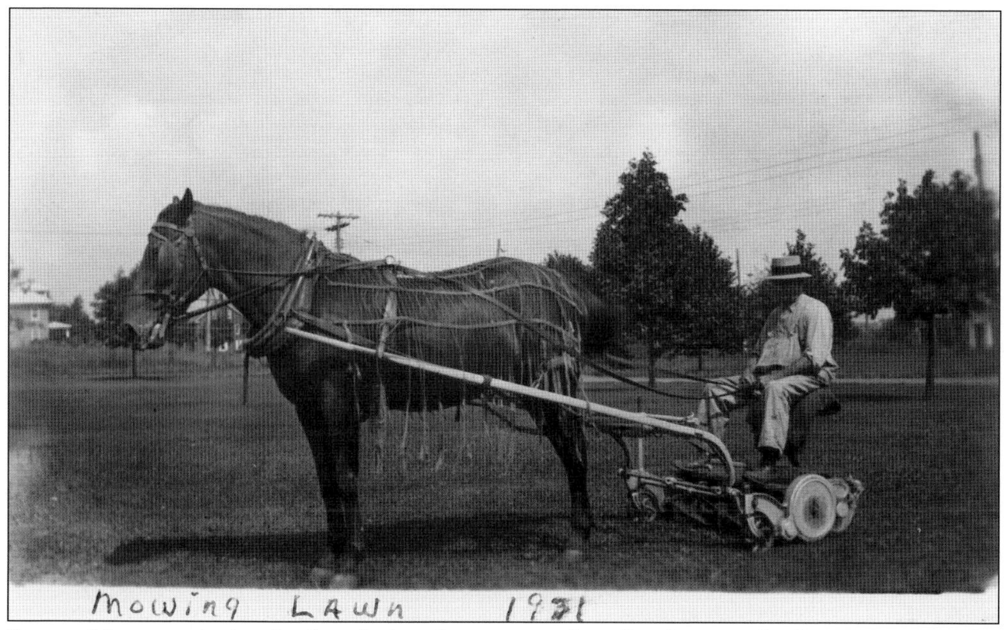

Pictured here might be the first "riding lawn mower" in Souderton, which was in use at the Eastern Mennonite Home. In 1985, the institution's name was officially changed to the Souderton Mennonite Homes. (Courtesy of Souderton Mennonite Homes.)

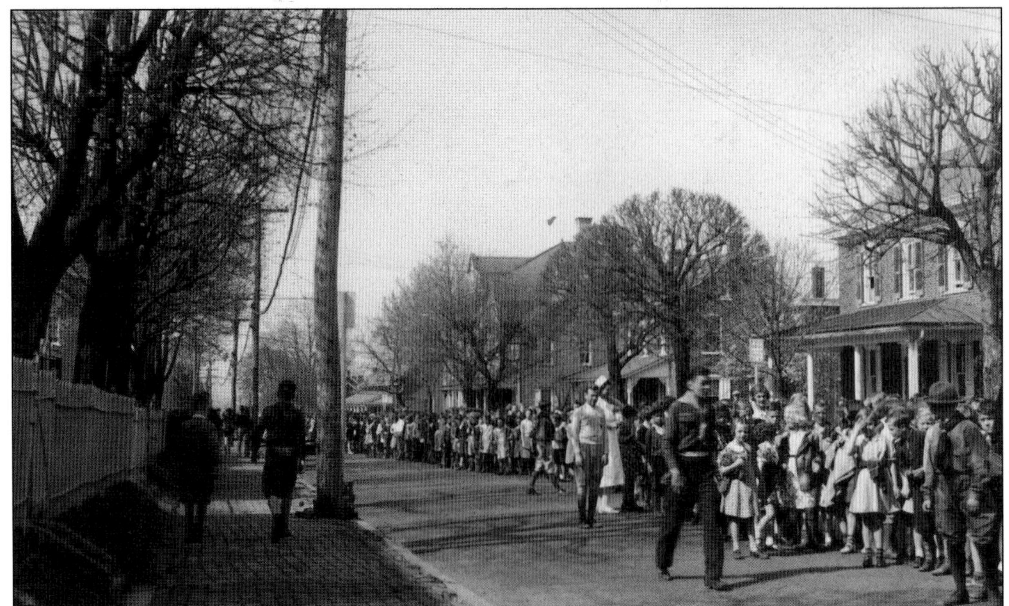

Many volunteer civic groups have helped create the Souderton community. For decades, these special volunteers have contributed to beautifying the town and providing help and recreation for the citizens. Among their many activities, the Souderton Lions were known for sponsoring the annual Easter egg hunt and parade. Here, over 1,000 children walk down Chestnut Street to a secret location to search for over 6,000 eggs and pieces of candy. (Courtesy of Del Muse.)

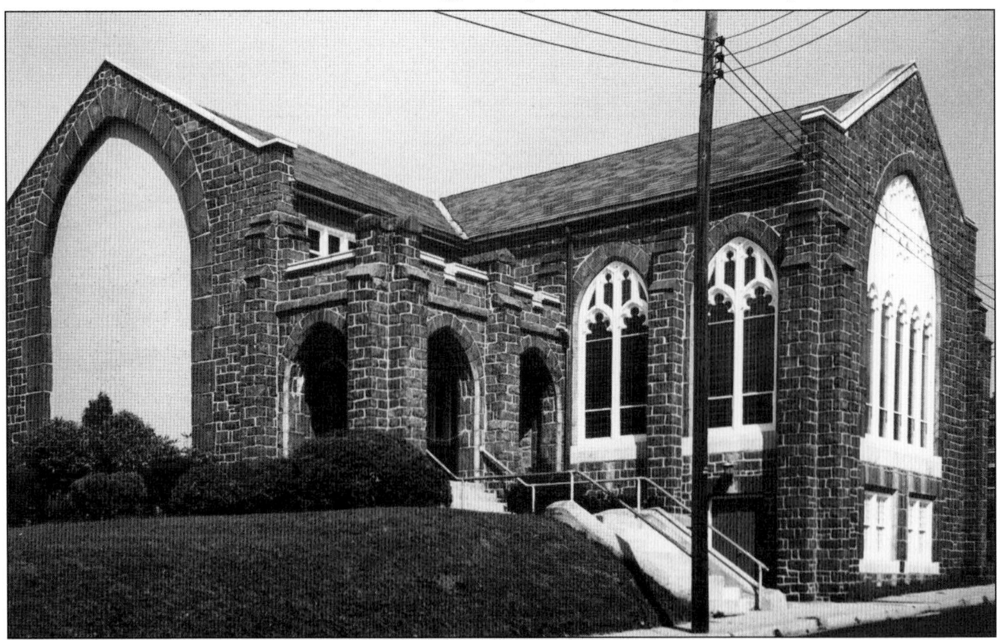

The MacCalla Lodge No. 596 of Free and Accepted Masons began in 1892 and met in Sellersville until 1967. This photograph of Zwingli United Church of Christ at Main and Church Streets became the home of the Masons after the congregation moved to their new church on Wile Avenue. The Masons stand for worshipping God, truth, justice, fraternity, philanthropy, enlightenment, and civil, religious, and intellectual liberty. (Courtesy of Gary Albright.)

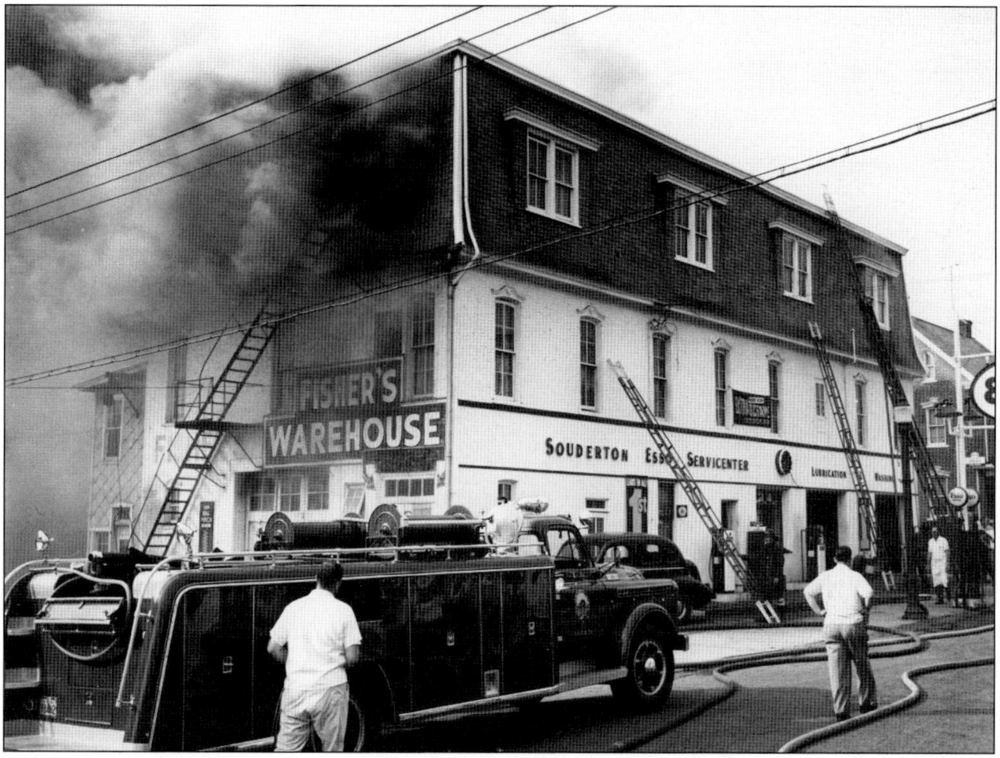

Freed's Hall, originally Liberty Hall, on East Broad Street was always a hub of activity. Civic and religious groups met in the community rooms. In the 1890s, fairs and exhibitions of talking machines and kinetoscopes drew crowds. Even a tightrope walker performed here in May 1885. In 1904, the third story was added and later saved by the Perseverance Fire Company, shown here. (Courtesy of Gary Albright.)

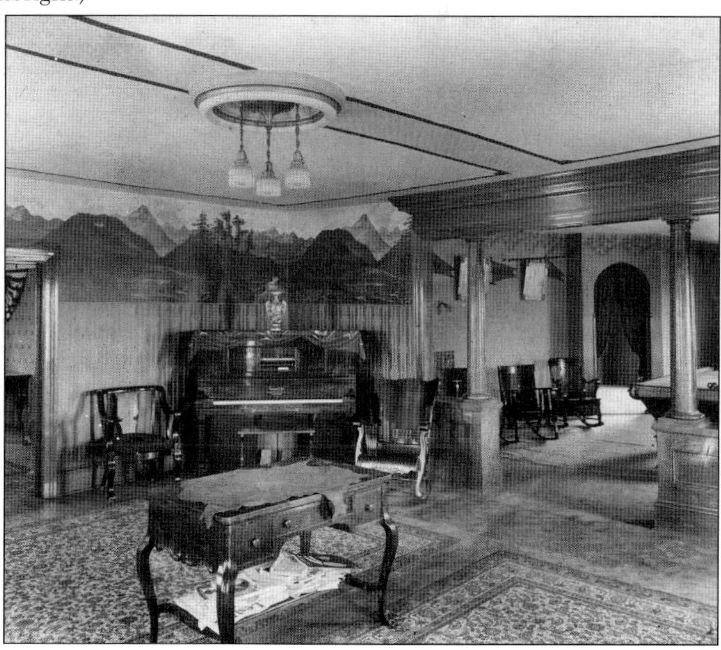

Souderton's residents enjoyed a variety of recreational pursuits. Adult men gathered at the New Century Club above the former Hunsberger Hardware Store on East Broad Street, where they could smoke, box, shoot pool, or swing Indian clubs. Young adults started a literary society in 1886, took sleigh rides, and attended corn huskings, where boys hoped to find a red ear of corn and kiss the girl of their choice. (Courtesy of Karl Fox.)

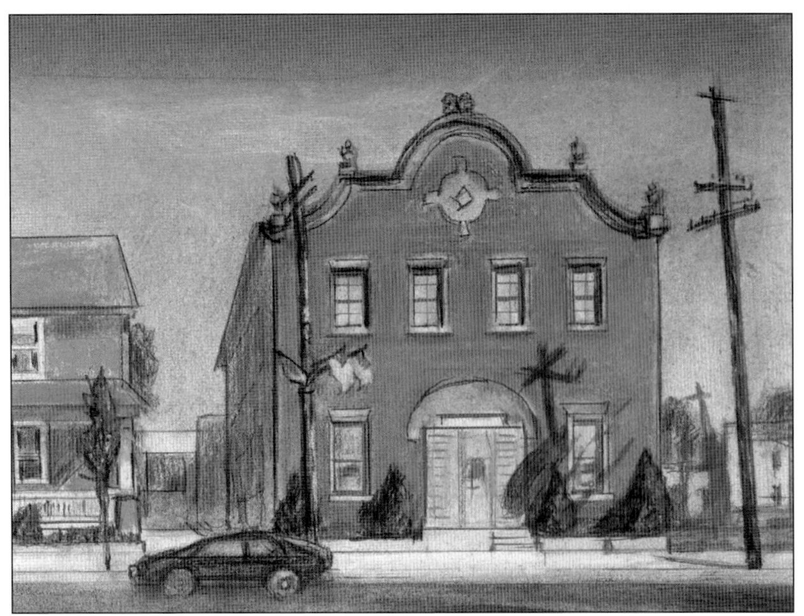

The Electric Mirror Moving Picture House on East Broad Street, later known as the Mirror Theatre, was built and operated by Andrew N. Leidy, opening in December 1911, with seating for 240 people. General admission was 10¢; reserved seating cost 15¢. (Artwork by Theodore Hallman, courtesy of Jeffrey Landis.)

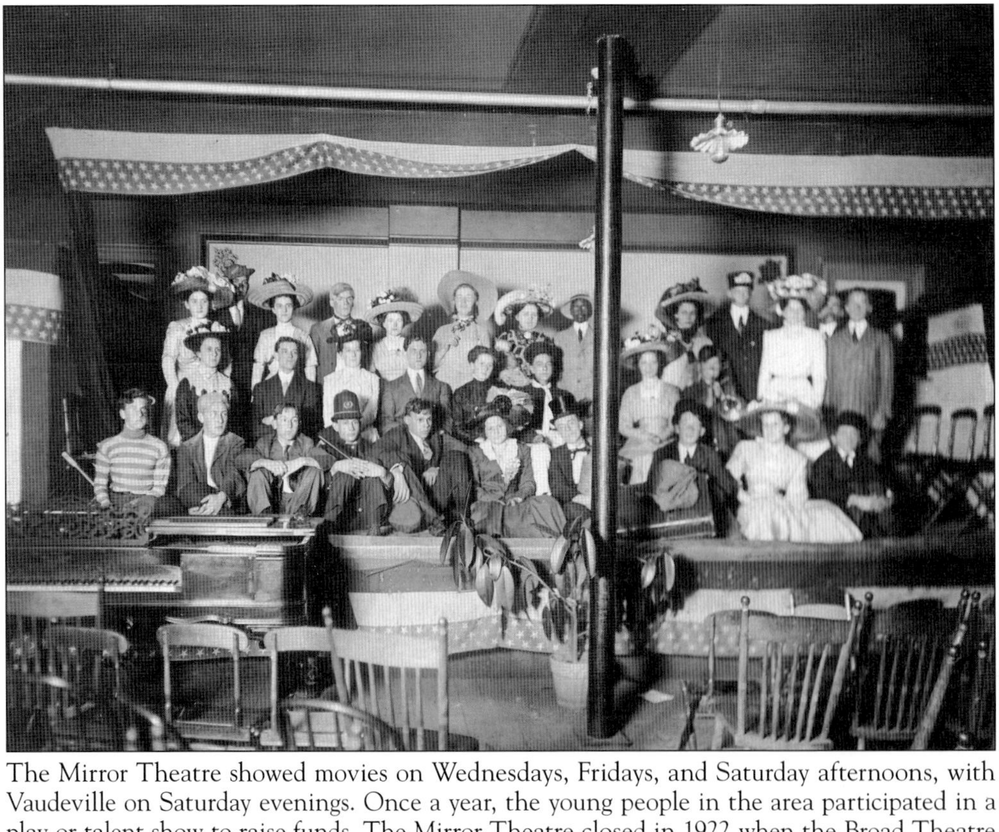

The Mirror Theatre showed movies on Wednesdays, Fridays, and Saturday afternoons, with Vaudeville on Saturday evenings. Once a year, the young people in the area participated in a play or talent show to raise funds. The Mirror Theatre closed in 1922 when the Broad Theatre opened. (Courtesy of Karl Fox.)

Five

An Enterprising Community

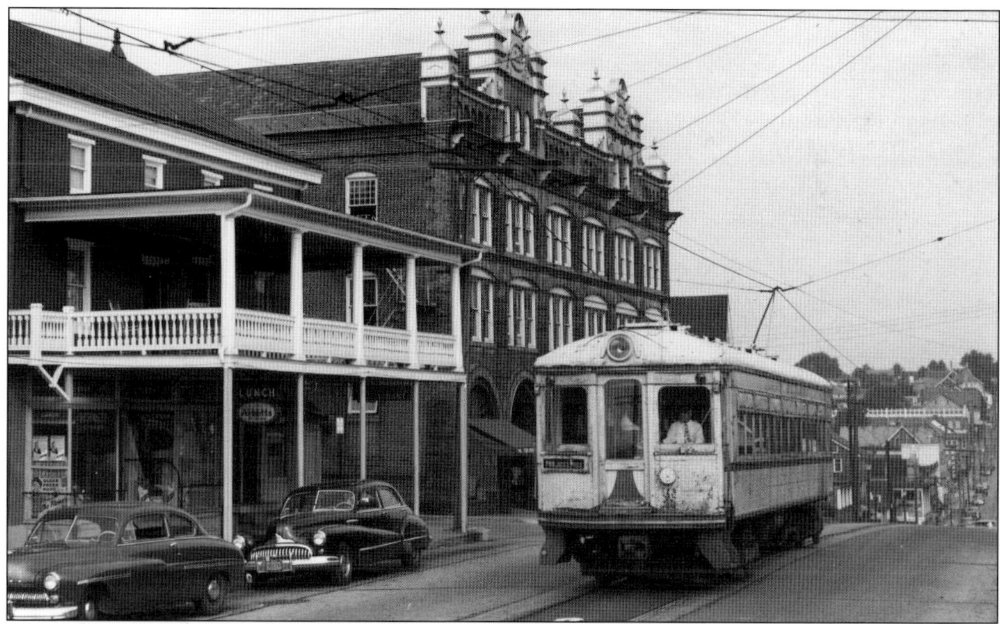

In 1899, the Inland Traction Company began laying its southward trolley line from Perkasie to Lansdale. Completed in 1900, the line ran through Souderton from East Summit Street down Main Street to Broad Street, continuing to Penn Avenue and on to Hatfield. Trolleys now ran from Philadelphia to Allentown. Here, a later 1916 Liberty Bell Limited series 700 car passes in front of the post office and the twin stores. (Courtesy of David Wismer.)

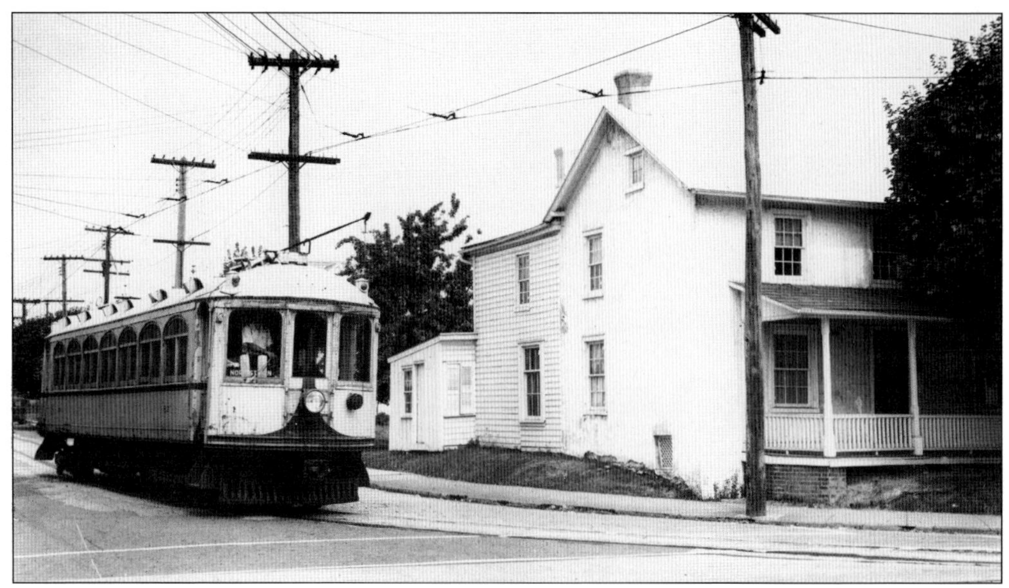

For a brief time, the Inland Traction Company became part of the Philadelphia and Lehigh Valley Traction Company, which reorganized in 1905 as the Lehigh Valley Transit Company. In 1902, a small tripper car, named "Dinky," ran between Souderton and Telford. By 1907, the Allentown to Philadelphia route became known as the "Liberty Bell Route." Here, an 800 series car, built around 1912, is rounding the corner from Summit onto Main Street. (Courtesy of Evelyn Wismer.)

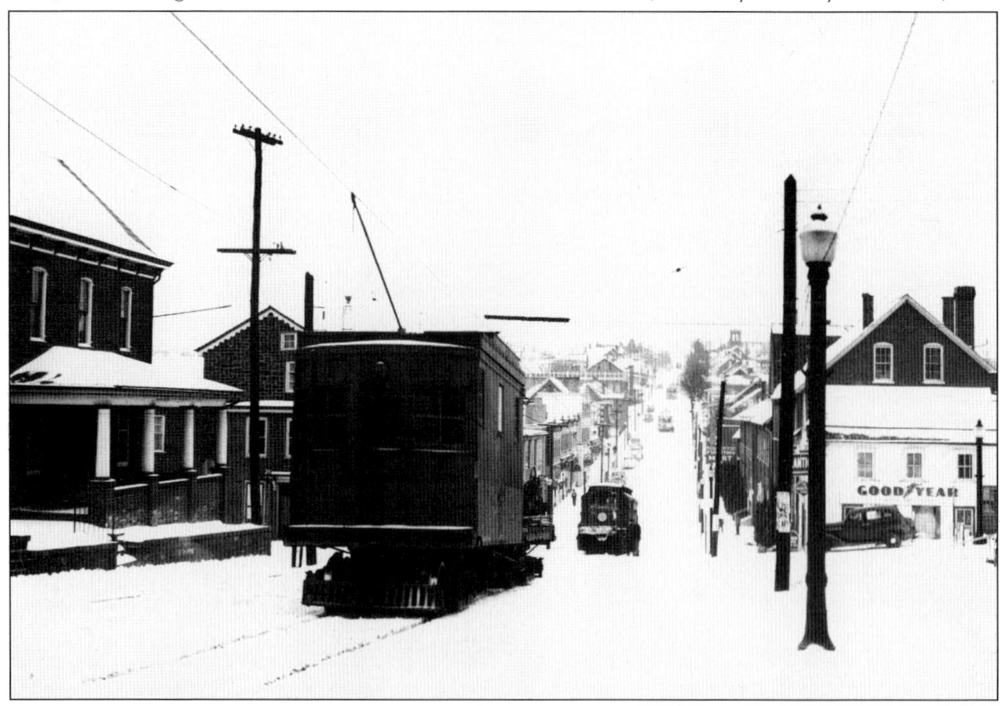

Heading down Main Street into the hollow is a snowplow, approximately five feet in height, attached to the front of a maintenance car, clearing snow from the tracks. A sweeper car with revolving brushes on the underside follows, removing snow before it becomes packed and causes a derailment. (Courtesy of Evelyn Wismer.)

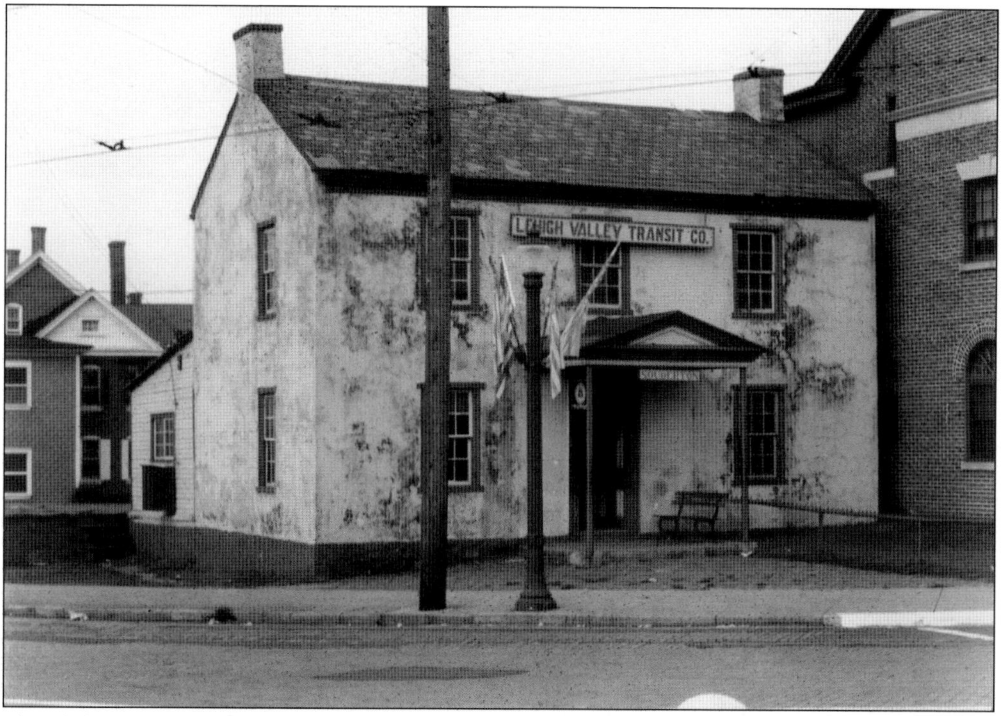

Shortly before the railroad came through in 1857, Henry O. Souder built his second home at the corner of Main and West Broad Streets, photographed around 1900. Later his home became the trolley station for Lehigh Valley Transit with a ticket window and a few benches. (Courtesy of Gloria Brandis.)

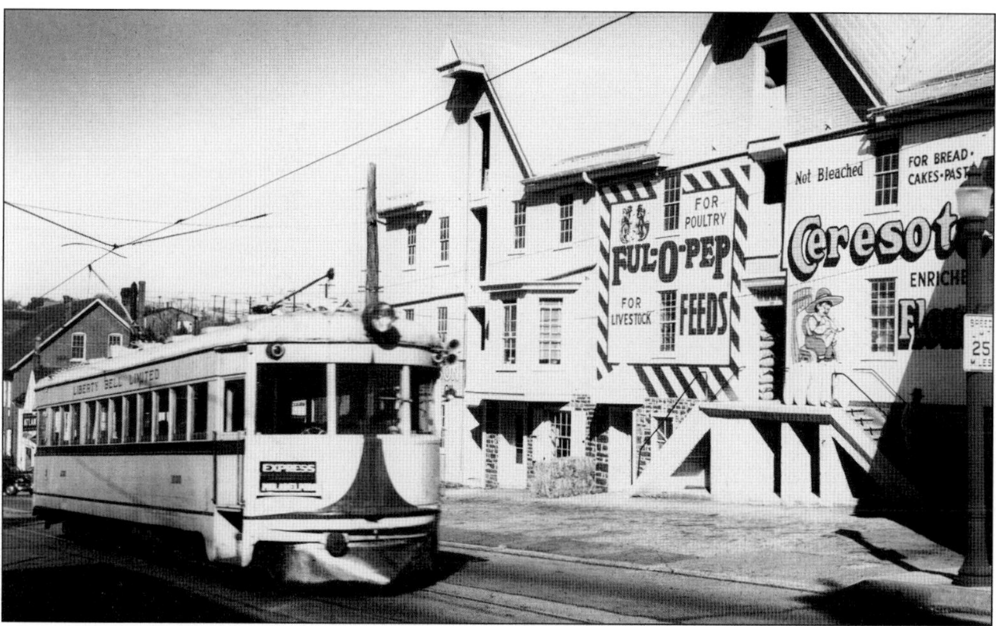

In the 1950s, Moyer & Son advertised its flour, feed, grain, seed, coal, cement, and fuel oils on the front of its mill. A 1000 series car is on its way toward the trolley station. (Courtesy of Evelyn Wismer.)

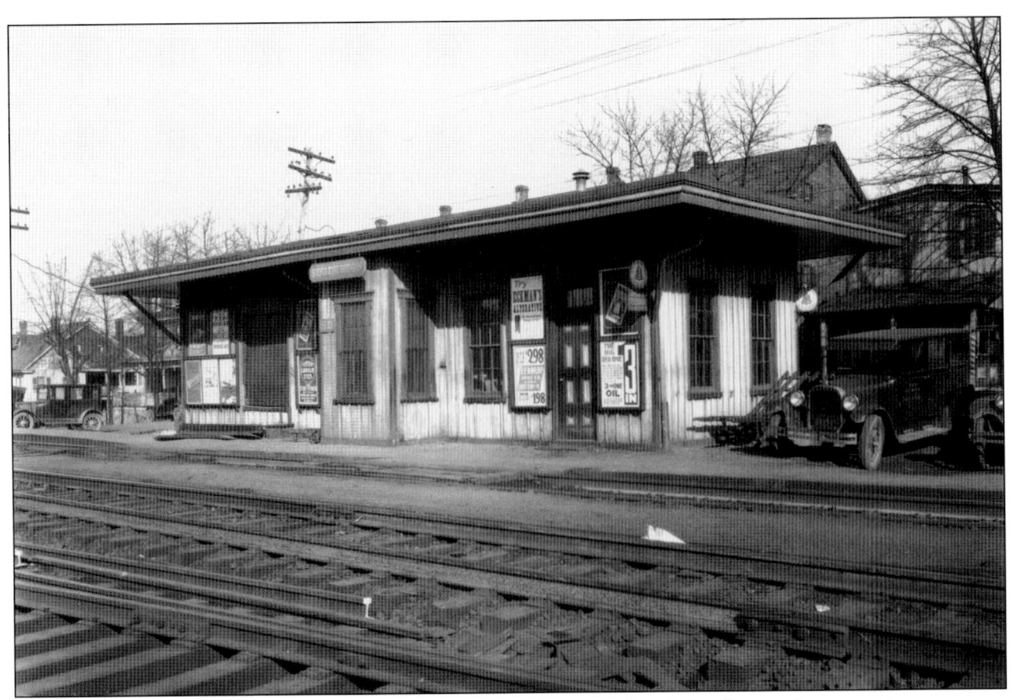

This photograph of the first railway station built along North Front Street was taken shortly before its removal in 1928. The original section of this building was built in 1865. (Courtesy of STMS collection.)

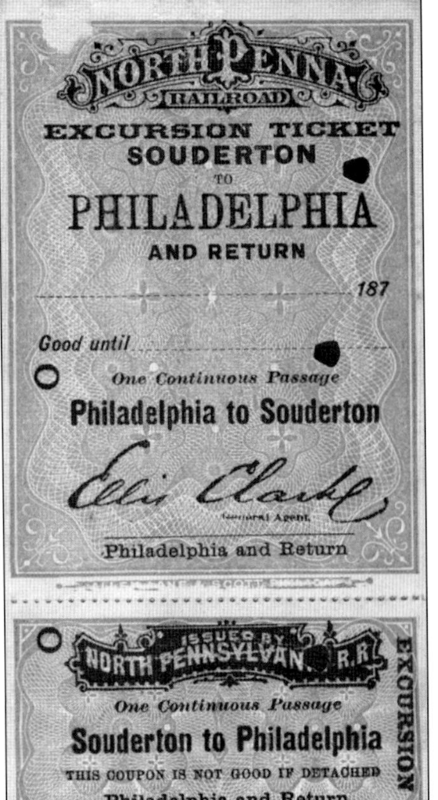

A North Pennsylvania Railroad excursion ticket, like this one, could be bought at the old railway station by passengers traveling between Philadelphia and Souderton. (Courtesy of Kurt Scherzberg.)

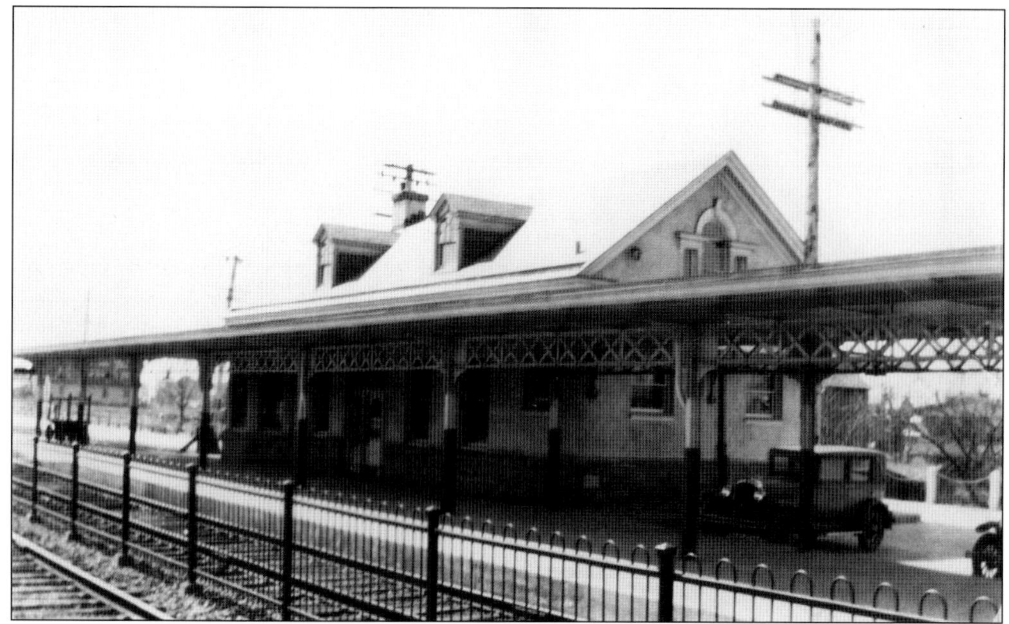

When the Souderton Chamber of Commerce was formed in 1924, the members immediately began encouraging the Reading Railroad Company and the Souderton Borough Council to collaborate on a new railway station and platform, and eliminate the dangerous Broad Street crossing. This new station, located diagonally across Broad Street from the original platform, opened on January 1, 1928. (Courtesy of James Shelly.)

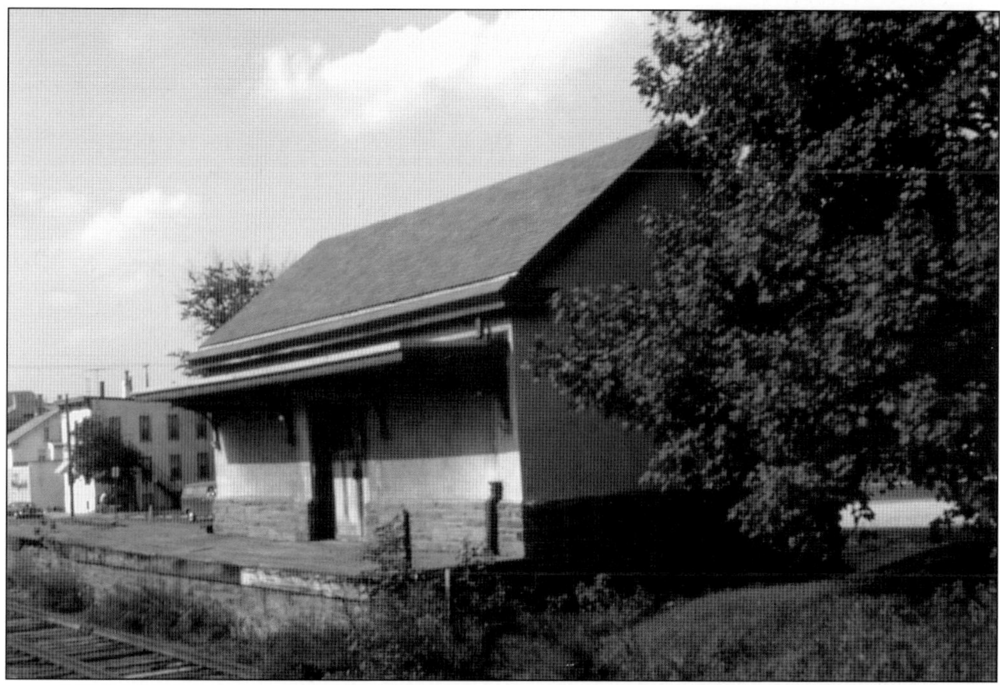

Also in 1928, this new freight station opened, a few hundred feet south and opposite the new rail station. Included on the northbound side was a covered arrival platform. Only a remnant of the platform remains. (Courtesy of Ron Alderfer.)

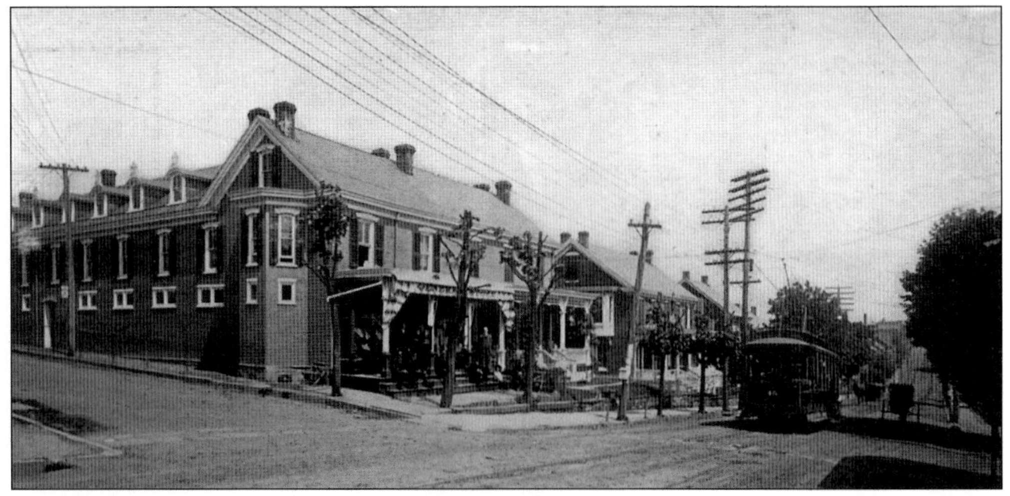

Despite the rapid growth of large supermarkets, distinctive corner markets still existed in the 1980s. In 1882, Jacob G. Leidy and Benjamin D. Alderfer started the Central Store on the corner of Main Street and Central Avenue as a general store. By 1918, Ervin G. Yocum ran it predominantly as a grocery store. An early Inland Traction Company electric trolley moves past the store, sharing the road with horses and buggies. (Courtesy of STMS collection.)

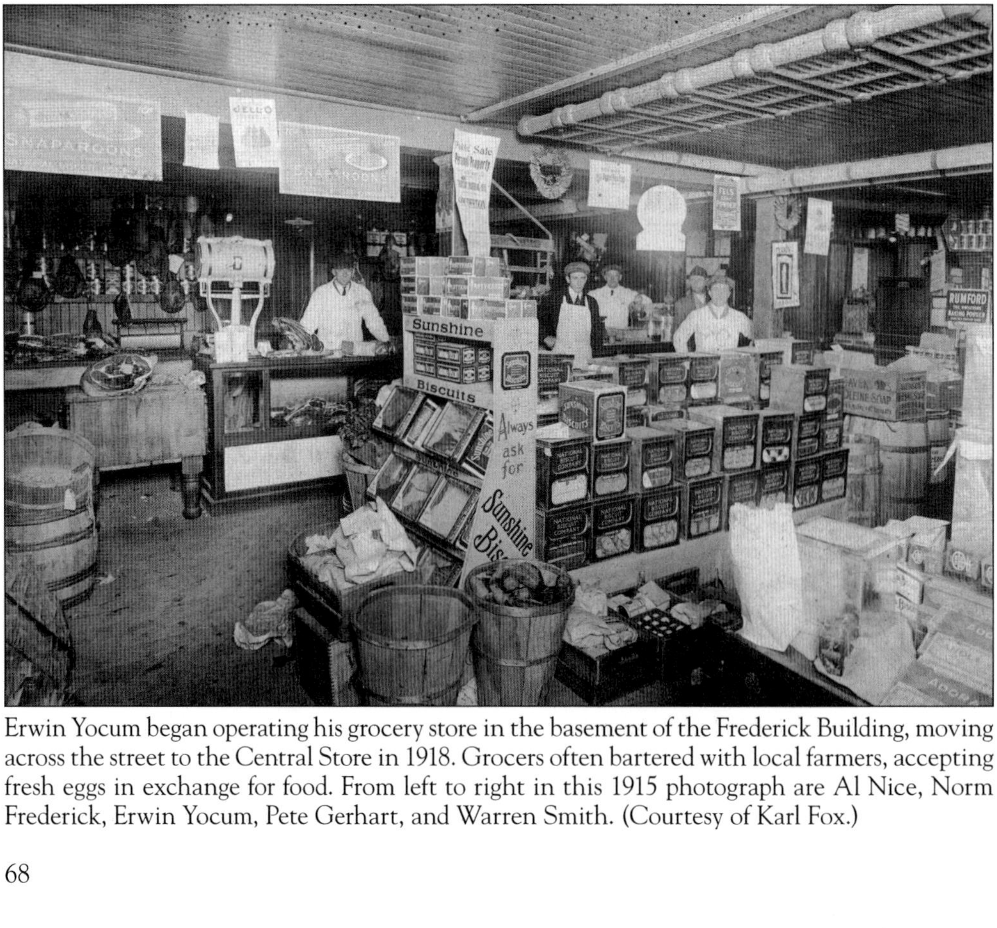

Erwin Yocum began operating his grocery store in the basement of the Frederick Building, moving across the street to the Central Store in 1918. Grocers often bartered with local farmers, accepting fresh eggs in exchange for food. From left to right in this 1915 photograph are Al Nice, Norm Frederick, Erwin Yocum, Pete Gerhart, and Warren Smith. (Courtesy of Karl Fox.)

Milton S. Frederick owned the same grocery store on Main Street three different times, starting in 1895. The last time, Milton partnered with son Norman M. Frederick. If patrons could not pay, their word was all Milton needed to extend credit. Here, Milton advertises Freihofer's Sonny Boy bread. (Courtesy of Brent Conver.)

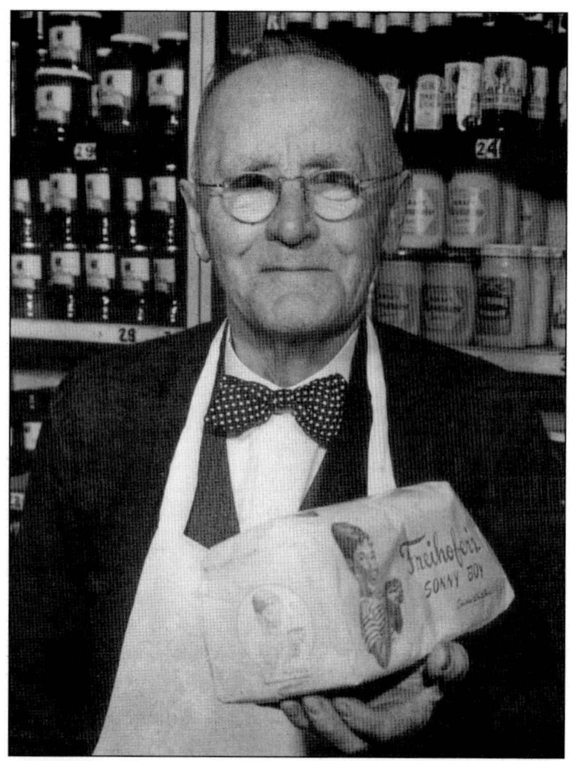

Frederick's Grocery Store was in the basement of this building, which later became Connie's Market, known for its peanut machine and personable third generation owner, Norman Conver. Above the store was Dr. Bunting's pharmacy. On Saturdays, Dr. Bunting always slipped candy into a young shopper's bag, remembering a piece for every child in that family. Eventually, the Towne Answering Service purchased and beautifully restored this well-known building. (Courtesy of Gary Albright.)

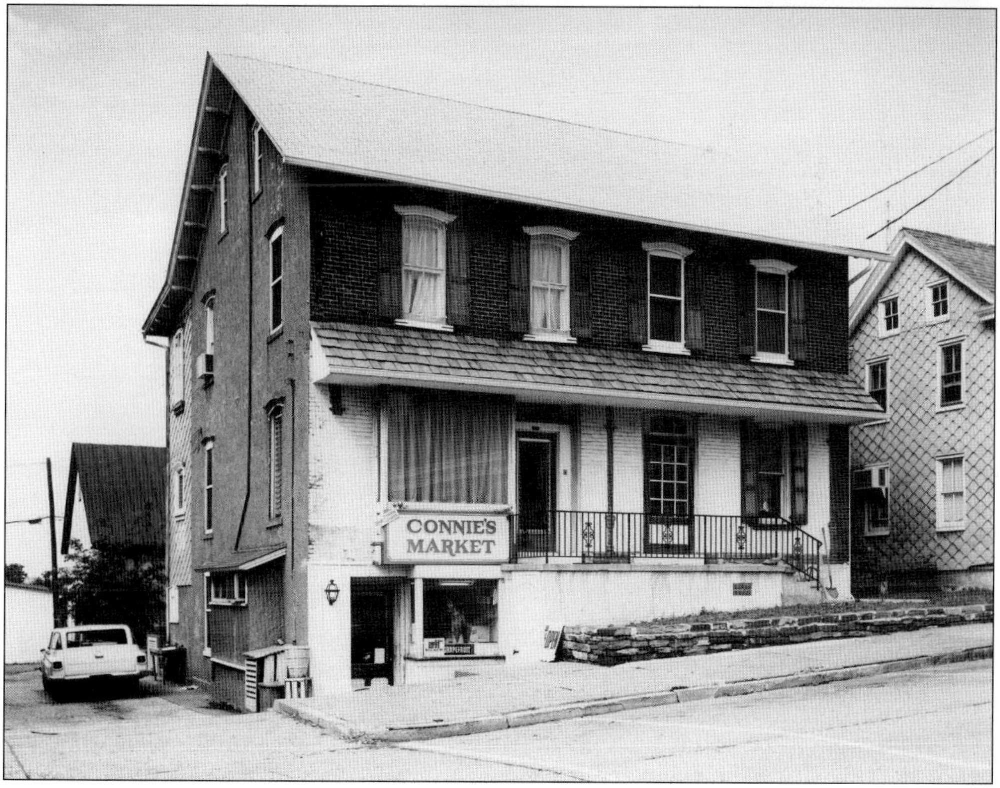

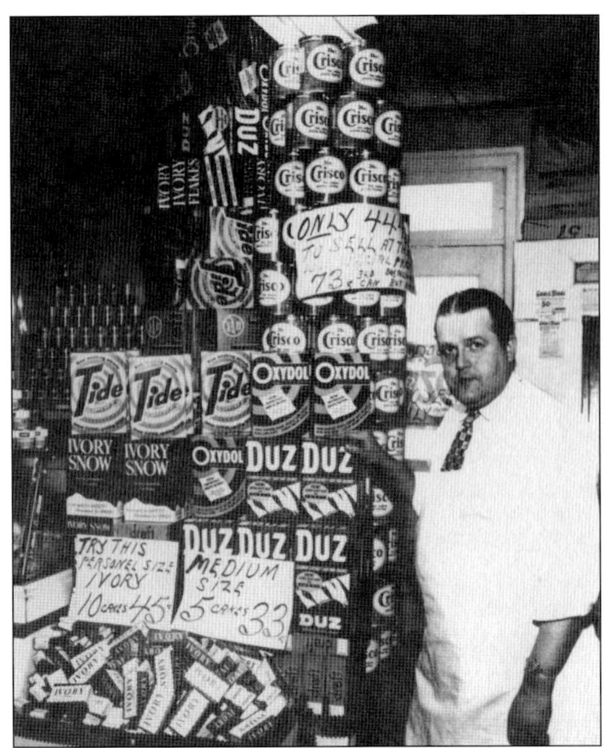

Lawrence Daub, pictured, started Daub's Market in the mid-1930s as a fish market, expanding into a full-service grocery in the 1940s. Despite two later owners, Joe Musselman and Keith Pierce, the store was still known as "Daubies" and remained at its original location on Second Street. (Courtesy of STMS collection.)

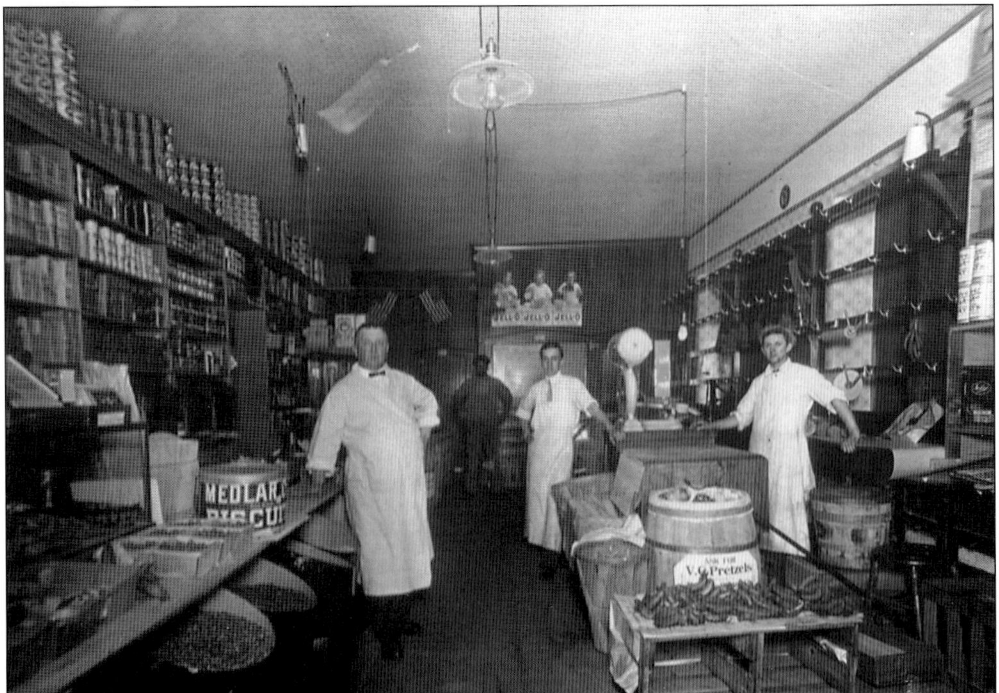

Claude Eck boasted a walk-in refrigerator and roasted peanuts weekly in his West Broad Street and Penn Avenue grocery store, which he bought in 1926. Pictured from left to right are Claude Eck, Henry D. Sell, unidentified, and William D. Sell. (Courtesy of STMS collection.)

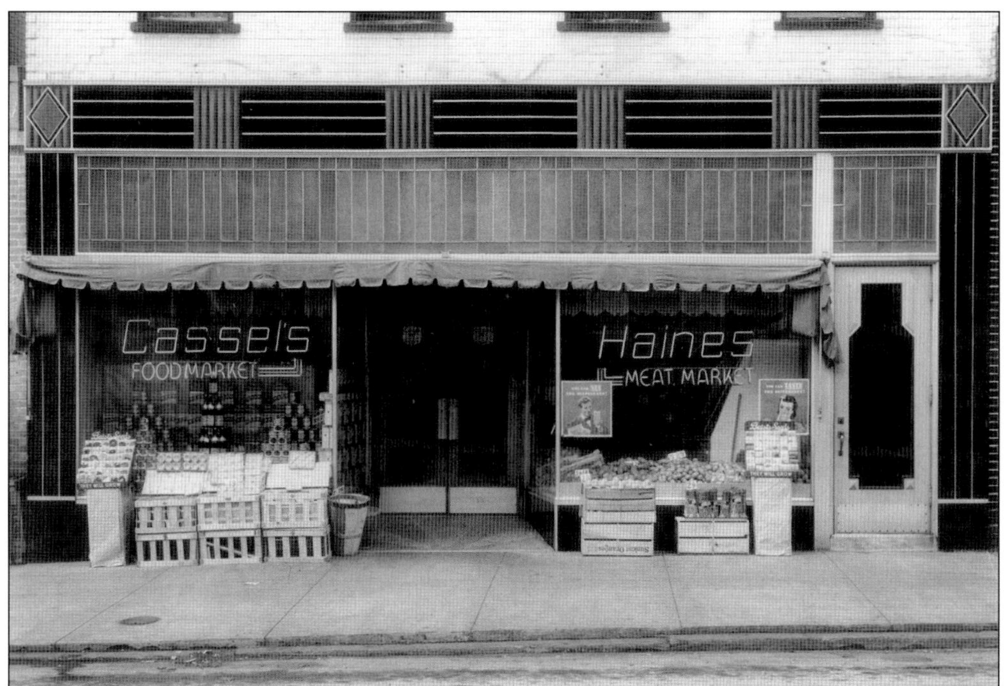

Cassel's Grocery Store opened in Souderton in 1921. Starting in 1935, Norman K. Haines Meat Market and Cassel's Grocery Store occupied the same building on Main Street, seen here. Throughout the 1930s and 1940s, proprietors of complementary services often shared space in the same building. (Courtesy of Mennonite Heritage Center.)

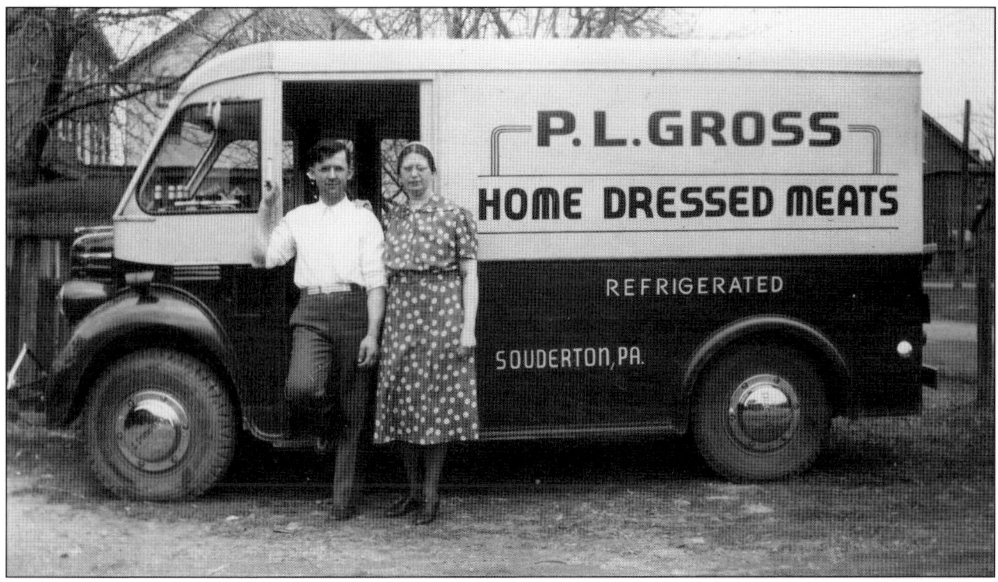

When butcher Norman K. Haines vacated Cassel's Grocery Store, Phares L. Gross and wife, Kathryn H. Gross, set up shop. Phares and Kathryn Gross lived on Cherry Lane where they would butcher their livestock and transport their "Home Dressed Meats" in a refrigerated delivery truck to sell at their Main Street store. (Courtesy of D. Jeffrey Gross.)

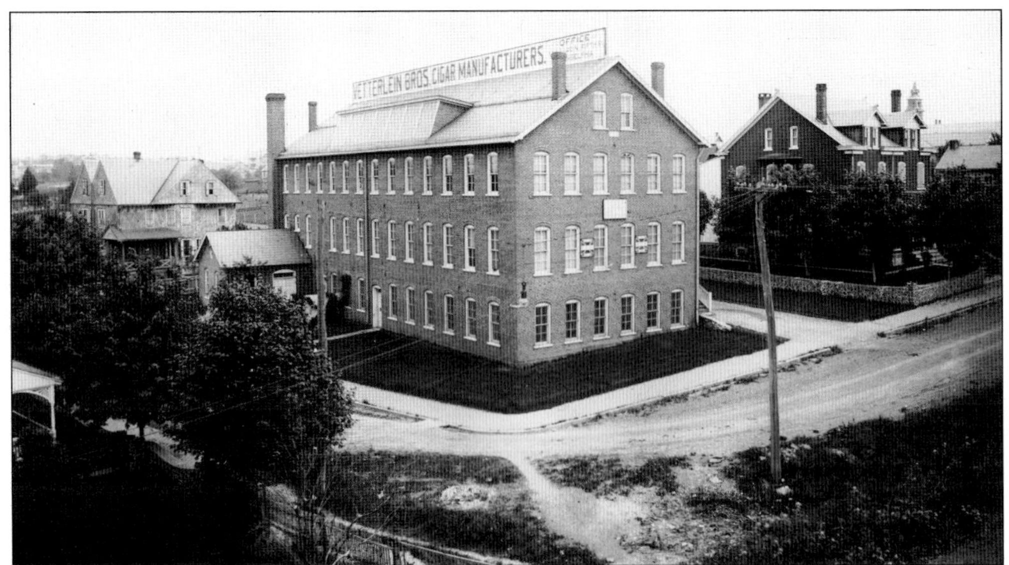

In 1895, the Vetterlein brothers moved their cigar factory from Main Street to Front and Water Streets, suspending operations in 1913. J. Schoeneman opened a clothing factory in the Vetterlein Building, and after 1920, the Hemsing Manufacturing Company built fine furniture there. By the time Clemmer Moving and Storage finally occupied it, the rope elevator that needed the strength of three men to operate challenged employees daily. (Courtesy of Phil Ruth.)

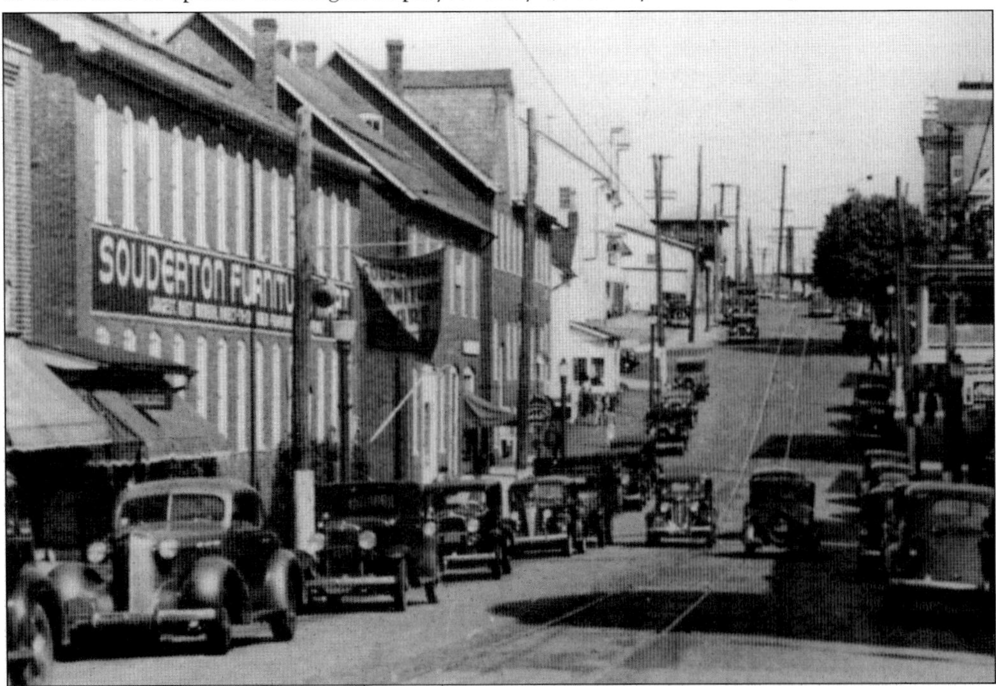

In 1899, Theobald and Oppenheimer opened a cigar factory in this Main Street building, photographed in 1937. After the manufacturing of cigars was discontinued in 1914, several owners took possession of the building, each bringing another new and successful business to Souderton. At one time, the building had been used as a towel factory. Later the well-known Souderton Furniture Mart occupied the space. (Courtesy of Souderton Family Restaurant.)

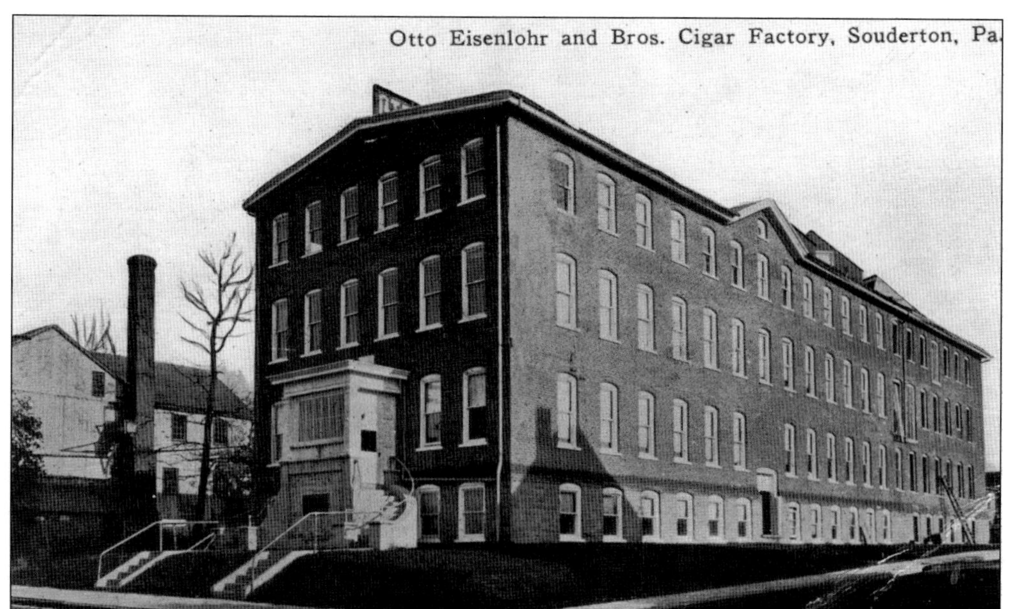

In 1907, Otto Eisenlohr built the largest of all the cigar factories at Chestnut Street and Penn Avenue, discontinuing in 1921. J. Schoeneman, clothing manufacturer, occupied this building from 1922 to 1924. After Clemmer Moving and Storage vacated the Vetterlein Building, they gratefully occupied this space, appreciating its electric elevator. It became the Ferris Shoe Manufacturing Co., Peerless Footwear, and Fox Bindery. This building has since been razed. (Courtesy of STMS collection.)

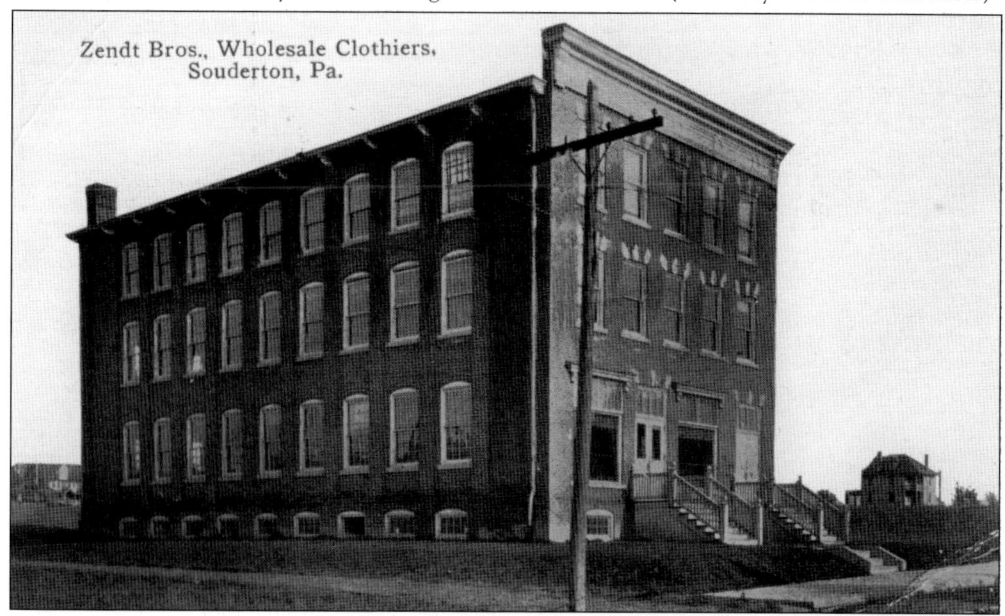

As cigar manufacturing moved south, textiles eventually became the dominant industry in Souderton. The Zendt brothers, Penrose, George, and Norman, opened a clothing factory, operating from the post office building in 1893. In 1910, they built this factory on Penn Avenue, which later became home to Markey Paper and Packaging, Inc. In 1927, the Zendt brothers operated their factory in conjunction with the Biberman brothers' dress factory on Washington Avenue. (Courtesy of Kurt Scherzberg.)

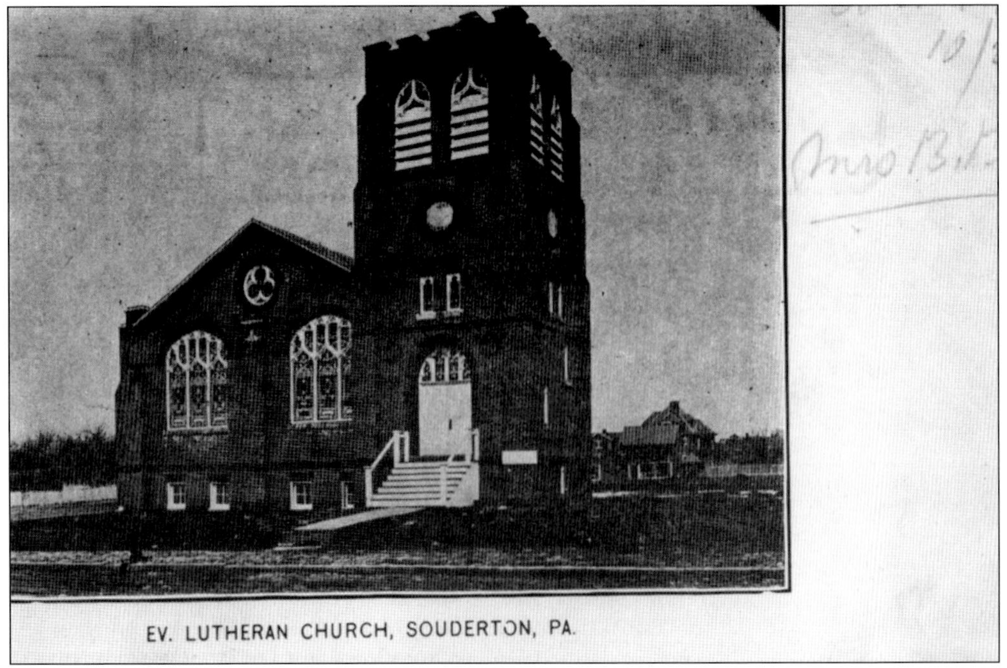

In 1894, Lutheran members of Immanuel Leidy's Church started a Mission League, holding services in the Strasser Building on Main Street. Jonas M. Landis, of J.M. Landis & Co., donated two lots on West Broad Street for the erection of Emmanuel Lutheran Church, shown here at its dedication in 1904. In 1926, a new church and Sunday school were built. The cemetery at Leidy's is still jointly owned. (Courtesy of Gloria Brandis.)

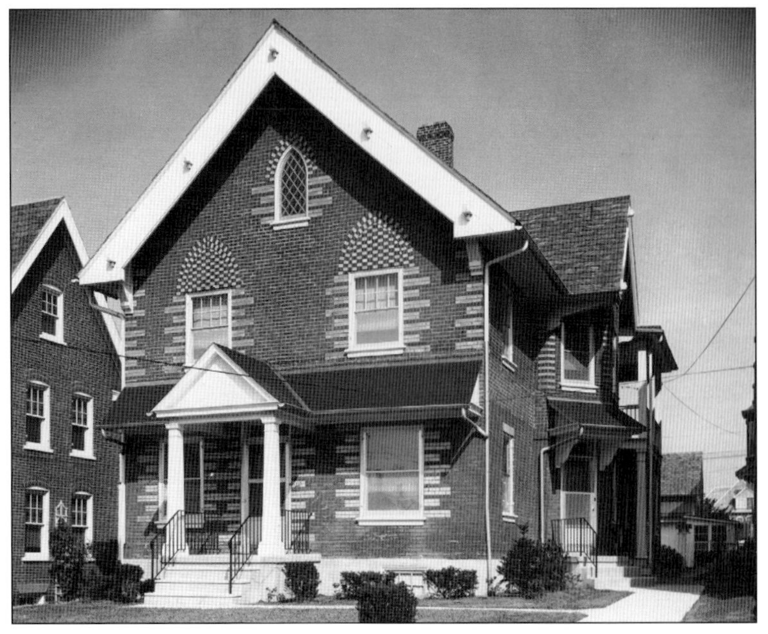

In 1921, this unique and beautiful parsonage was built and donated to Emmanuel Lutheran Church by Jonas M. Landis, part owner of J.M. Landis & Co. Today, it still stands to the left of the church on West Broad Street. (Courtesy of Gary Albright.)

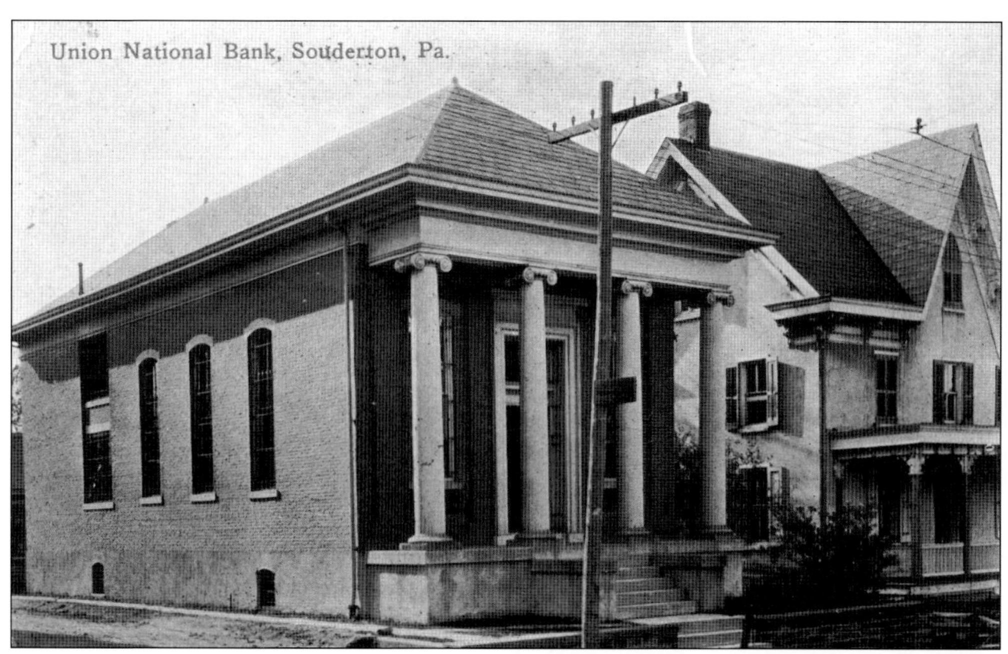

To keep up with the changing times, Souderton's first bank, the Union National Bank of Souderton, located on Main Street, received a face-lift. In 1909, the bank was expanded and given a more modern facade. In 1928, the name was changed to Union National Bank and Trust Company. (Courtesy of James Shelly.)

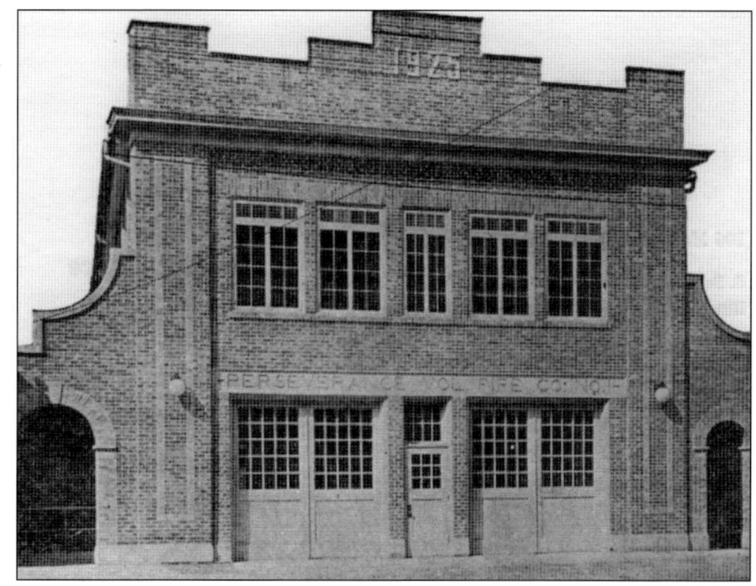

The Perseverance Fire Company No. 1, originally located in Souderton Borough Hall, moved to its new building across Main Street in 1925. Firemen supplied most of the labor during its construction. In 1947, a single overhead door was added, and the second floor was converted into a banquet and meeting room. (Courtesy of Perseverance Fire Company.)

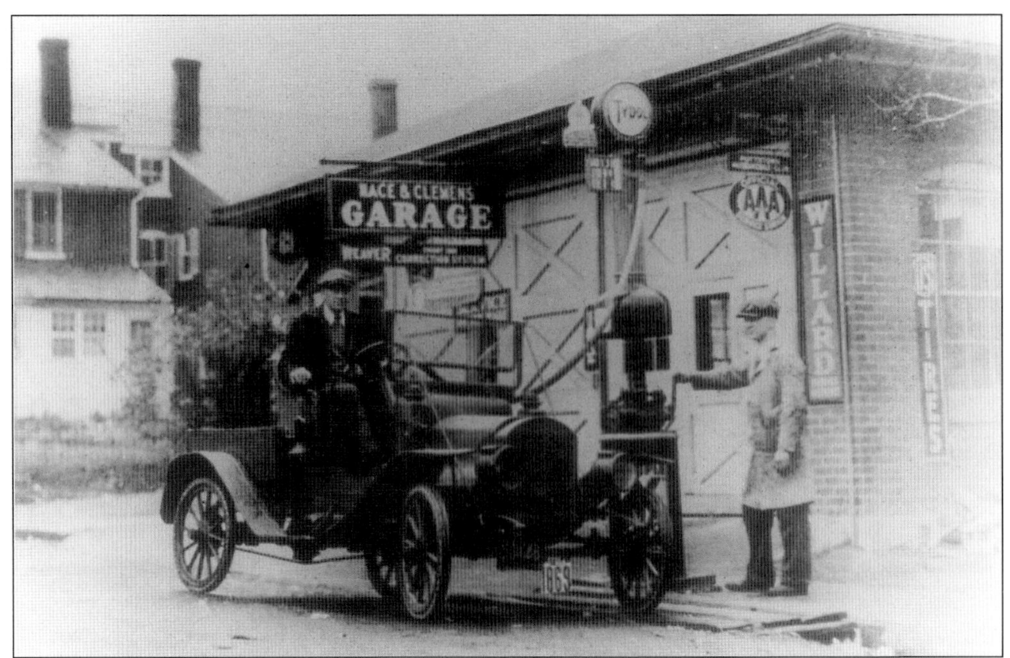

The Nace & Clemens garage on Third and Broad Streets pumped Tydol gas, which was sold on the East Coast. A visible gas pump allowed the customer to see how much clean gas he was getting. It was pumped manually out of the ground into the cylinder and would flow by gravity down the hose and into the car. (Courtesy of John Derstine.)

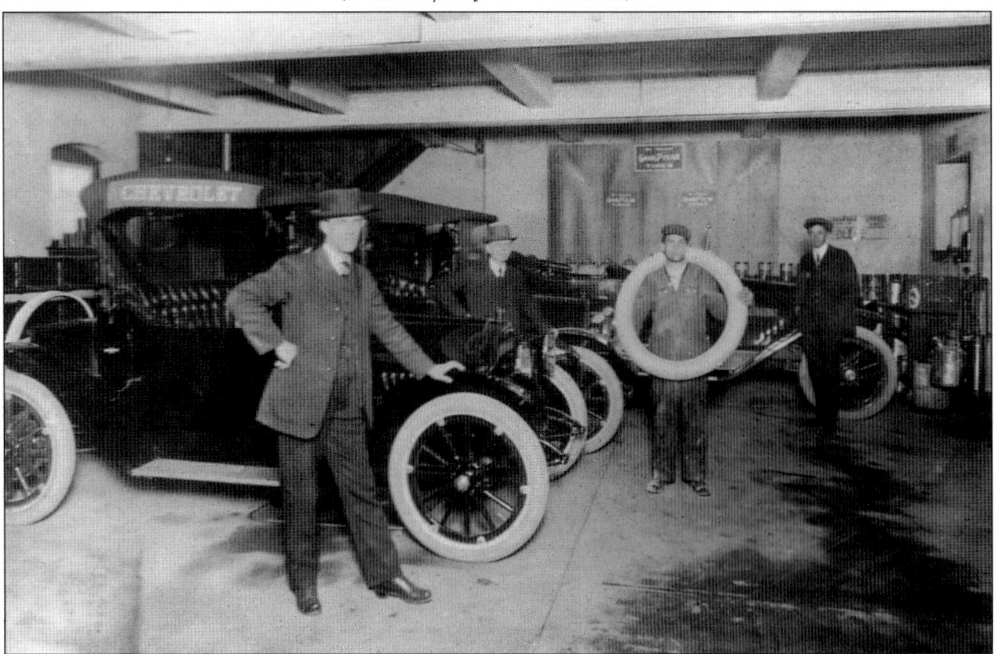

Elwood H. Stover, pictured here with a tire around his neck, opened the first garage and auto repair shop in town in 1911 on Chestnut Street. He sold it to the Cressman Motor Company, which expanded the business, adding a sales room, a used car building, and, eventually, gas pumps. (Courtesy of STMS collection.)

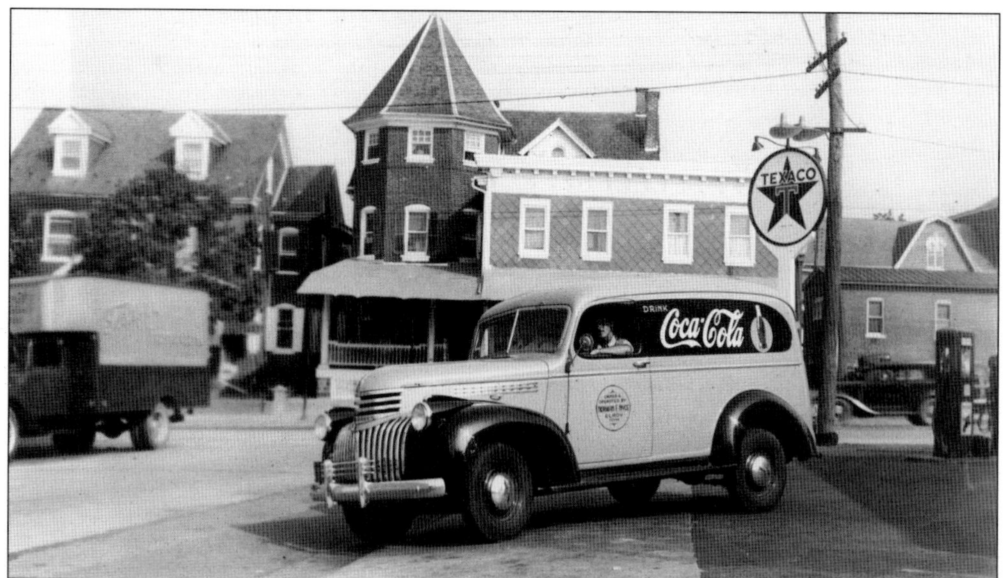

A Norman E. Nyce Coca-Cola distributor truck from nearby Elroy, Pennsylvania, is pulling out of the Texaco station on the corner of Washington Avenue and West Broad Street. Later, an outdoor fountain was installed on this corner, and the Union National Bank, now Univest, added a drive-up window for convenient customer service. (Courtesy of Del Muse.)

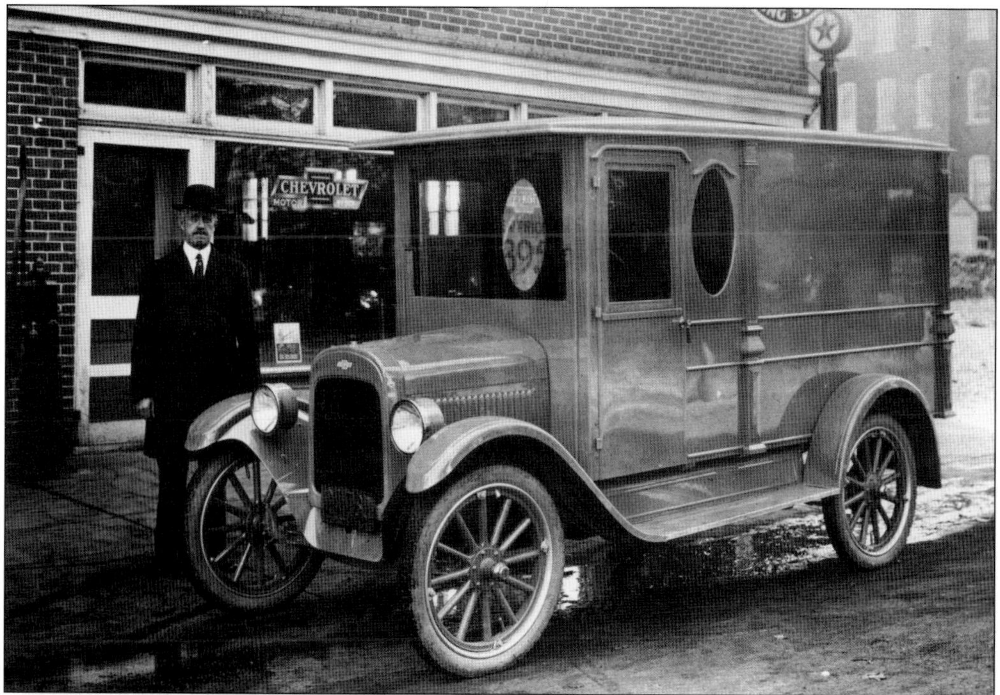

In 1894, the Hillside Cemetery on Hillside Avenue, one of the few public cemeteries in the area, opened. Pictured is an early automobile hearse with an unidentified undertaker outside the Cressman Motor Company. It was known that if a child died during the school year, his school desk and chair were draped in black for the rest of the year as a constant sad reminder of the child's passing. (Courtesy of Gary Albright.)

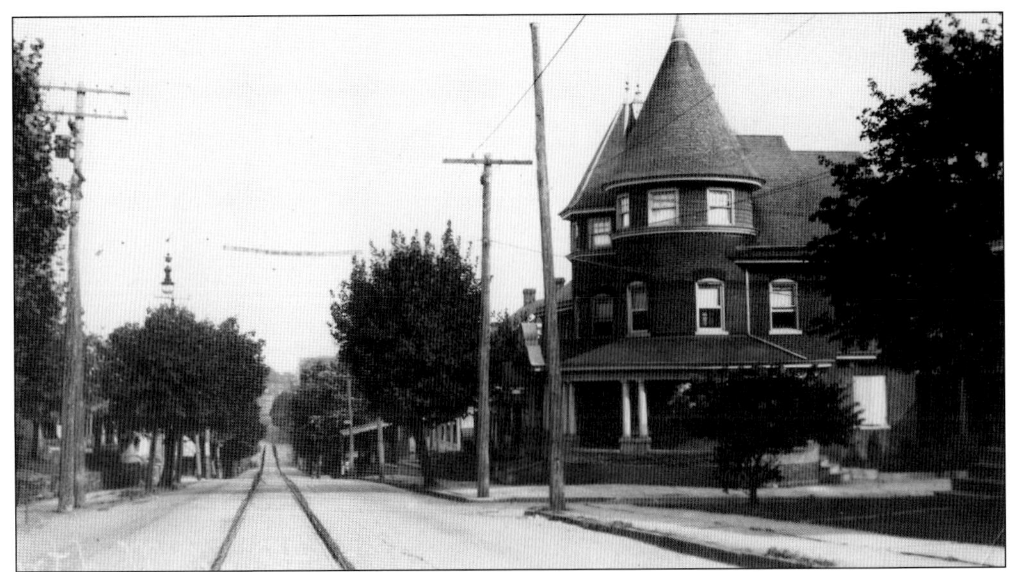

Wesley J. Moyer began his undertaking business in 1921. Later, his son Robert joined him, both being graduates of the Eckles School of Embalming in Philadelphia. Robert opened his funeral home on Main Street in the former mansion of cheese factory owner Theodore Holly. (Courtesy of Kurt Scherzberg.)

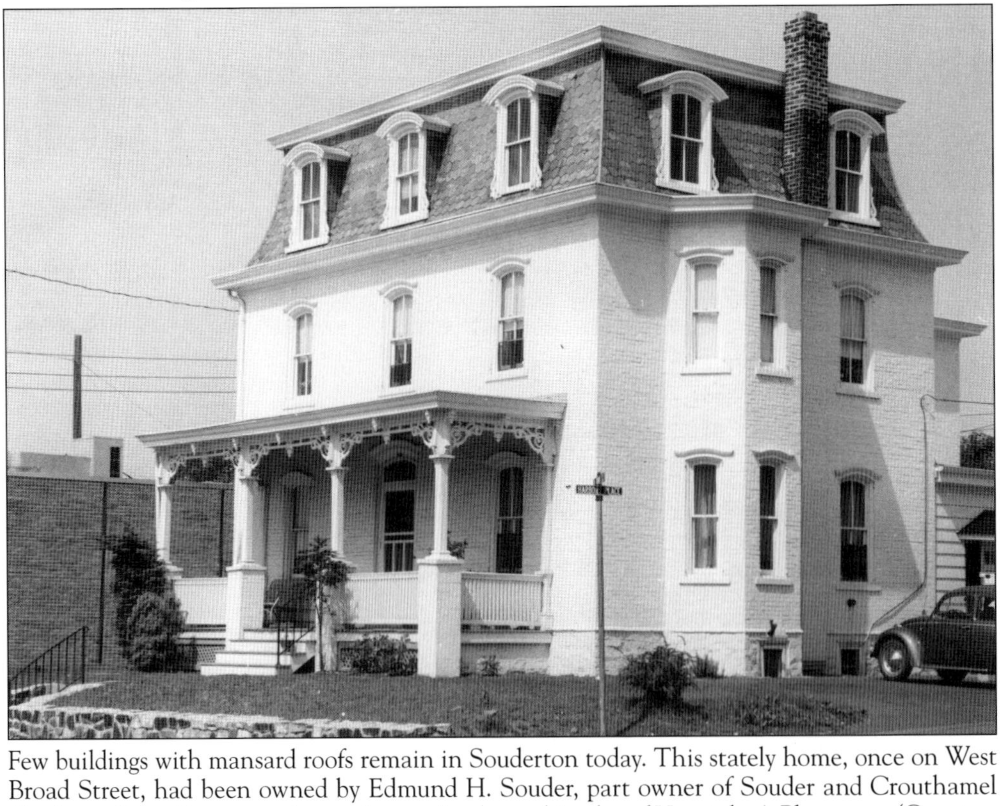

Few buildings with mansard roofs remain in Souderton today. This stately home, once on West Broad Street, had been owned by Edmund H. Souder, part owner of Souder and Crouthamel Hardware Store. It was razed to make way for the parking lot of Hunsicker's Pharmacy. (Courtesy of Gary Albright.)

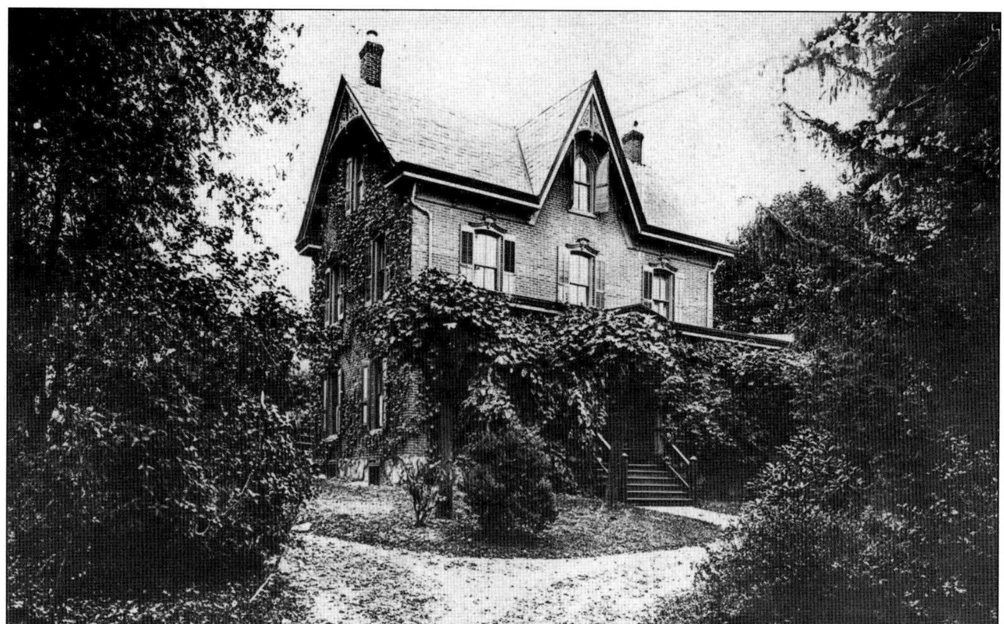
William B. Slifer, Henry O. Souder's son-in-law, built this home at Cherry Lane and Front Street. Painted four shades of brown, the estate boasted a dumbwaiter in the house and a carriage elevator in the barn. In a business venture with Daniel, a supposedly trusted brother, William was grievously robbed in 1885 and lost all. Eventually, the house became the parsonage of Zion Mennonite Church. Only the barn remains. (Courtesy of Gloria Brandis.)

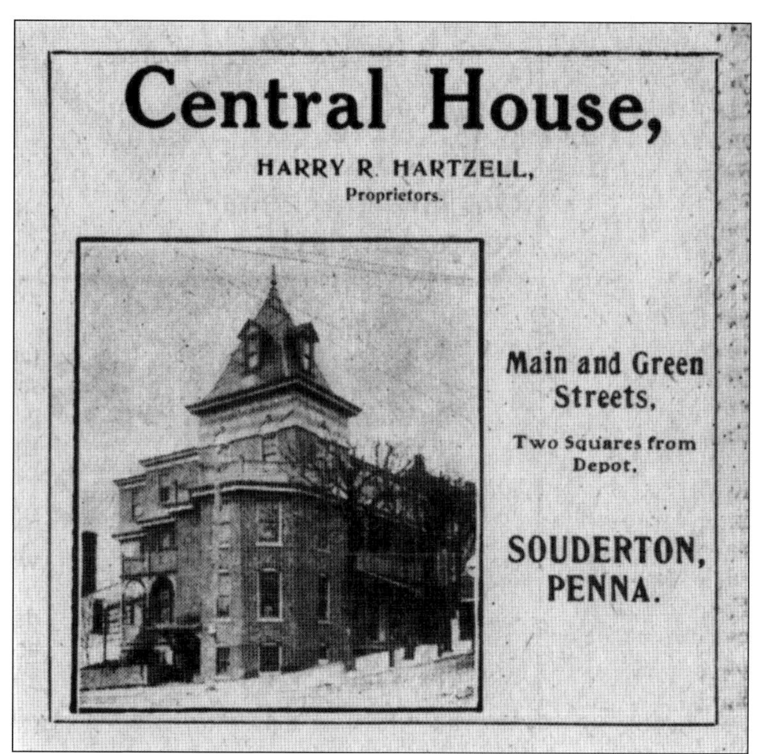

Over the years, renovations to the Central House at Main and Green Streets created quite an impressive building. In 1905, Harry R. Hartzell bought the establishment, conducting an extensive livestock trade in connection with the hotel. Taxi service ran from the train station, and the trolley passed by. At various times, a meat store, livery, wheelwright, and even a dentist shared this space. (Courtesy of Gary Albright.)

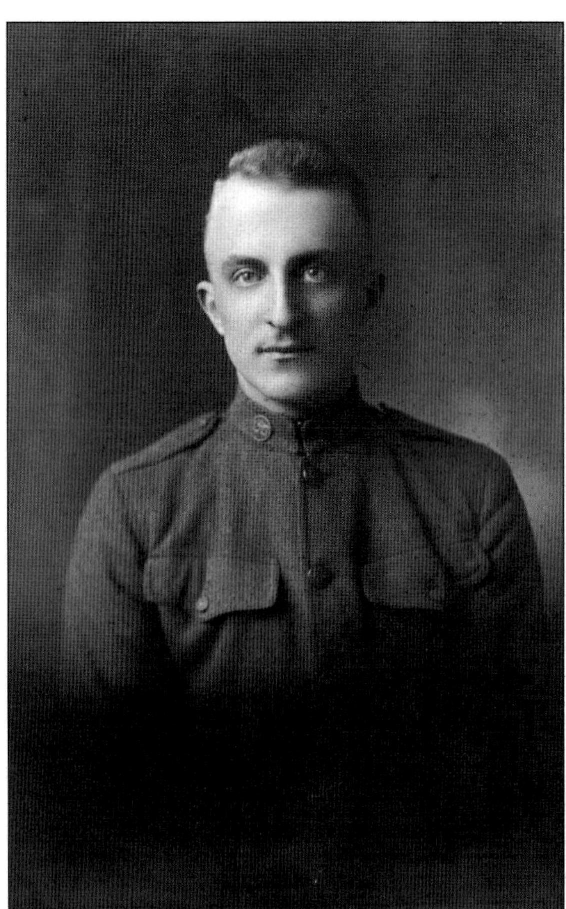

Souderton men and women have served in all of the wars, both on the battlefield and in alternative services for conscientious objectors. John Carroll Souder served in World War I. (Courtesy of Susan Long.)

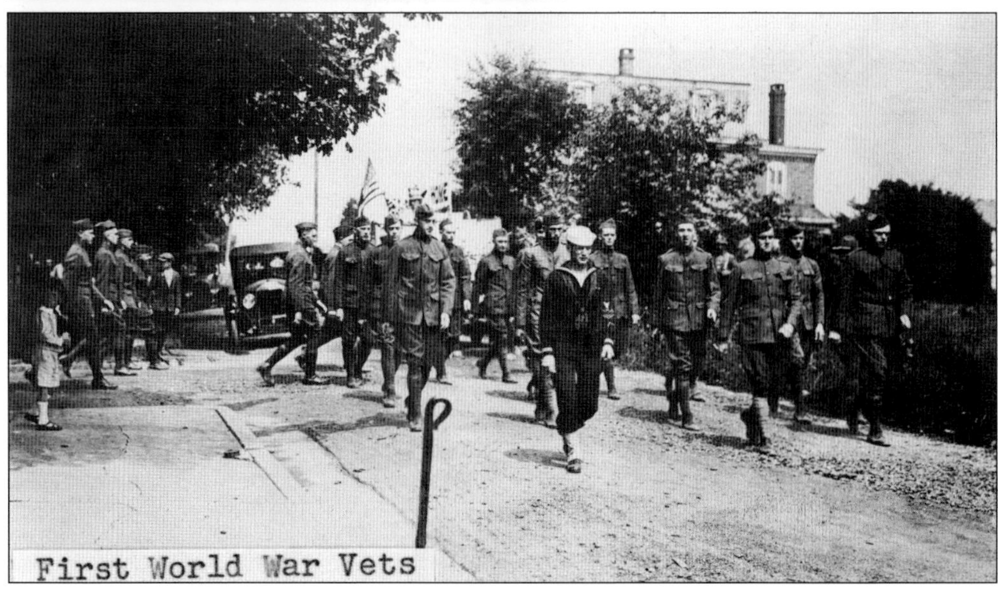

In 1919, when all the men and women had returned from World War I, Souderton held a grand parade to welcome them home. (Courtesy of STMS collection.)

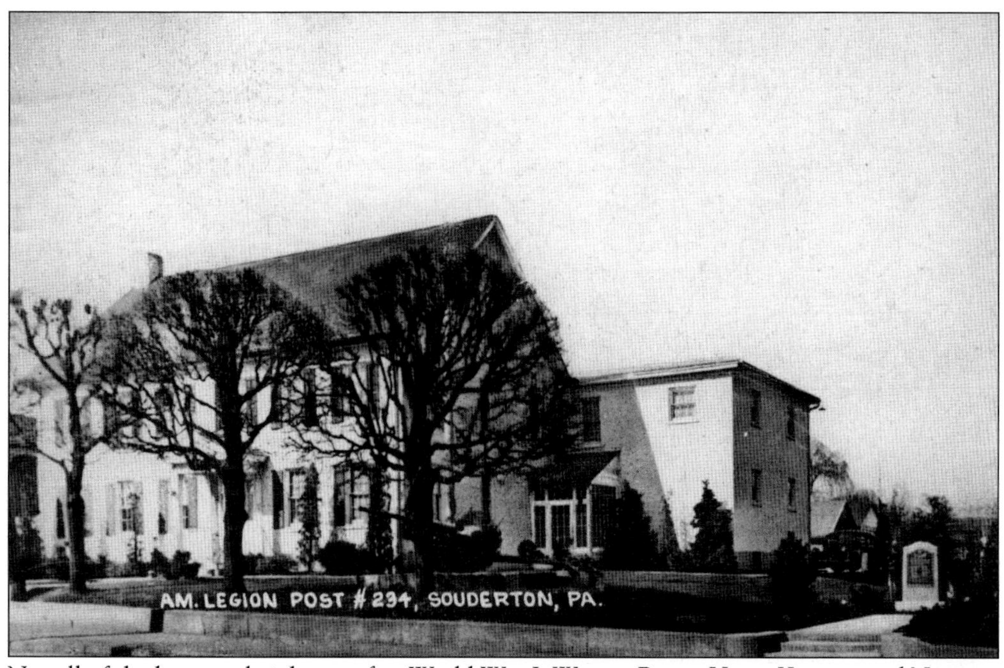

Not all of the boys made it home after World War I. Warren Royer, Harry Kramer, and Norman Egolf were all killed in action. The Warren Royer Post No. 234 American Legion began in the borough hall in 1919 and moved to its present location on Main Street in 1940. The members of the American Legion promote the welfare of the community and contribute to its well-being, always remembering their fallen comrades. (Courtesy of Kurt Scherzberg.)

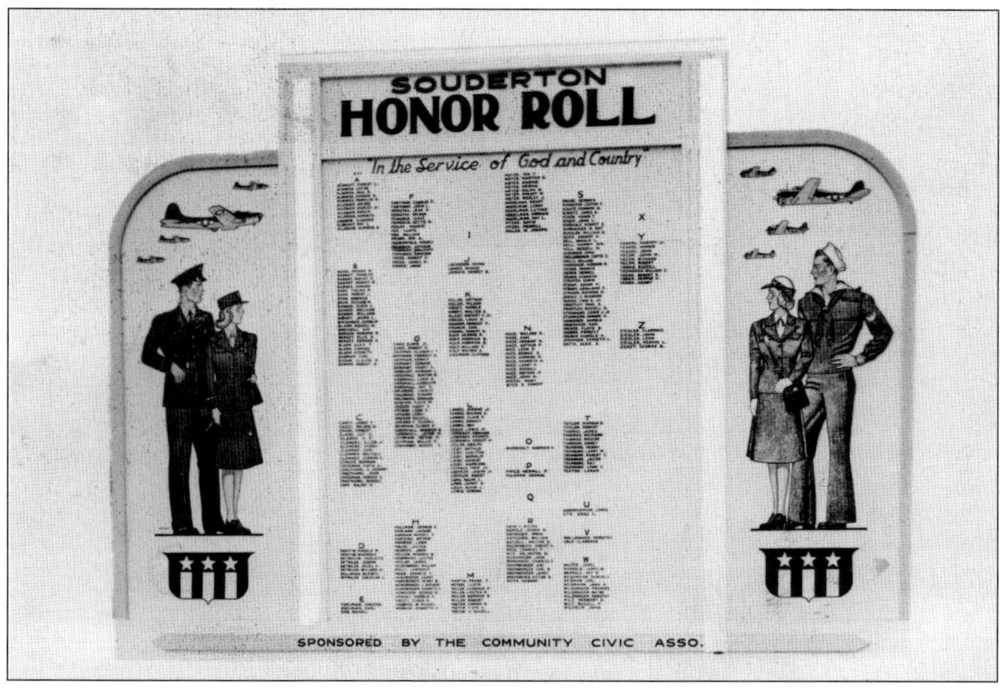

The World War II Souderton Honor Roll, sponsored by the Community Civic Association, alphabetically listed all those who served. (Courtesy of Kurt Scherzberg.)

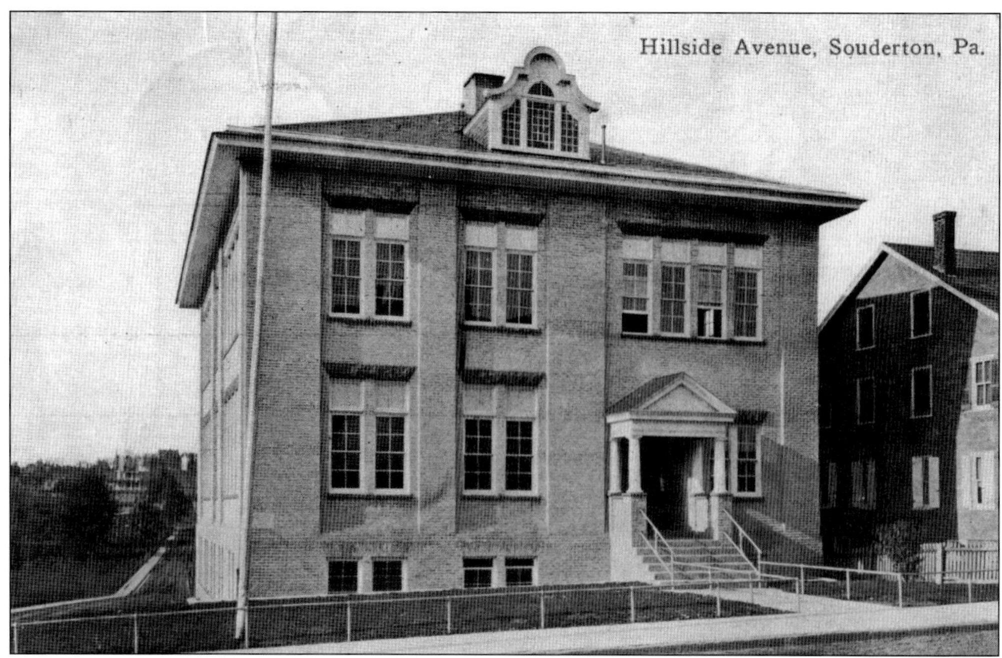

Incorrectly noted as Hillside Avenue in the photograph, the first high school was built in 1911 on Chestnut Street. This "modern" building featured efficient ventilation and excellent lighting. The water in the fountain was cooled by passing over coils in an ice box. By 1914, high school had gradually increased from two to four years, though many Souderton children left school after the eighth grade. Razed in the 1960s, the site is now a park. (Courtesy of James Shelly.)

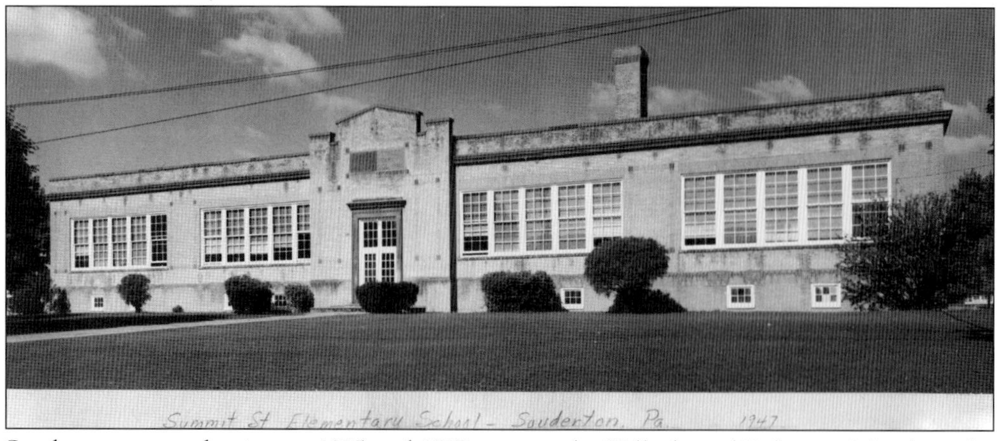

Souderton annexed twice, in 1915 and 1917, putting the Hillside and Reliance Schools under the jurisdiction of the Souderton School Board. In 1921, the Summit Street Elementary School, shown here, opened, and the Hillside and Reliance Schools were closed. In 1982, this school was closed due to declining enrollment. It was sold, renovated, and became the Souderton Borough Hall. (Courtesy of Gary Albright.)

Six

A Bright Future

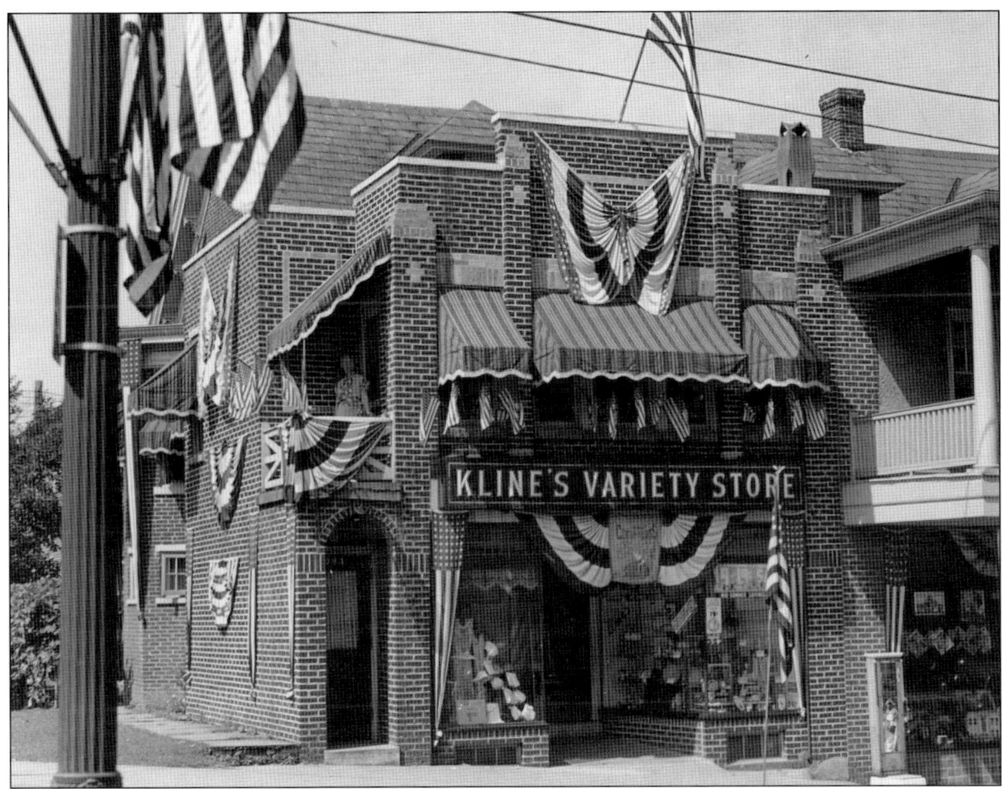

In 1927, R.W. Kline purchased the old Hemsing homestead on Main Street and remodeled it into a five-and-dime, known as Kline's Variety Store. Here, a child could happily spend his allowance on a game of jacks, rubber ball, or a Big Little Book. In 1934, the store was enlarged to accommodate a corsetiere, a tailor who made women's corsets. (Courtesy of STMS collection.)

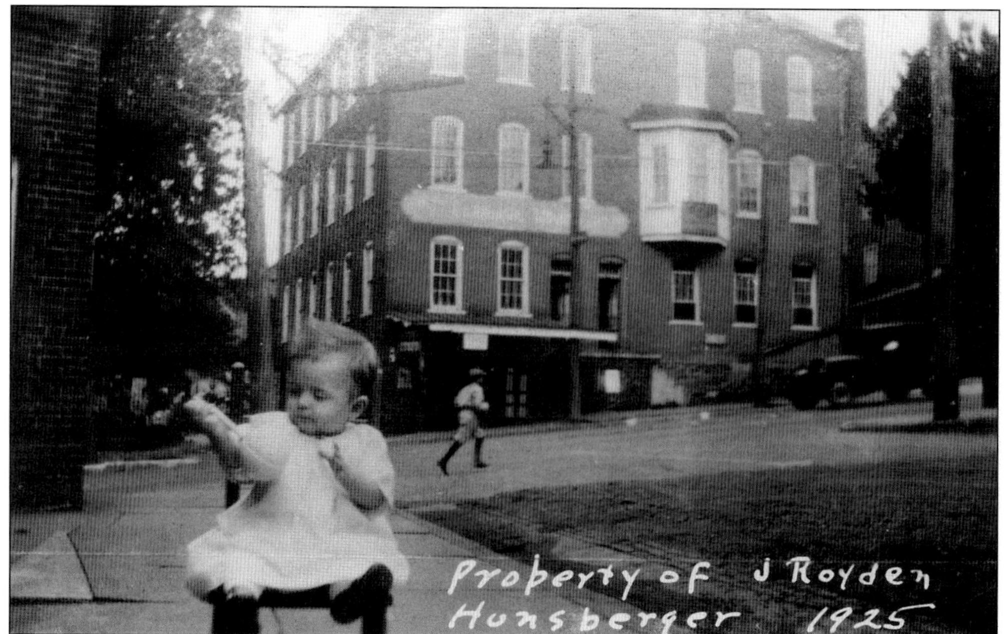

In 1892, a spark from a passing locomotive ignited a fire that took E.W. Strasser's establishments. He then erected the large three-story building, pictured in the distance, at the same site on Main Street where he continued his carriage building trade and blacksmithing. He rented space for a grocery store, first to John Springer, then to C.S. Freed, and space for a harness shop to Daniel L. Gehman. (Courtesy of Ron Landis.)

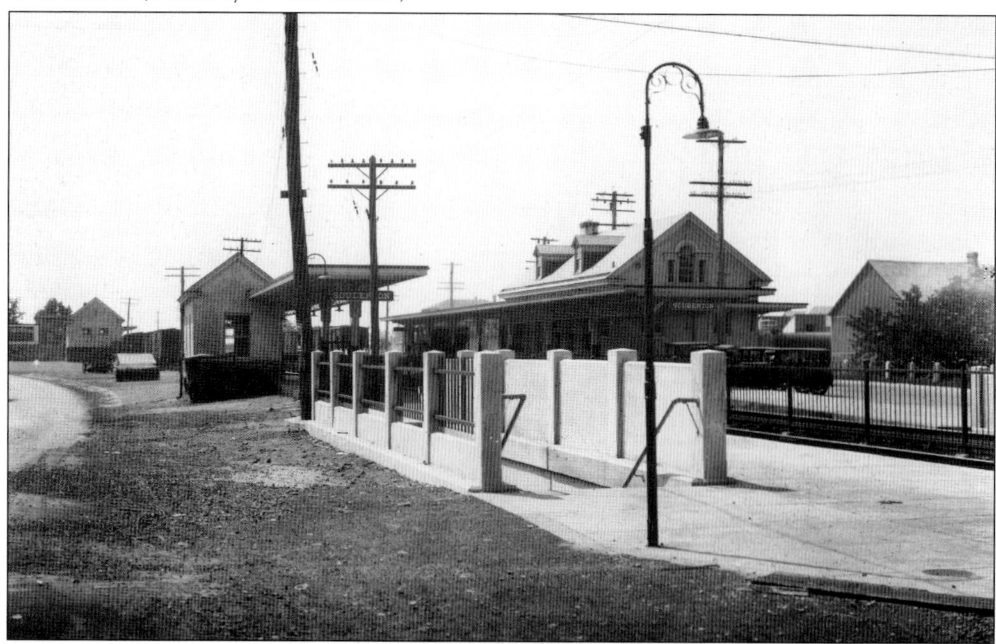

With an average of 51 trains passing through Souderton each day, a number of accidents and fatalities occurred, resulting in the closing of the Broad Street crossing. In 1928, a pedestrian underpass, called the foot tunnel, was built, which crossed underneath the tracks and was illuminated by three electric lights. (Courtesy of Harold Yocum.)

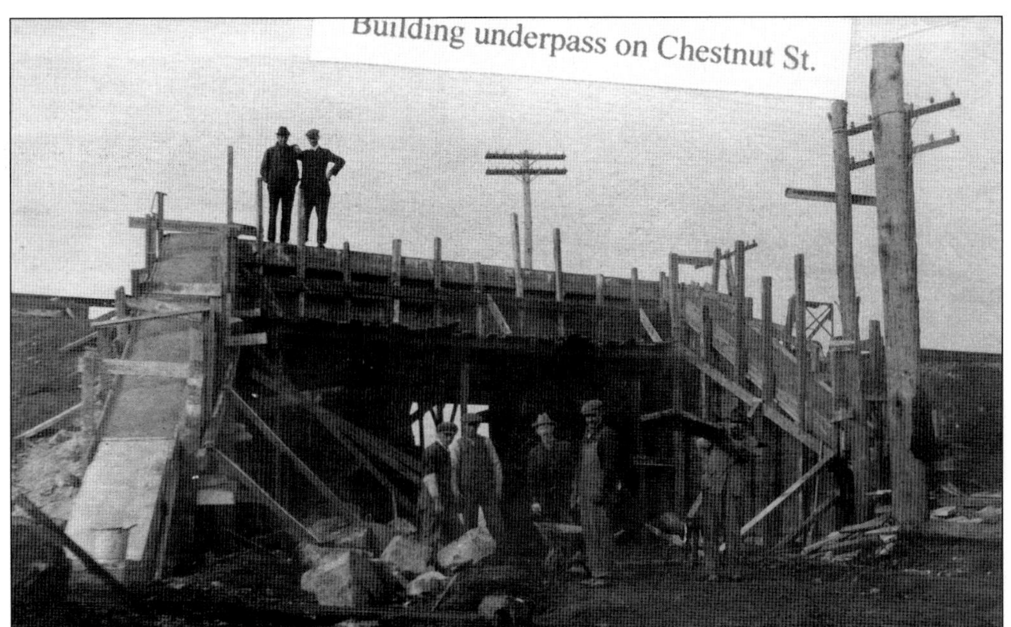

Originally, Water Street connected to Main Street but was closed off by the railroad embankment. In 1926, E.W. Strasser's blacksmith building was condemned and razed so that an automobile underpass could be built, once again connecting the two streets. (Courtesy of Harold Yocum.)

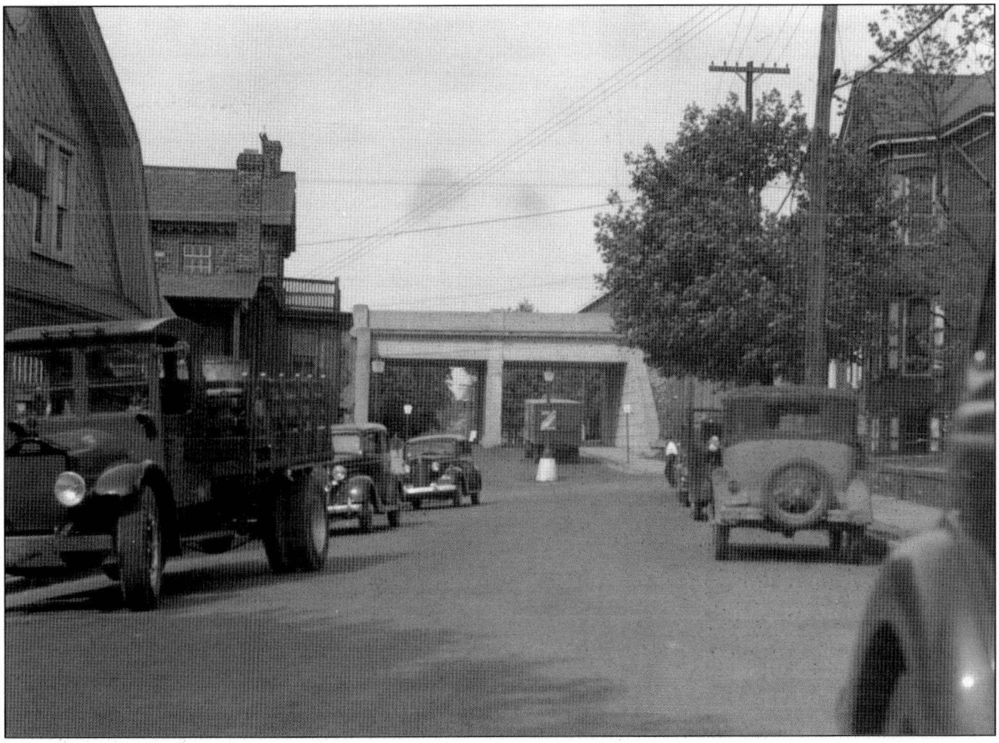

In 1928, both underpasses were complete, the Broad Street crossing was closed to pedestrians and vehicular traffic, and Water Street was later renamed East Chestnut Street. (Courtesy of Mennonite Heritage Center.)

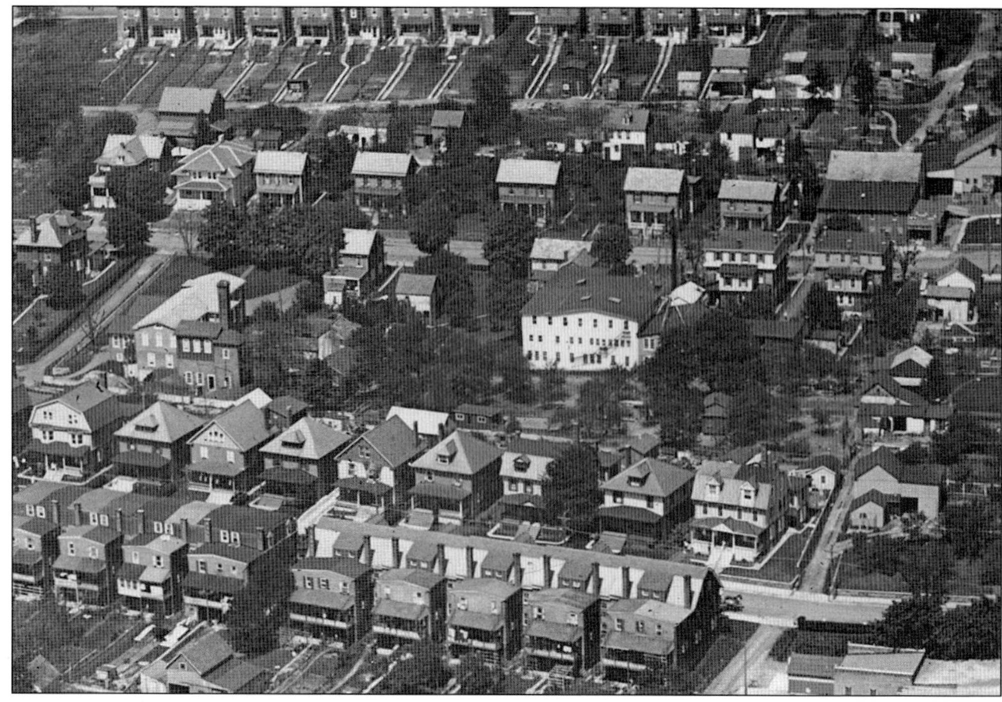

Harvey Souder continued to expand the Excelsior Cigar Box Factory on Green Street with larger boilers and more additions. In 1904, he raised the roof of his two-story brick factory, adding a third floor. His 5:00 p.m. whistle was heard throughout the town, signaling the children to return home for supper. One Sunday morning in 1934, the factory burned to the ground, putting 55 people out of work. (Courtesy of STMS collection.)

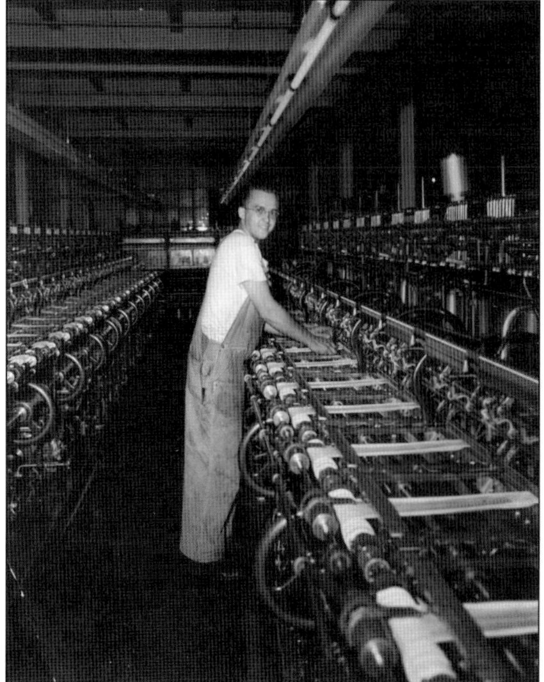

The M.B. Bergey Company on Green Street, one of the oldest hosiery mills in the country, acquired the Granite trademark in 1935. With full automation, an operator could turn out 90 dozen pairs of ladies' silk stockings per day. By 1937, Granite Knitting Mills employed 180 people and was one of Souderton's largest employers. In 1944, Henry Price, seen here, was one of 80 employees producing nylon hose. (Courtesy of Dennis Price.)

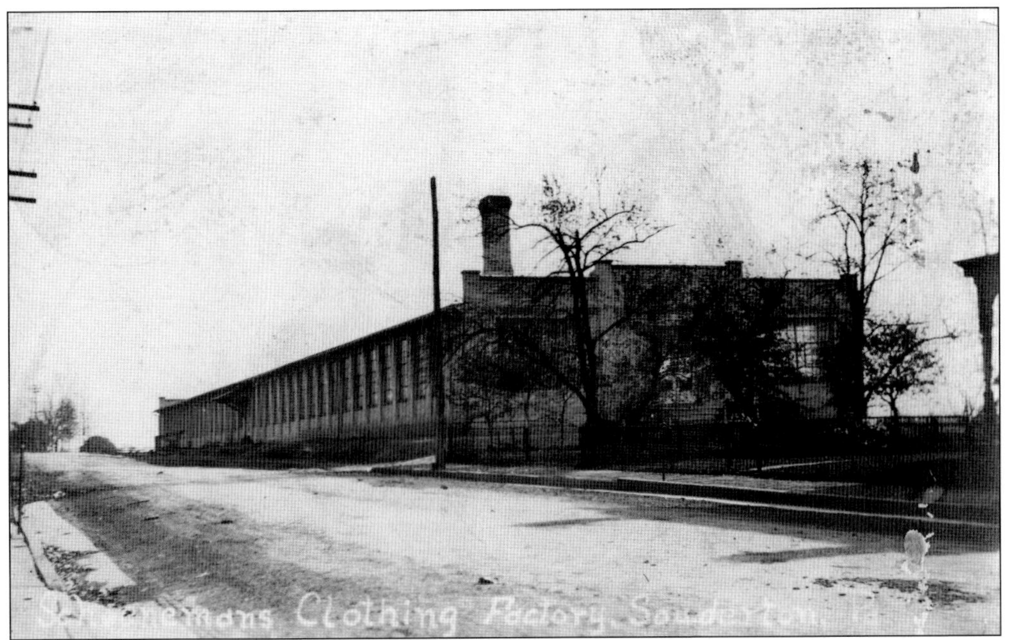

J. Schoeneman, a Philadelphia businessman, erected a factory in 1924 on South Front Street after first renting out space in three other facilities. Operating under the name Sun-Lite, Schoeneman manufactured men's coats and pants for wholesale to area stores. (Courtesy of Gloria Brandis.)

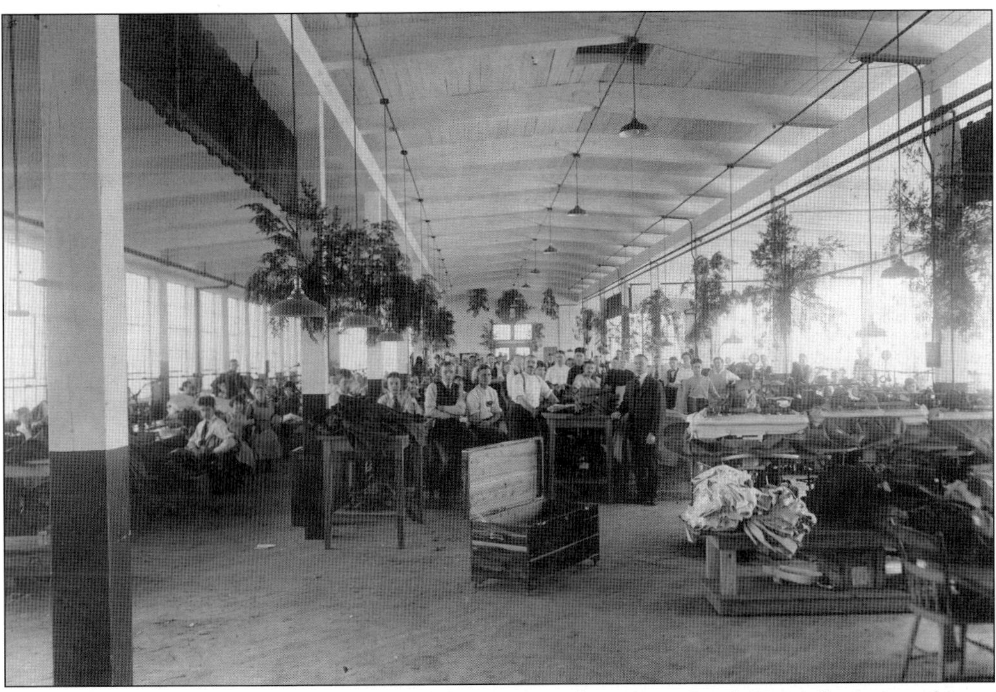

In this 1925 photograph of the interior of the Sun-Lite factory on South Front Street, employees presented their foreman with a Christmas gift of a cedar chest. The Sun-Lite factory advertised as "the busy plant." (Courtesy of Kurt Scherzberg.)

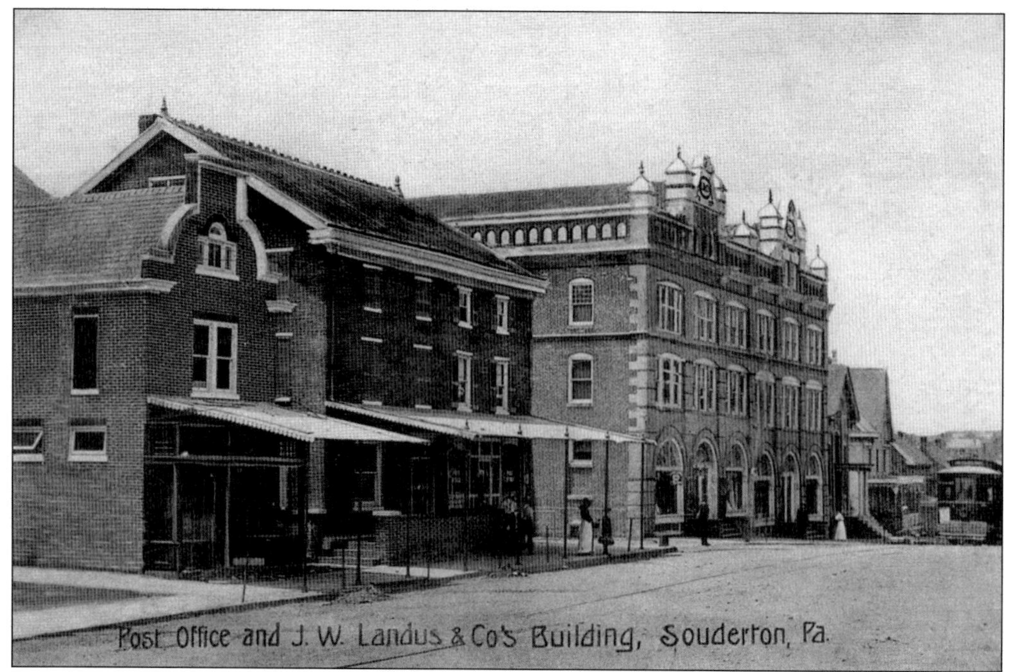

Several buildings in town have been renovated so many times that one would be hard-pressed to recognize any semblance of the original structure. In 1870, Henry O. Souder built a three-story brick house on Main Street next to his second home. This was his final home, where he died in 1897. The building, with at least one addition, is seen at far left. (Courtesy of STMS collection.)

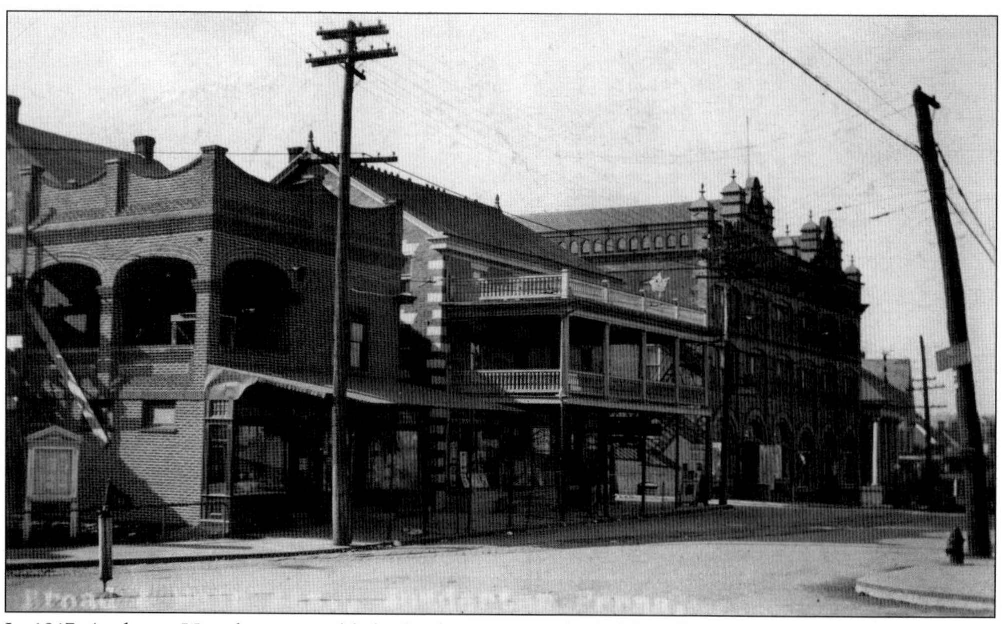

In 1917, Ambrose Hunsberger established a drugstore in the left-hand side of the old Souder home on Main Street. In 1928, Harry S. Kratz opened a watch and jewelry store in the right-hand side. The roof of the original house can still be seen above the addition. (Courtesy of STMS collection.)

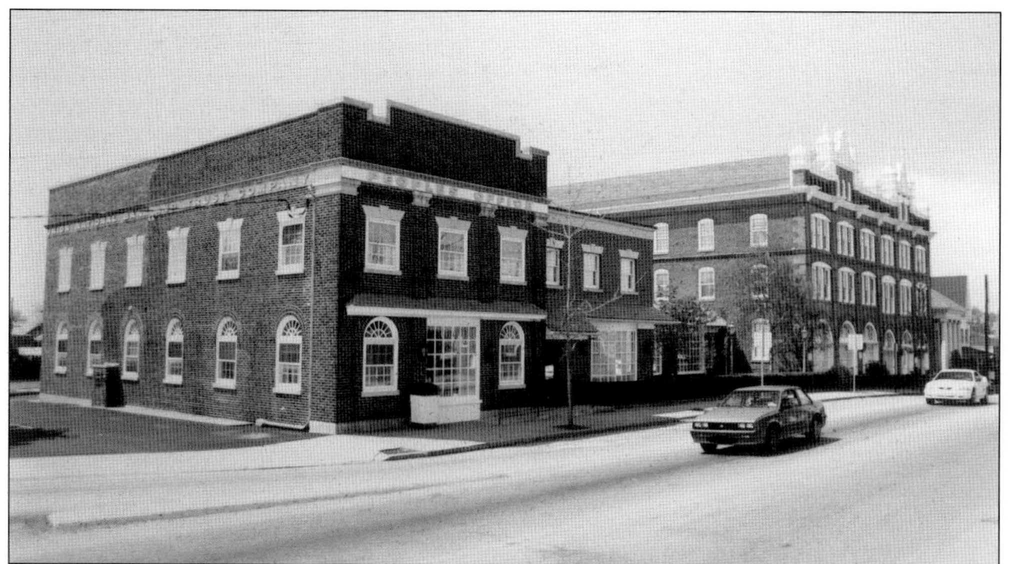

In 1928, a group of citizens concluded that the town's growth and progress warranted another bank. The Peoples National Bank was constructed by once again altering the old Henry O. Souder home on Main Street. The original house is still embedded in the middle. (Courtesy of Univest Corporation.)

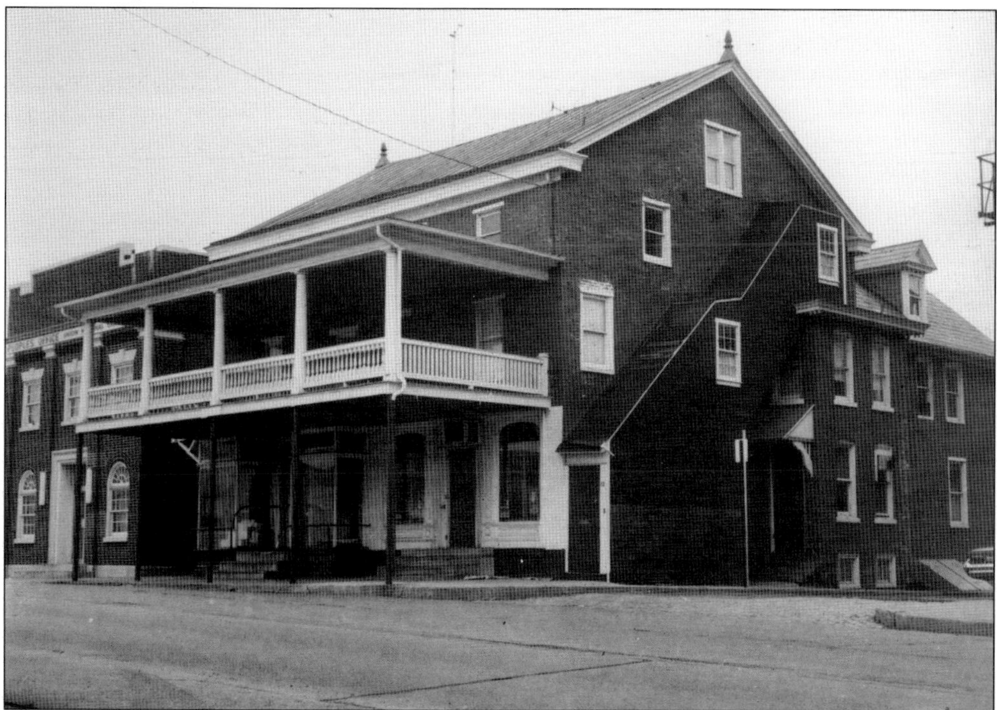

Gideon Haas purchased a poolroom and bowling alley, located in the original J.M. Landis & Co. building on Main Street, from Howard Freed in 1922. In the likelihood that reputations might be injured in this unwholesome atmosphere, the business of the poolroom was "conducted under the personal supervision of the owner." When the post office relocated in 1934, Haas established a restaurant in the formerly occupied rooms. (Courtesy of Univest Corporation.)

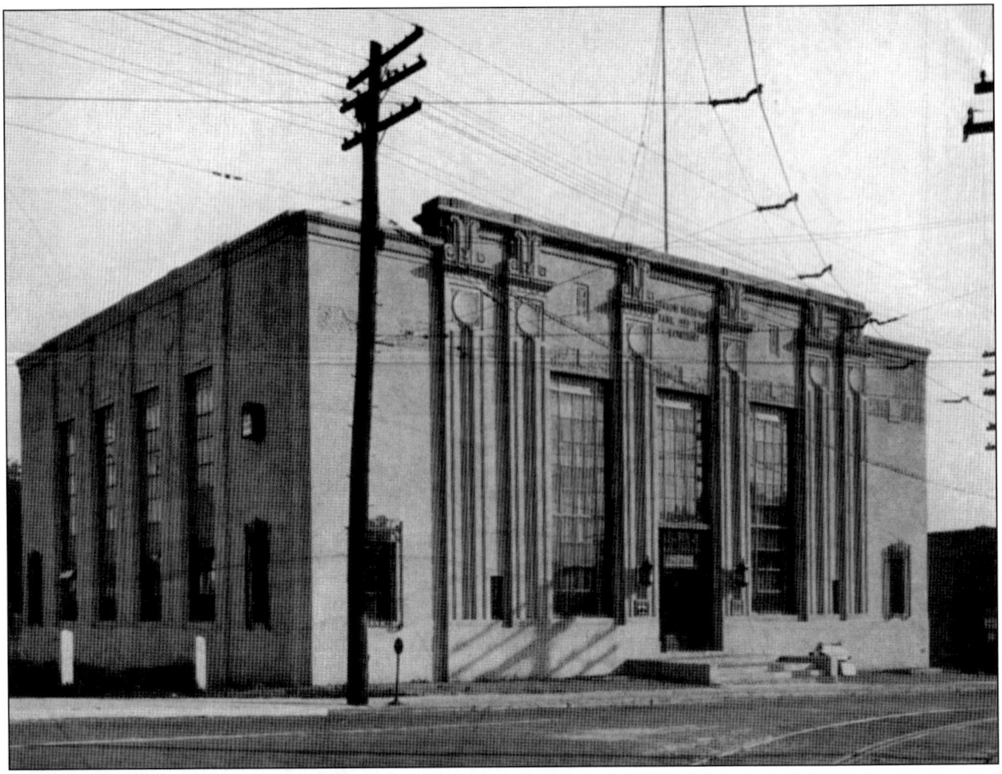

In the late 1920s, the Union National Bank and Trust Company outgrew its building on Main Street. In 1929, at the same time Peoples National Bank was being built, the new "progressive" Union National building at Main and West Broad Streets was also underway. Both banks had their grand openings in August of that year. (Courtesy of STMS collection.)

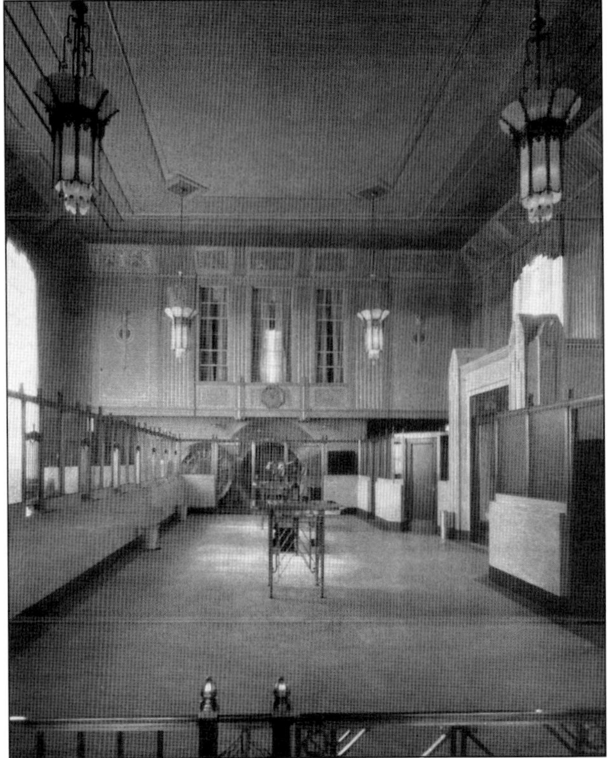

A photograph of the interior of the 1929 Union National Bank and Trust Company building, designed by architect Tilghman Moyer of Allentown, Pennsylvania, shows a building unlike any other in town. The new interior featured large bright windows, a stunning tan, gold, and blue color scheme, and gleaming finishes of bronze, marble, and crackled glass. (Courtesy of STMS collection.)

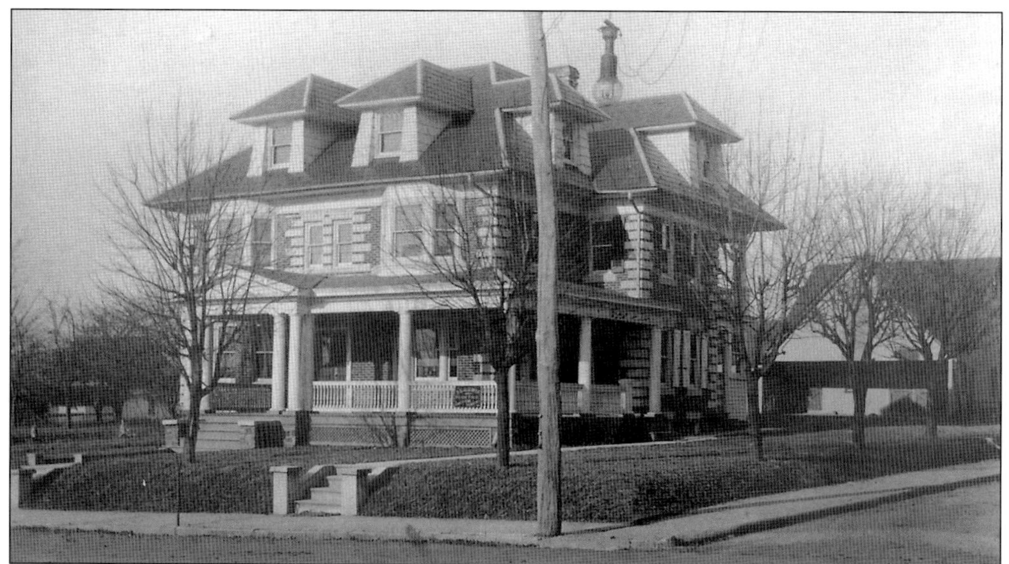

Wealthier Souderton residents built large homes along West Broad Street. Pictured here is the home of Benjamin D. Alderfer, built in 1904, in which he maintained a notary office. The extra labor needed to include the stained-glass windows, chestnut interiors, cement sills, and lintels certainly increased the overall cost. During Prohibition, Alderfer notarized the necessary papers for churches to purchase communion wine. (Courtesy of V. Steven Clemmer.)

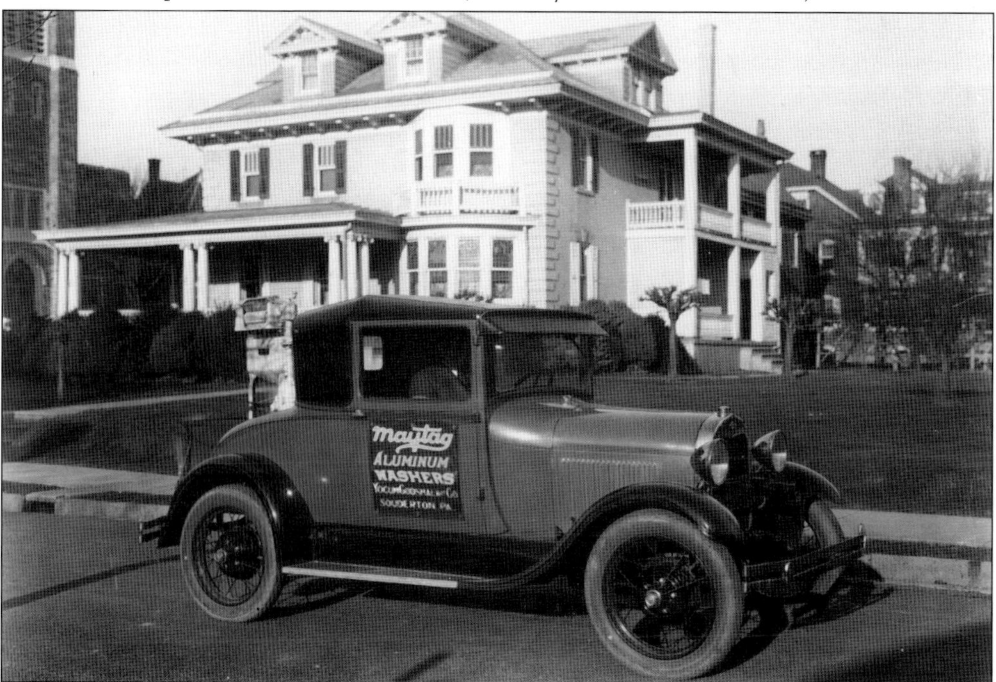

Competition not only existed between Souderton's families but also between business partners. In 1905, Jonas M. Landis had a new house built at the corner of West Broad Street and Franklin Avenue (above). Landis purposely constructed his home two feet wider and two feet longer than Ellis H. Souder, whose home was at West Broad Street and Penn Avenue. Landis and Souder were both partners of J.M. Landis & Co. (Courtesy of Harold Yocum.)

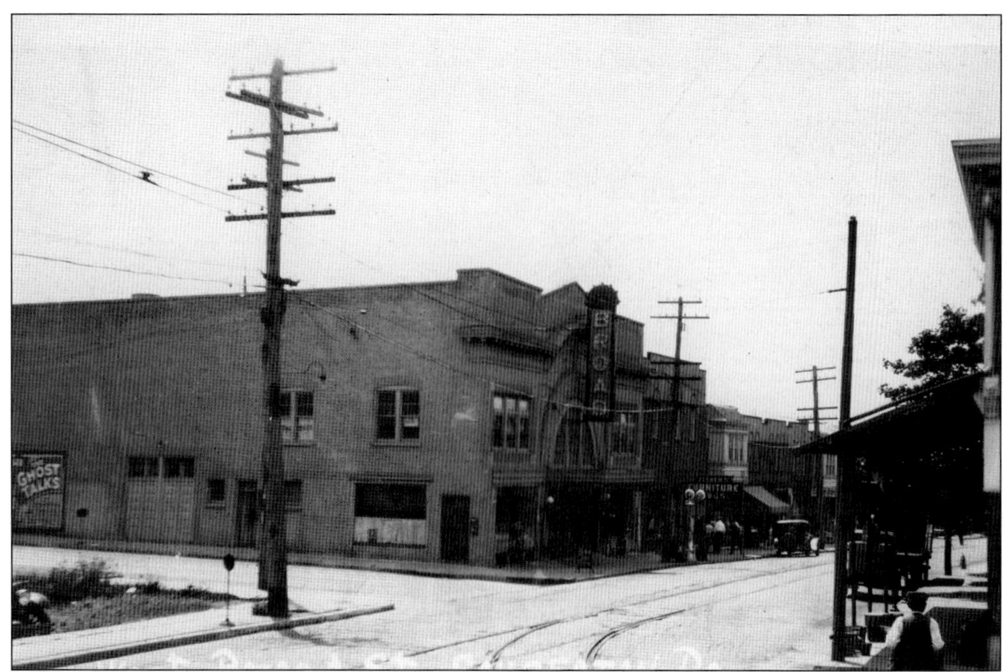

In 1922, the "palatial" Broad Theatre, designed by Souderton architect Jerome S. Landes, held its grand opening. More than 600 patrons watched Cecil B. DeMille's *Fools Paradise*, paying 30¢ for an adult admission. The gas pumps visible in the photograph are from the C.M. Cassel tire and accessory store next to the theater, which opened in 1925. (Courtesy of Susan Long.)

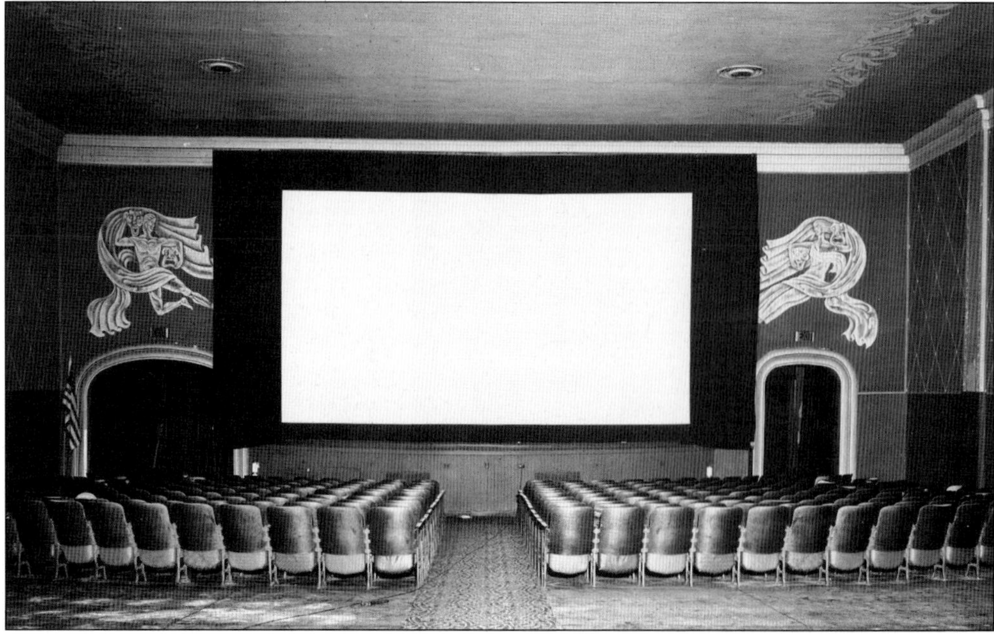

This 1934 interior photograph of the Broad Theatre, Souderton's first air-conditioned public building, highlights its lavish new decor, complete with spring cushion seats and lamps designed to give more restful light. Here, audiences enjoyed the latest Hollywood fare as well as entertaining vaudeville shows. (Courtesy of Gary Albright.)

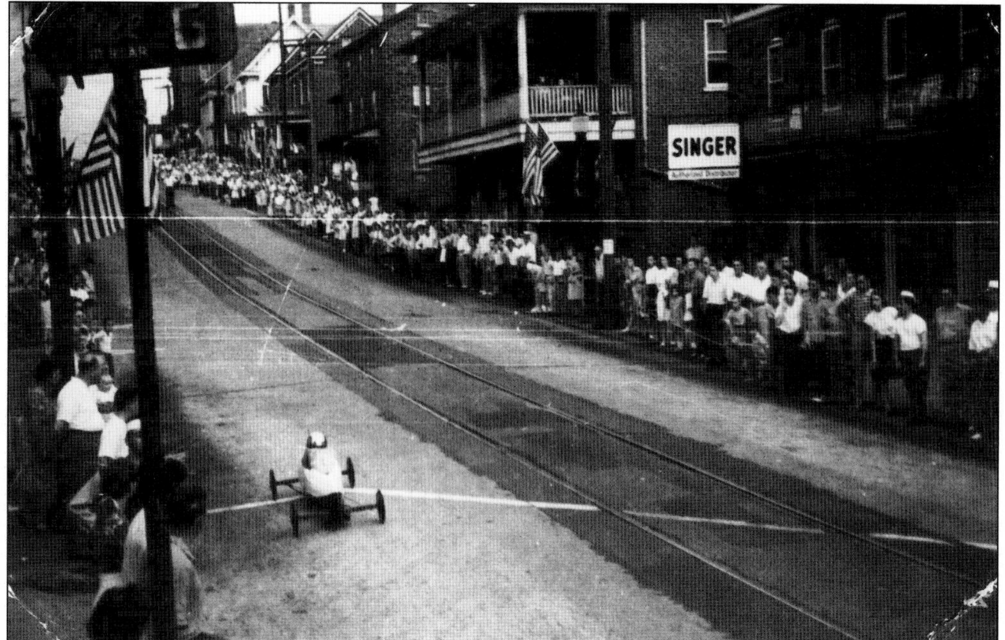

The first Souderton Coaster Derby was held in 1941. The Main Street of Souderton proved to be one of the best natural courses and attracted crowds of 5,000 or more. Suspended from 1952 to 1959 due to accidents, the derby resumed after the trolley tracks had been removed from the center of the street and stricter safety measures were enforced. (Courtesy of John Derstine.)

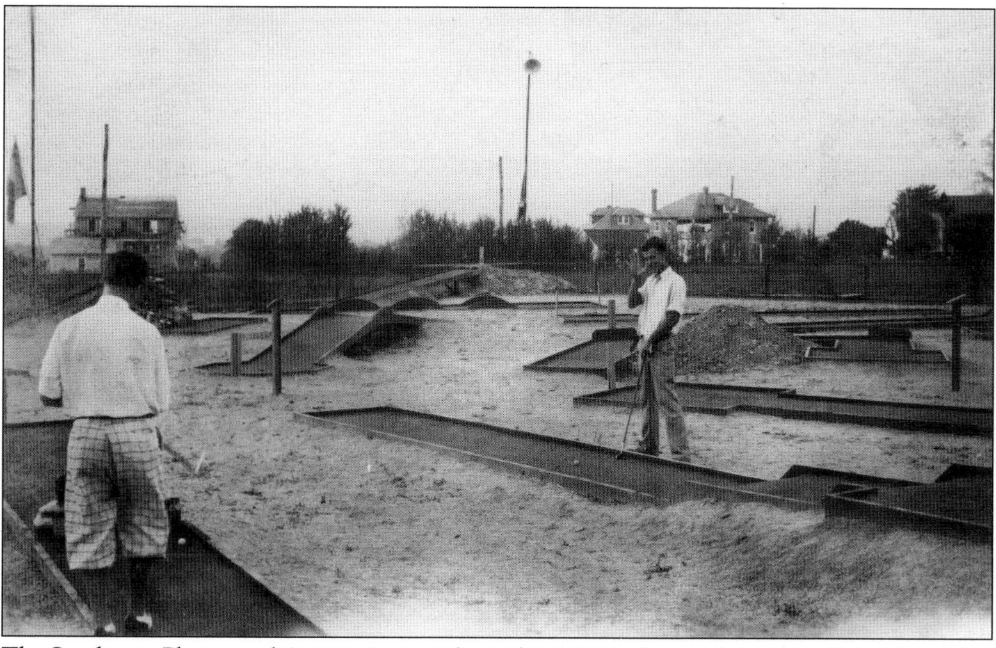

The Souderton Playground Association was formed in 1924 and opened the beautiful and versatile park at Reliance and Wile Avenues in 1925. This appropriately dressed man is playing a game of miniature golf in the location that was once a junkyard. The association later added several shuffleboard courts, a baseball diamond, and a grandstand. (Courtesy of Joslyn Kirsch.)

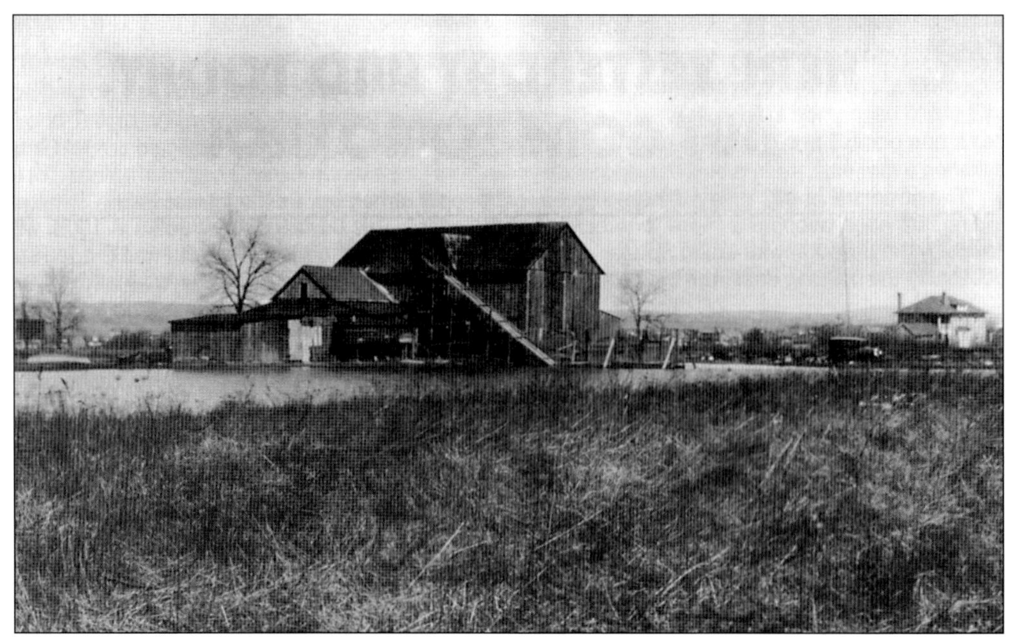

At the site of the former brickyard and clay pit on the corner of Wile Avenue and Reliance Road (above), neighborhood children enjoyed a swimming hole stocked with fish for their summer's recreation. During the winter months, ice from the pond was scored, pried loose, slid into the icehouse, and covered with sawdust. The ice would last all summer if properly stored. Preston G. Freed bought an ice cream factory and moved it to this location in 1916. In 1928, the Souderton Playground Association opened on this same site a large sand-bottom pool that was 300 feet in diameter (below). Freed then conducted a retail business, selling ice cream, soft drinks, cigars, and candy. (Above, courtesy of STMS collection; below, courtesy of Gloria Scheip.)

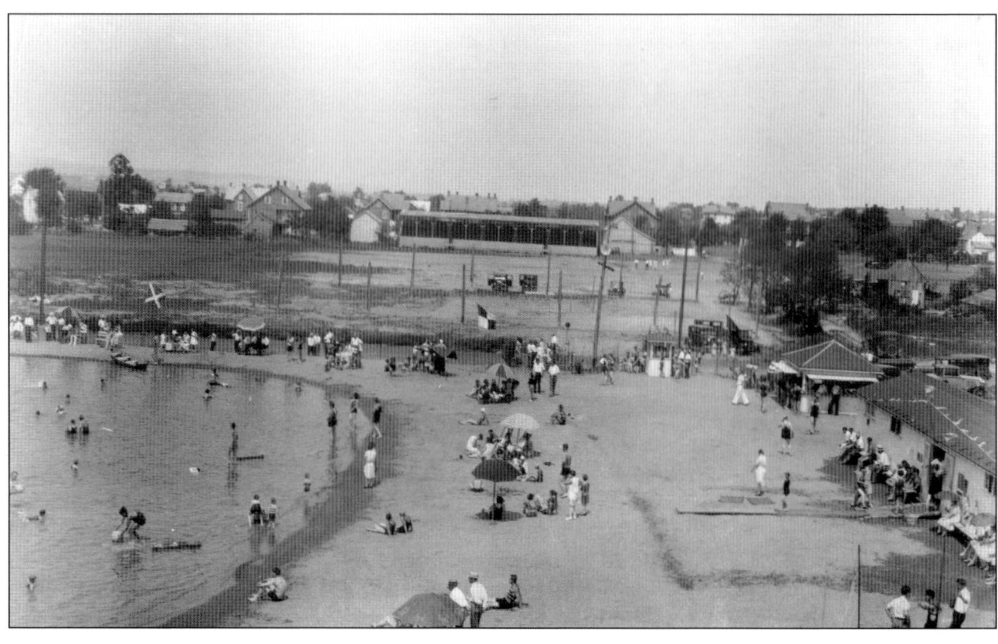

Complete with a diving platform (right), the sand-bottom pool at Wile Avenue and Reliance Roads was the best game in town. Not only did the people of Souderton congregate there, but folks from the surrounding areas flocked to swim and sunbathe on this sandy shore. In 1941, the board of health condemned the sand-bottom pool, and not until 1954 was the concrete swimming pool opened on the same spot (below). Ahead of its time, this recreational center offered a wading pool, a lap pool for competition, and one for general use. The pool opened at noon to only seniors, so that these residents could enjoy a quiet swim. The general public was admitted an hour later. In May 2010, the pool was closed for a complete renovation and rebuilding. (Right, courtesy of Gloria Scheip; below, courtesy of Gary Albright.)

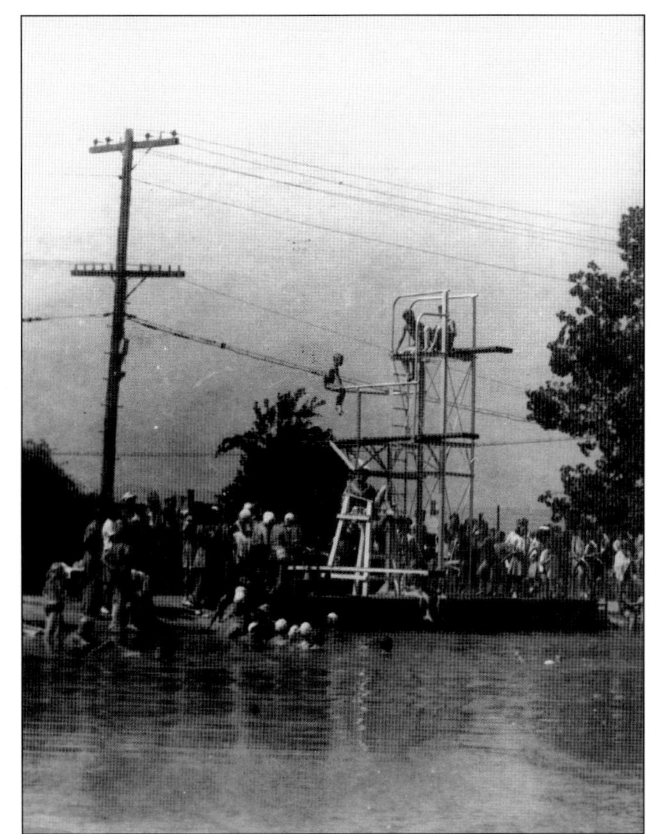

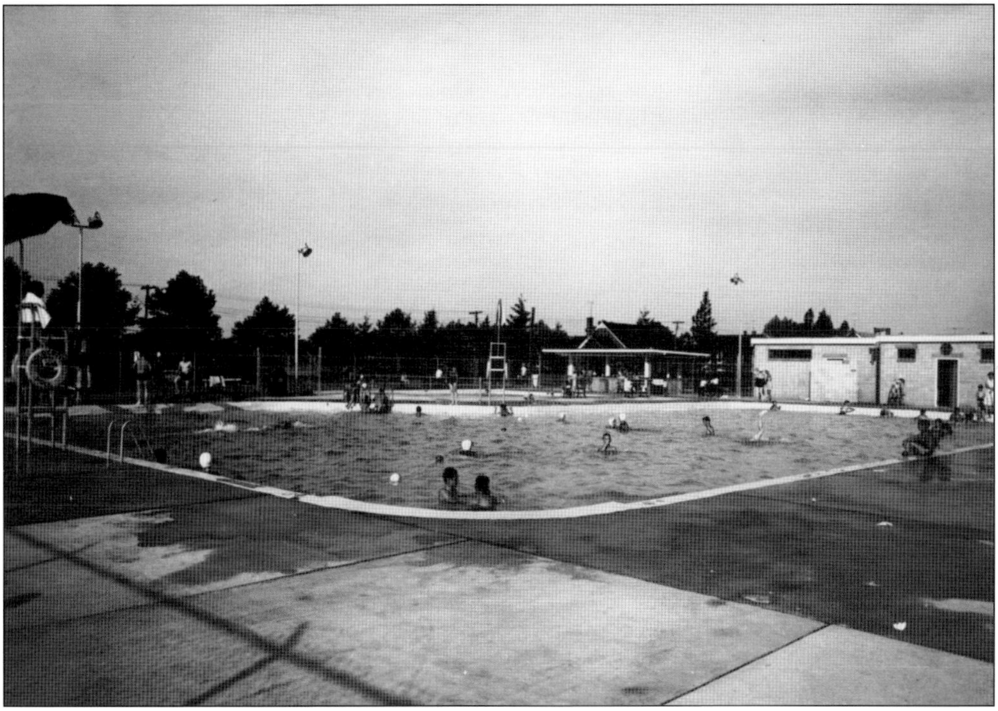

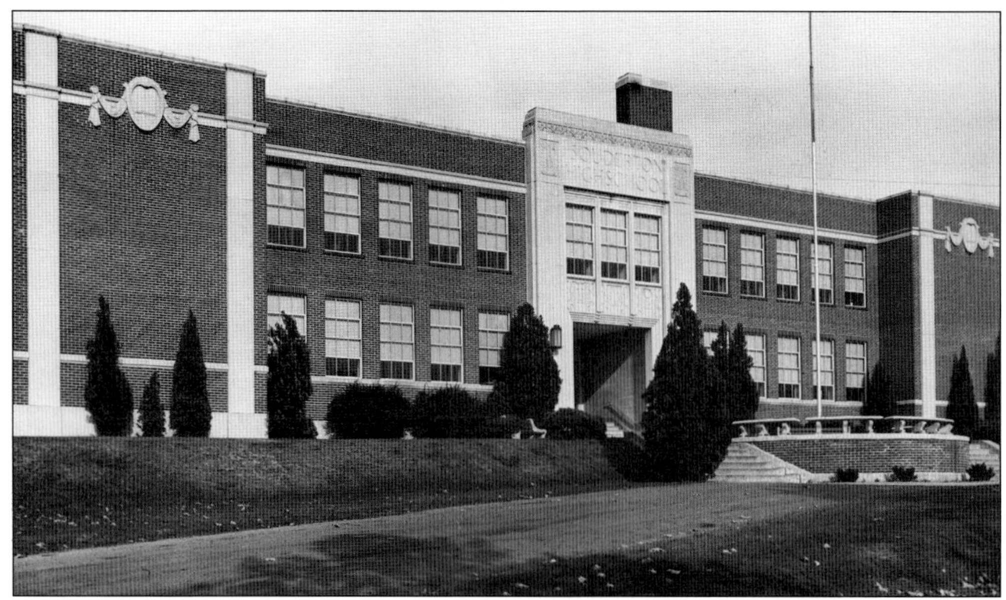

In 1932, the new junior-senior high school was erected on School Lane in the Art Deco style. The pride of the school was the 1,002-seat auditorium and unusually large stage that doubled as a gymnasium. Over the years, this building underwent several additions, including an Olympic-size pool and a wing of new classrooms, before closing its doors on the class of 2009. (Courtesy of Gary Albright.)

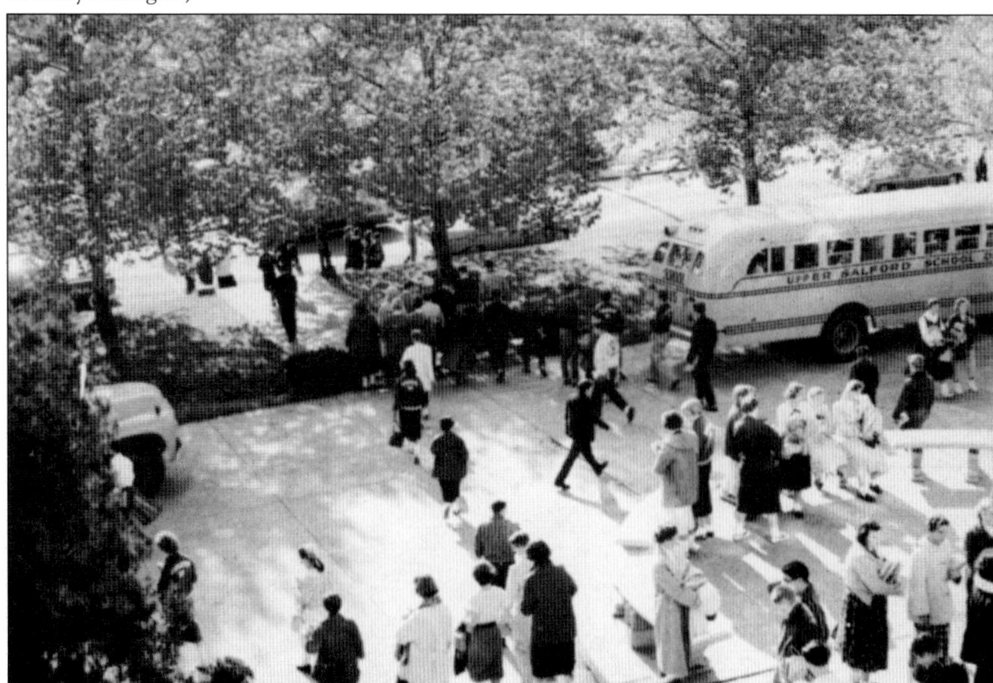

In 1936, Clarence G. Hagey, owner of Hagey's Bus Service, signed his first bus contract at $1.50 a day with the Franconia Township School Board. His business has been safely transporting the schoolchildren ever since. In 1970, when sold to his son Donald, the name was changed to Transportation Services, Inc. (Courtesy of Souderton Area School District.)

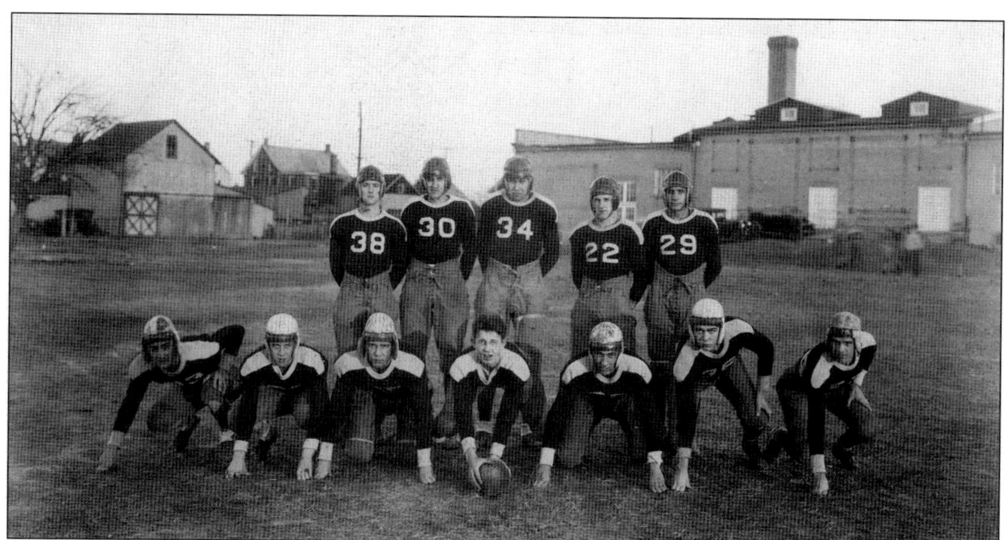

As members of the Bux-Mont Conference, the Souderton High School boys participated in football, baseball, and basketball. The 1932 football team practiced in the new park behind the Summit Street School. Standing are, from left to right, Leon Trumbore, ? Xander, John Seitz, Joseph Dillon, and ? Clemens. The rest are unidentified. (Courtesy of Fred Seitz.)

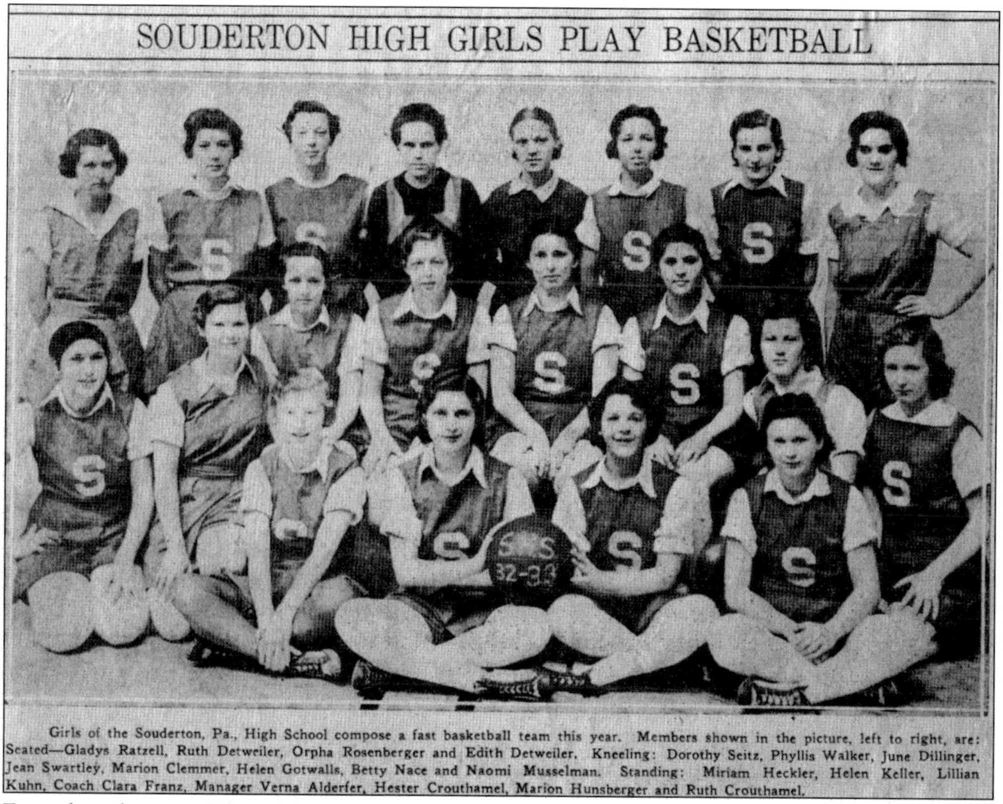

SOUDERTON HIGH GIRLS PLAY BASKETBALL

Girls of the Souderton, Pa., High School compose a fast basketball team this year. Members shown in the picture, left to right, are: Seated—Gladys Ratzell, Ruth Detweiler, Orpha Rosenberger and Edith Detweiler. Kneeling: Dorothy Seitz, Phyllis Walker, June Dillinger, Jean Swartley, Marion Clemmer, Helen Gotwalls, Betty Nace and Naomi Musselman. Standing: Miriam Heckler, Helen Keller, Lillian Kuhn, Coach Clara Franz, Manager Verna Alderfer, Hester Crouthamel, Marion Hunsberger and Ruth Crouthamel.

Even though most of the public's attention went to the boys' teams, the girls were ready to compete. The 1932 Souderton girls' basketball team must have appreciated the new basketball court on the stage in the auditorium. (Courtesy of Fred Seitz.)

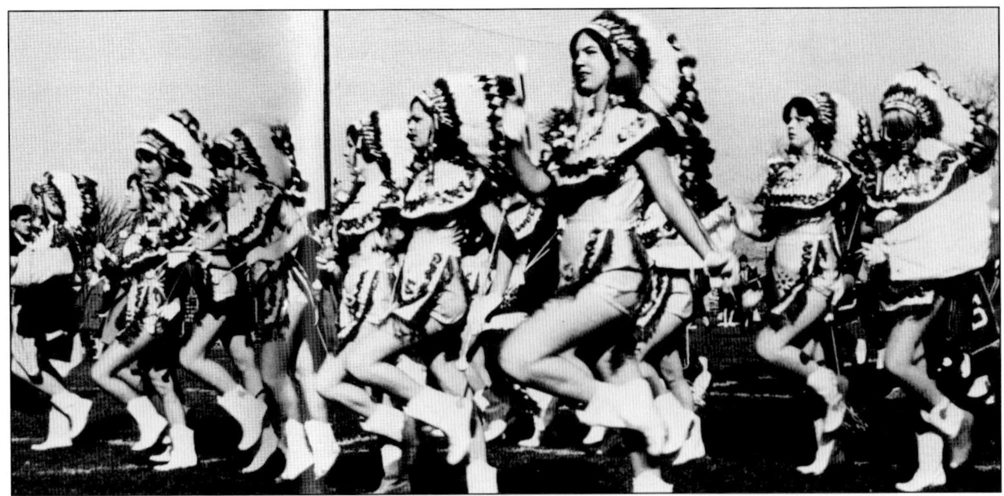

Souderton lies in the Indian Valley, the name given to the North Central section of Montgomery County. As would stand to reason, the new high school's sports teams chose the Souderton Indians as their name. In 1967, dressed in full headdress, the majorettes and drill team, dubbed the "Indianettes," performed their halftime show on the football field. (Courtesy of Souderton Area School District.)

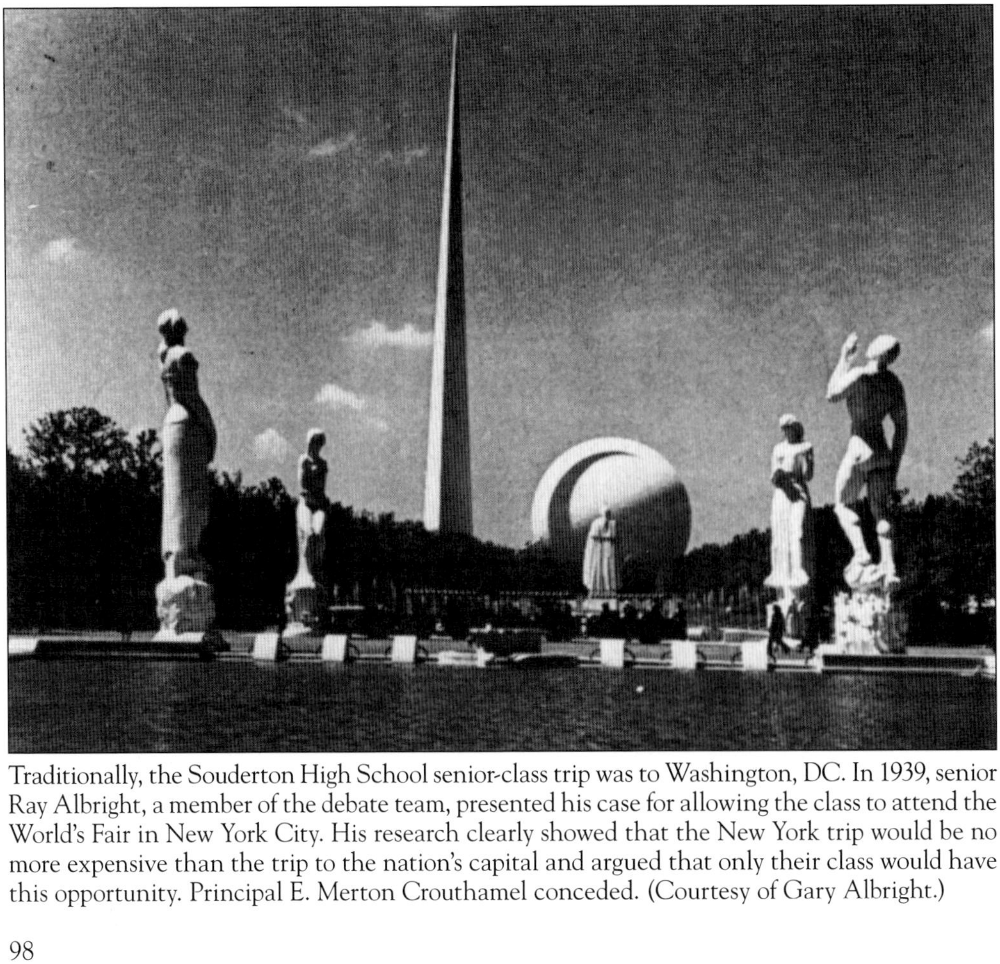

Traditionally, the Souderton High School senior-class trip was to Washington, DC. In 1939, senior Ray Albright, a member of the debate team, presented his case for allowing the class to attend the World's Fair in New York City. His research clearly showed that the New York trip would be no more expensive than the trip to the nation's capital and argued that only their class would have this opportunity. Principal E. Merton Crouthamel conceded. (Courtesy of Gary Albright.)

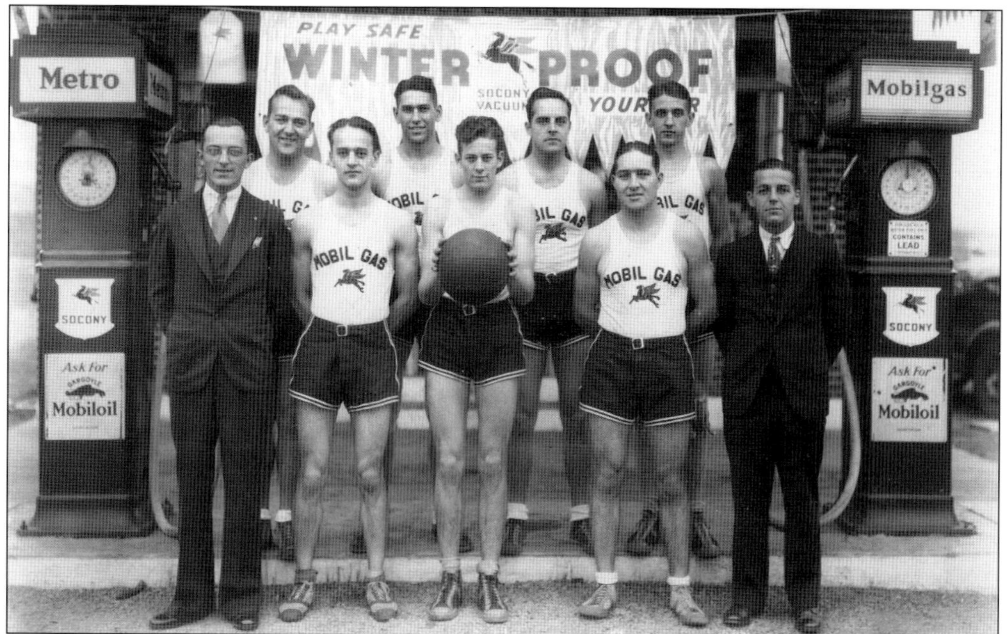

Also in 1932, Souderton High School alumni, most having lettered the previous few years, were involved in a men's semi-professional basketball team, sponsored by Metro/Mobil Gas. Pictured are, from left to right, (first row) Manager ? Shearer, Joe Diehl, "Mox," Setu Eshelman, and ? Moyer; (second row) Vic Frederick, John Seitz, "Turk" Landes, and "Junie" Landes. (Courtesy of Fred Seitz.)

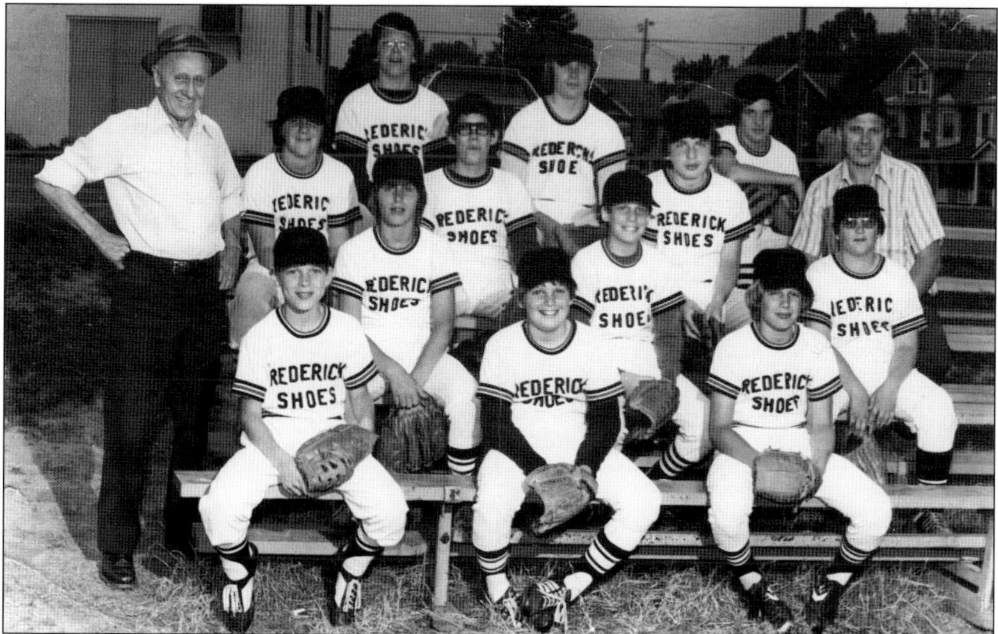

The smile on sponsor Jake Frederick's face (standing), of Frederick Shoe Store, makes it obvious that his 1975 junior little-league team of Souderton, photographed at the ball park on West Broad Street, Telford, won the championship. Frederick let each boy choose a free pair of shoes from his store. They all chose sneakers! (Courtesy of Dale Michener.)

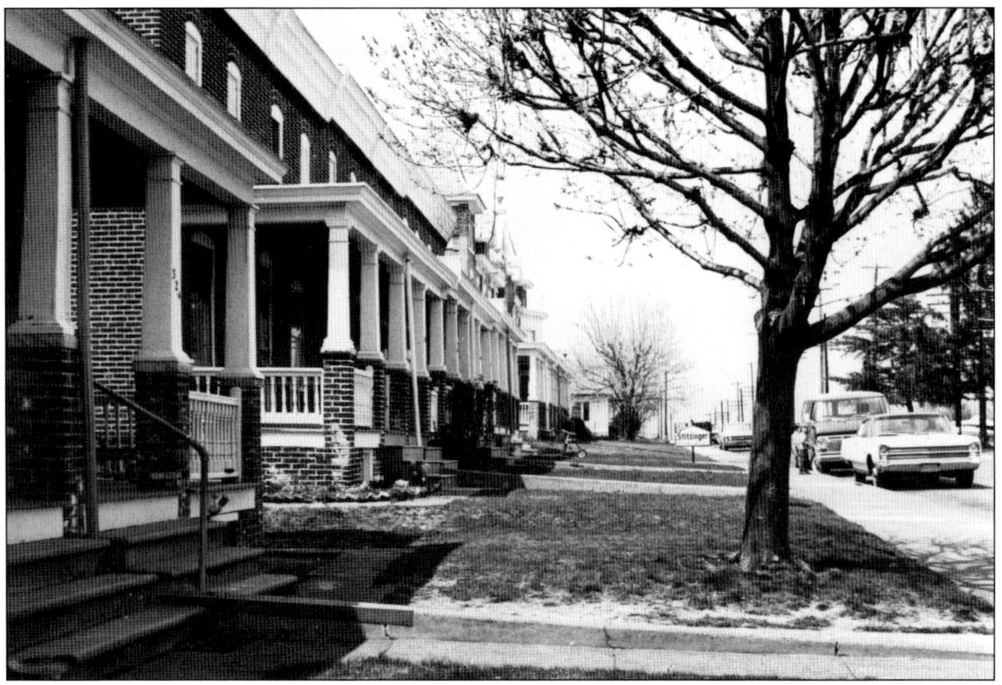

With businessmen like Otto Eisenlohr advertising positions for more than 100 workers at a time, the need for affordable in-town housing for the working class continued to be in great demand. One solution was the construction of row houses along Railroad Avenue, which offered comfortable homes on smaller parcels of land. (Courtesy of Gary Albright.)

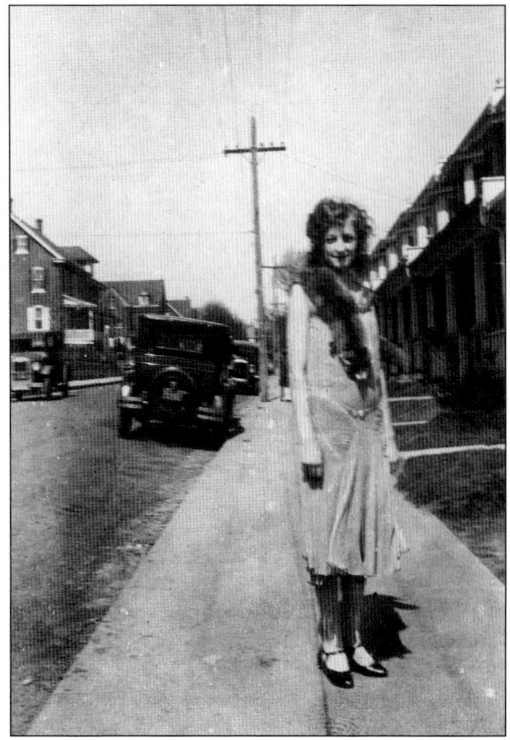

Wearing a fox stole, stylishly dressed Beulah Hackman is standing on Diamond Street. Row homes, tightly packed twin homes, and a few single dwellings created a comfortable neighborhood. Opened in 1896, the homes on this street were occupied by employees of many local businesses and remained affordable even during the Depression. (Courtesy of Betty Hackman.)

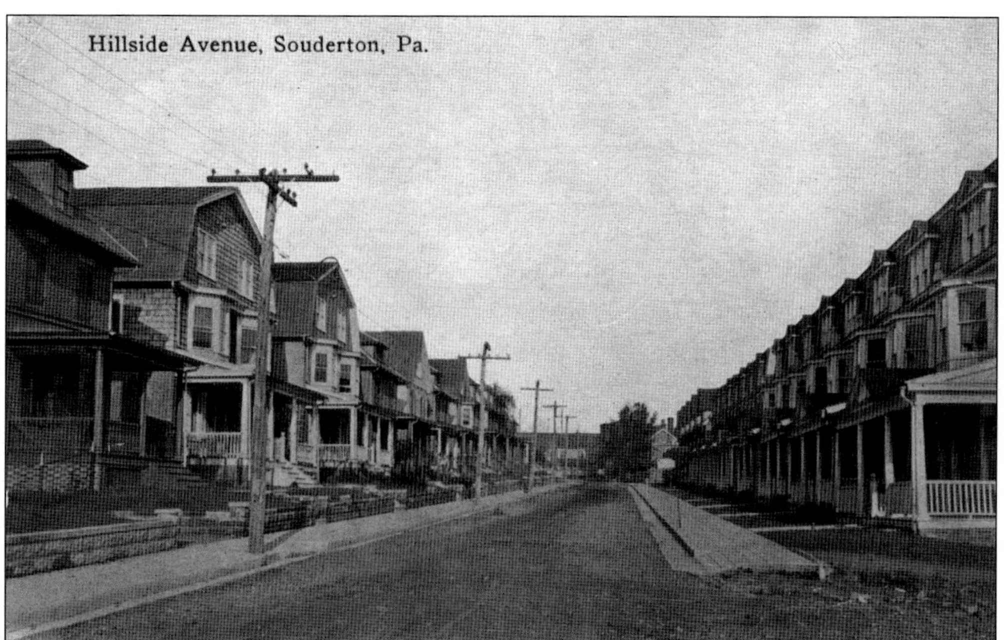

Hillside Avenue was opened in 1908, filling the last of the meadow and woods in the borough with more twins, singles, and row homes. (Courtesy of Gary Albright.)

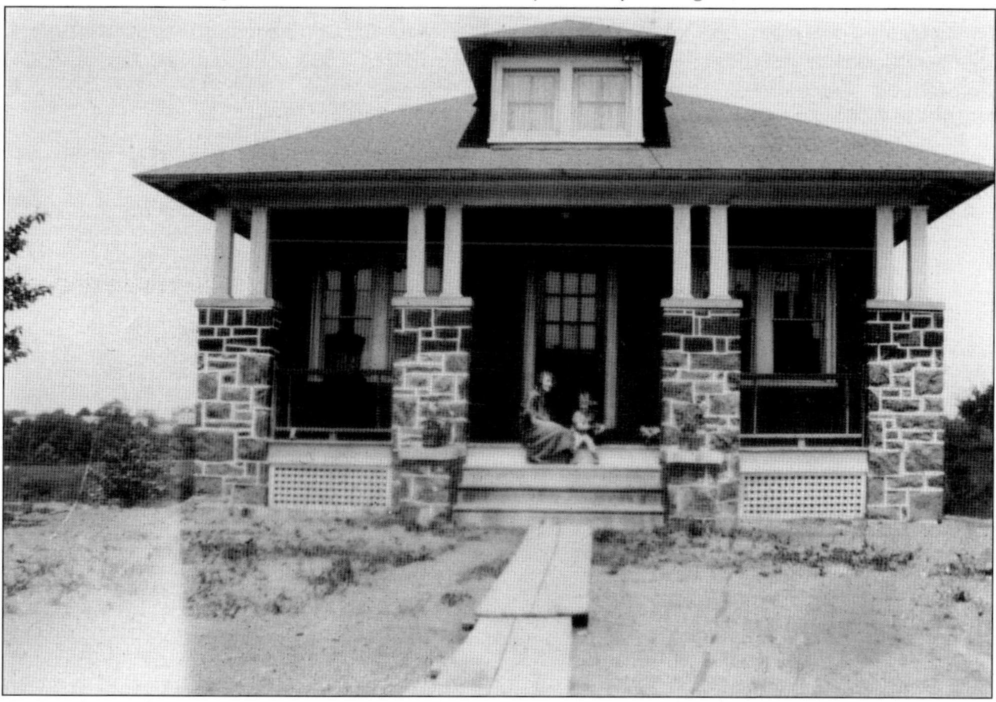

As Souderton became more industrialized, land in the borough grew more expensive. Families were now limiting their size, and therefore, the majority of house construction reflected smaller homes for the working class. Large homes were often converted to several apartments. J. Carroll Souder built this small, affordable home on East Broad Street in 1923 for his wife, Verna, and only child, John Carroll. Several businesses have since occupied this building. (Courtesy of Susan Long.)

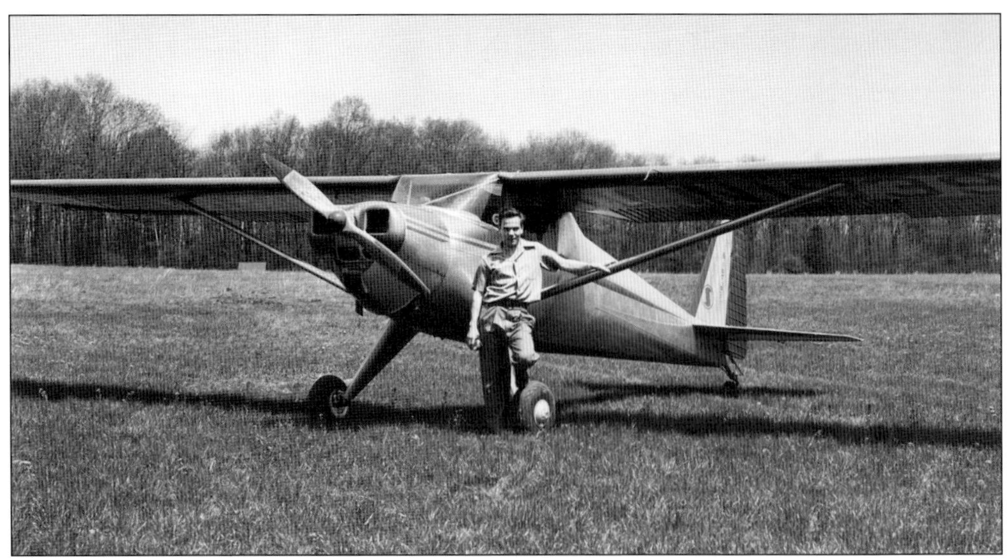

Souderton has been most fortunate to have so many photographers recording the visual history of the town. Daniel F. Ziegler, Tony Bova, and Ray Albright are among the most prolific photographers. Combined with his love of photography, Ray's passion for flying has provided a perspective of the town like no other. Standing beside his Luscombe Silvaire airplane and holding a Metalist I camera, Ray gets ready to take to the skies. (Courtesy of Gary Albright.)

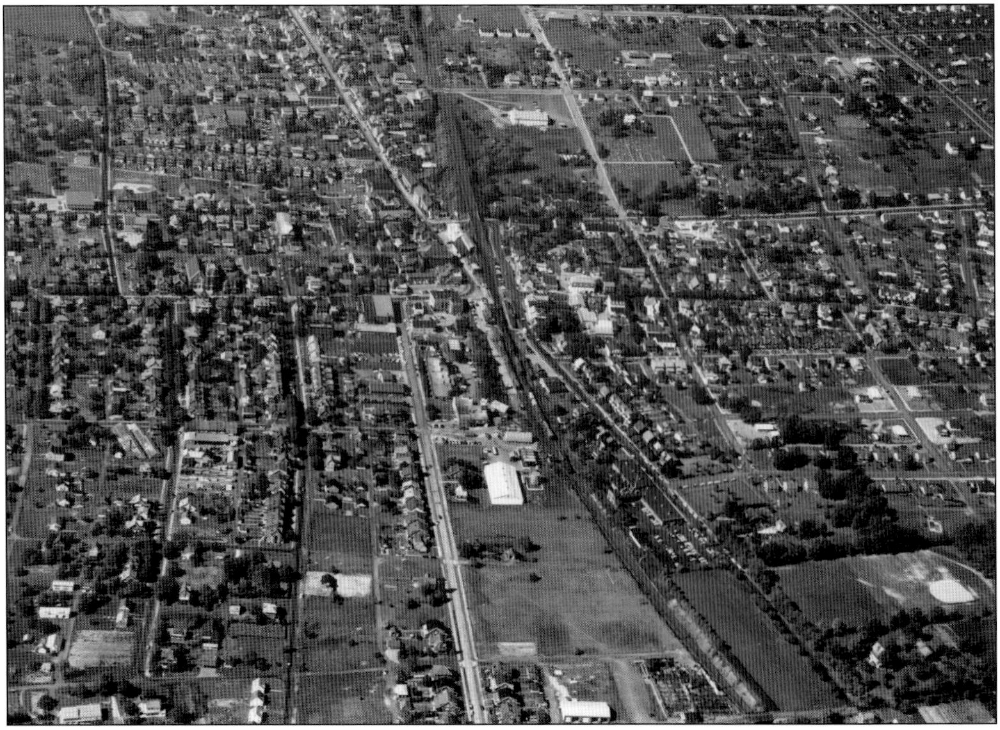

This aerial view of Souderton, taken in 1955, clearly shows the robust results of Henry O. Souder's visionary decision to approach the Philadelphia, Easton & Water Gap Railroad with his offer of free land, leading to this remarkable transformation of Souder's corner in Franconia Township. (Courtesy of STMS collection.)

Seven

Souderton's Collective Memories

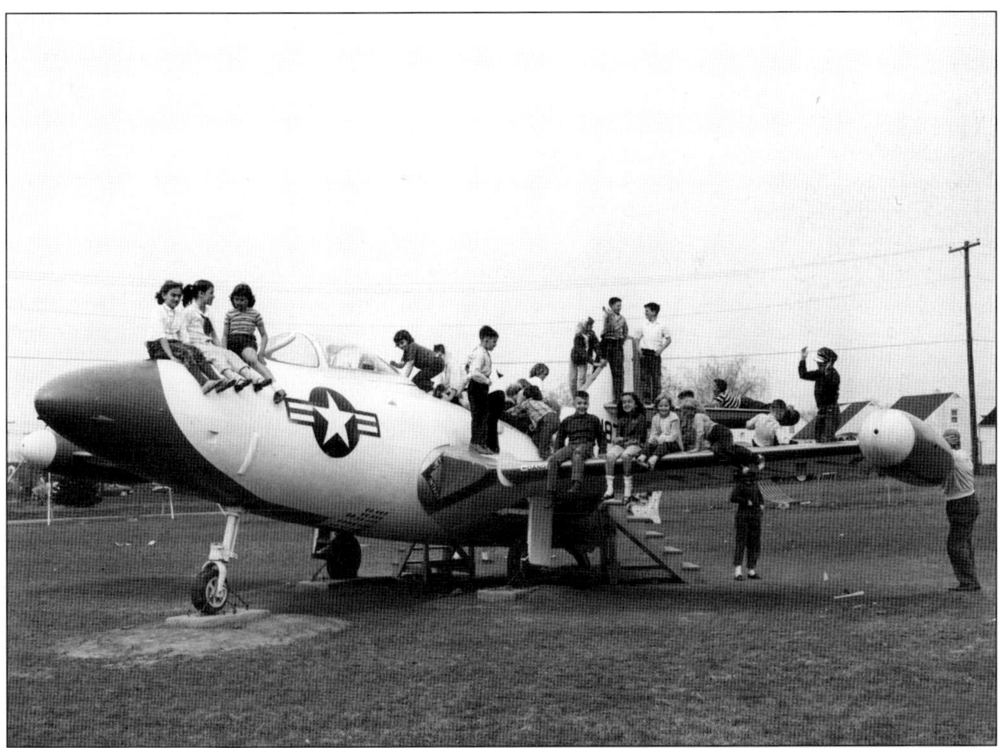

Not many parks provide an F9F-2 Panther jet for children to explore. In 1961, the Summit Avenue Park at Summit and School Lane, in neighboring Telford, installed this Korean War–era airplane from Johnsville Air Development Center. Before nearby citizens realized that the plane had been brought to the park in pieces for reassembling, they were somewhat dismayed to think that a plane had crashed in their neighborhood. (Courtesy of Gary Albright.)

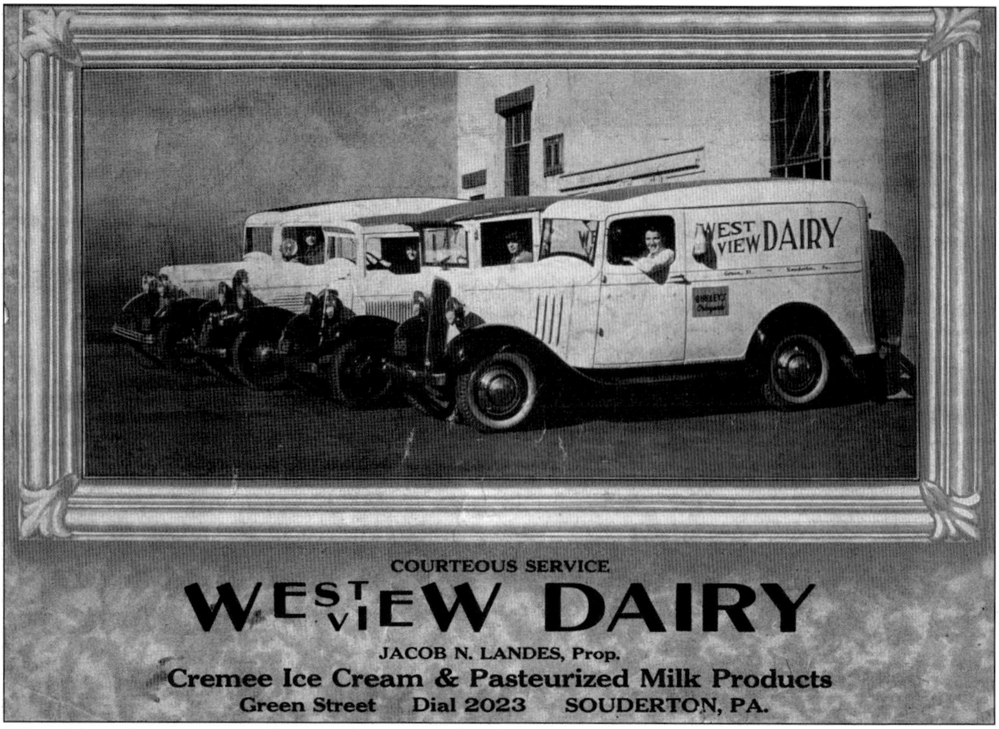

COURTEOUS SERVICE

WEST VIEW DAIRY

JACOB N. LANDES, Prop.

Cremee Ice Cream & Pasteurized Milk Products

Green Street Dial 2023 SOUDERTON, PA.

West View Dairy, owned by Jacob N. Landes, began as a milk route started by J.K. Clemmer in 1905. Souderton area farms provided the milk. Located on Green Street, the business kept expanding, and trucks (above) replaced horses and wagons. In 1932, Landes began manufacturing ice cream, eventually opening the Frostie Cup ice cream shop on Old Bethlehem Pike. During the 1950s, a route helper could earn $4 a day, working from 4:00 a.m. to 2:00 p.m. One summer, the West View Dairy, crediting George Washington as being the first to introduce ice cream to America, gained customers by giving out numbered fans (below). Every week numbers were displayed on the dairy's delivery trucks. If the number on a customer's fan matched the number on the truck, the lucky patron received a free quart of ice cream! (Above, courtesy of Robert Greenwood; below, courtesy of John Urich.)

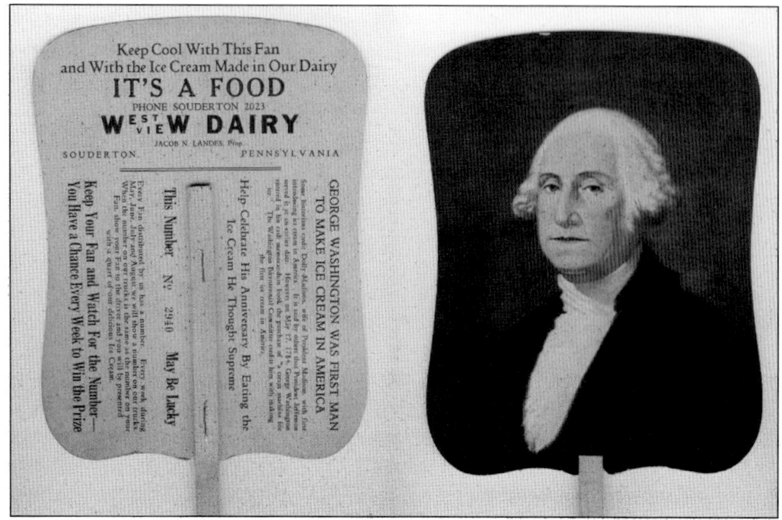

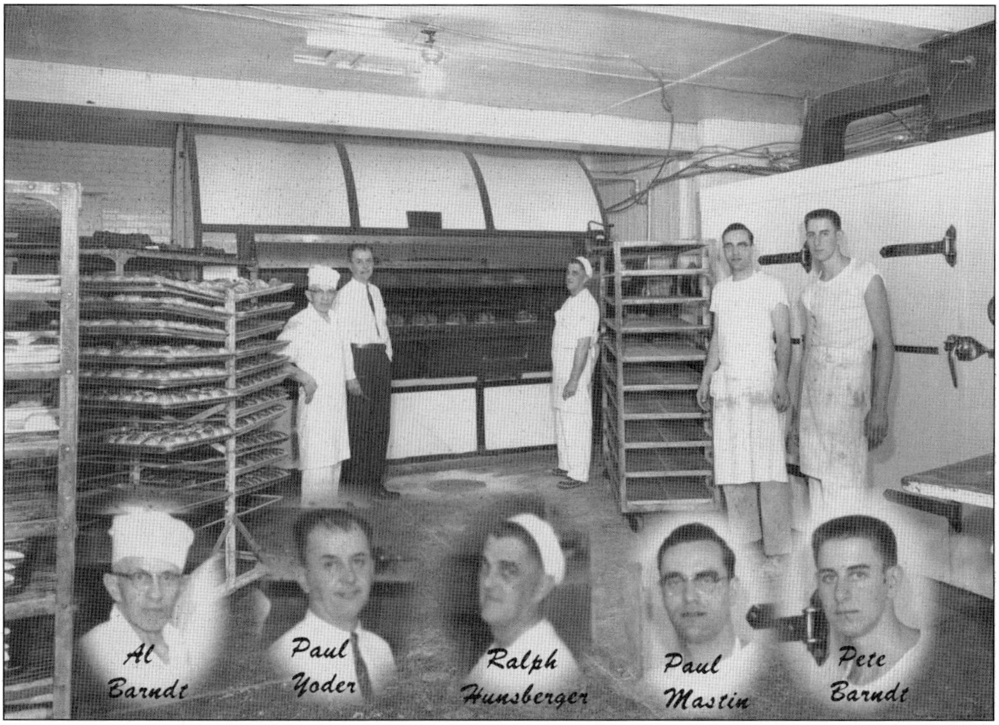

Al Barndt
Paul Yoder
Ralph Hunsberger
Paul Mastin
Pete Barndt

Established in 1883 and having a number of previous owners, this bakery on Main Street (above) was purchased by Drissel & Diehl in 1916 and renamed Souderton Baking Company. The outdoor bake oven had already been replaced by modern machinery, and by 1937, owner Paul Yoder had 27 employees who baked delicious rye bread and sold bags of broken pretzels for 1¢. Even after closing time, a knock at the basement door would be answered by a friendly baker willing to sell a few more donuts. In 1937, Souderton Baking Company advertised their special Dan-Dee Bread on their delivery trucks (below.) With a fleet of 11 trucks, the bakery served residents within a radius of 15 miles of Souderton. (Both, courtesy of Joslyn Kirsch.)

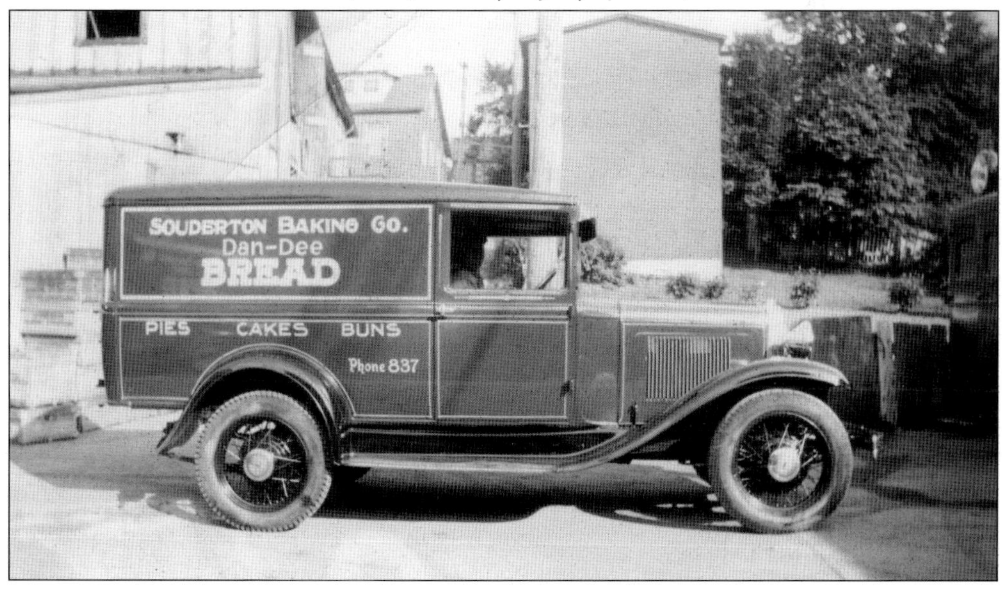

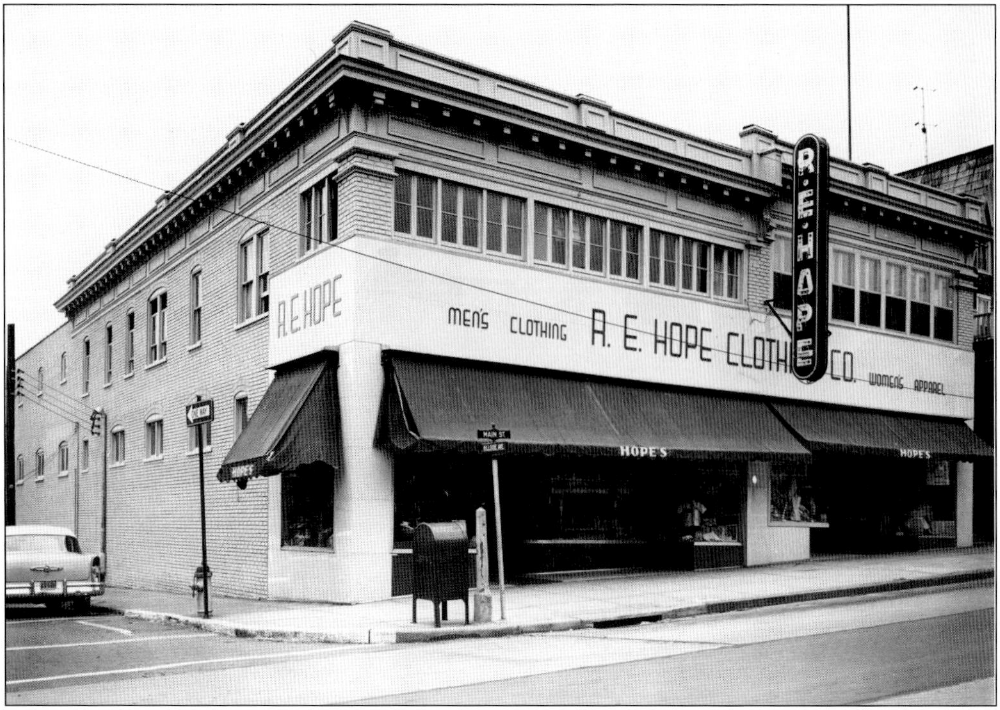

Beginning his career as a pattern designer for Zendt Brothers clothing manufacturers in 1908, Rudolph E. Hope established this factory and store on Main Street in 1923. He specialized in custom-made men's and boys' clothing, including plain coats for Anabaptists and a variety of ready-made clothes. By 1926, he added women's clothing. Hope allowed his customers to buy on credit, even stopping by their homes to collect installment payments. (Courtesy of Gary Albright.)

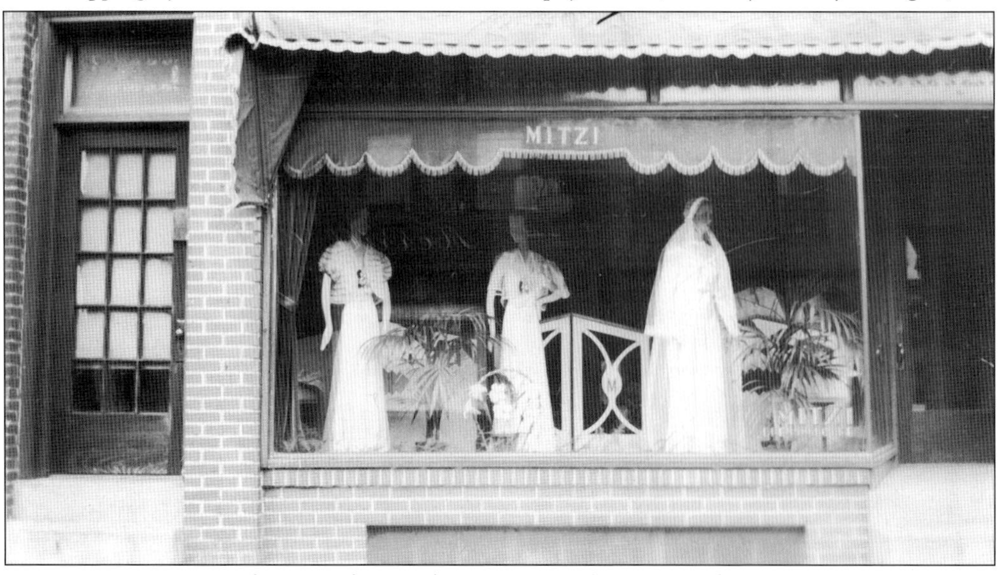

In 1933, seamstress Martha Hartzel opened Mitzi's Dress Shop on North Front Street. A year later, she made Pearl Fox a partner and moved to larger quarters on Main Street, shown here. Martha had a good eye for fashion and often traveled to New York to purchase the latest creations. By 1940, the partnership dissolved, and Fox owned the shop independently. (Courtesy of Gerald Hartzell.)

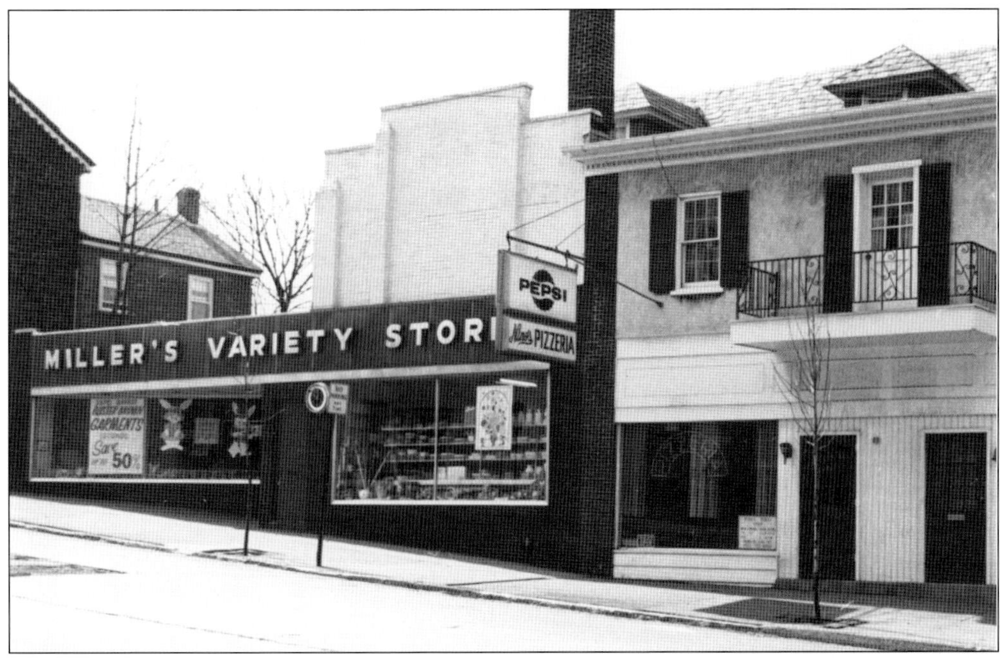

Harvey L. Miller purchased Kline's Variety Store, a five-and-dime, on Main Street in 1948. He changed the name to Miller's Variety Store and, in the late 1950s, added the large windowed portion seen in the photograph. Eventually the store was owned by former stock boy John Butterwick and salesclerk Shirley Gerhart, who met at Miller's and married in 1957. If newer stores didn't carry a favorite item, a customer could always find it at Miller's! (Courtesy of Gary Albright.)

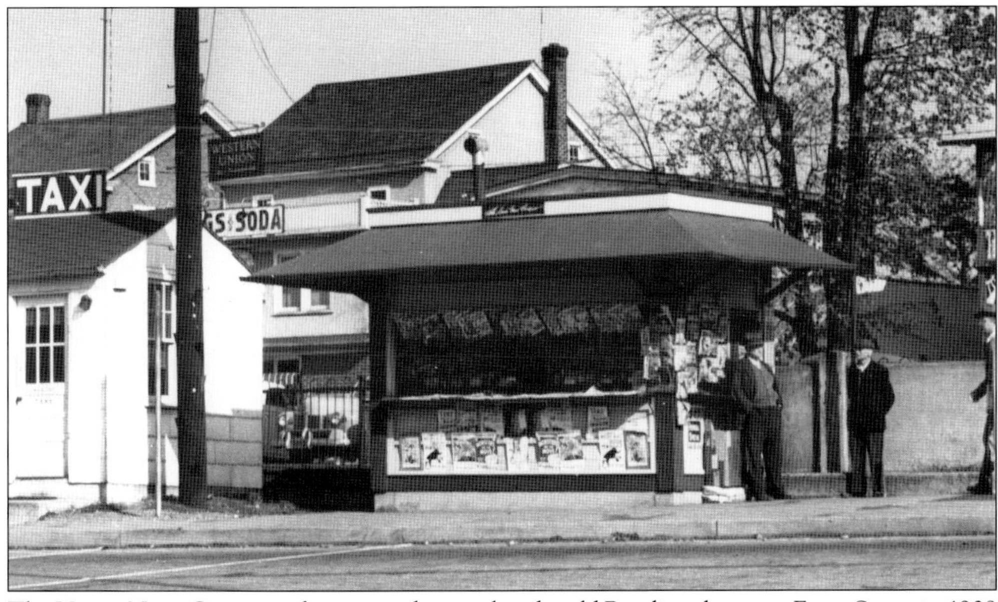

The Union News Company first opened a stand at the old Reading depot on Front Street in 1908 with Joseph Musselman in charge. When the new depot opened in 1928, the stand, pictured here, was built on Main Street across Broad Street from the depot. Since 1925, proprietor Emil Straude, who had lost both legs in a train accident, sold everything from the *Souderton Independent* to magazines, comic books, and candy. (Courtesy of Evelyn Wismer.)

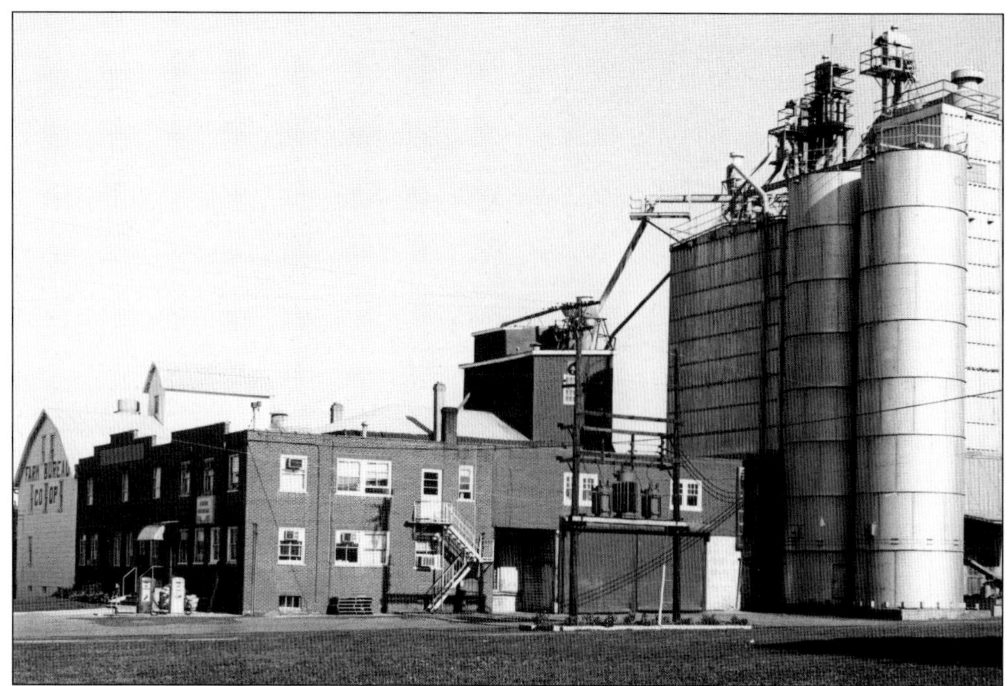

The Montgomery-Bucks Farm Bureau Cooperative Association on Washington Avenue was originally owned entirely by area farmers, who sold supplies, feed, and petroleum for farm use. A Pottsville man purchased the nearby railroad siding in the 1980s after Agway had bought the farm bureau. He announced that six feet of Agway's building was on his land, and he wanted $265,000 for the property. Since sales were declining, Agway simply tore down the building. (Courtesy of Gary Albright.)

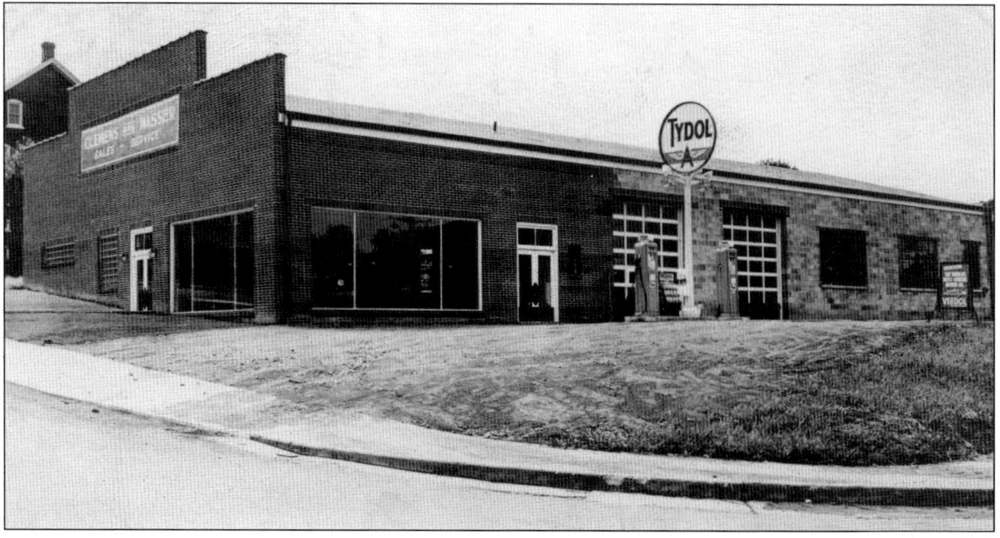

Located on the corner of East Chestnut and Second Streets, the Souderton Motor Company was established in 1948 by George S. Clemens and Irwin F. Wasser. In 1954, the proprietors incorporated as a Dodge-Plymouth agency. A faith-driven aspect of their business was their sales to missionary and evangelical organizations and members of the ministry who served throughout the United States, Ecuador, and Africa. (Courtesy of Kurt Scherzberg.)

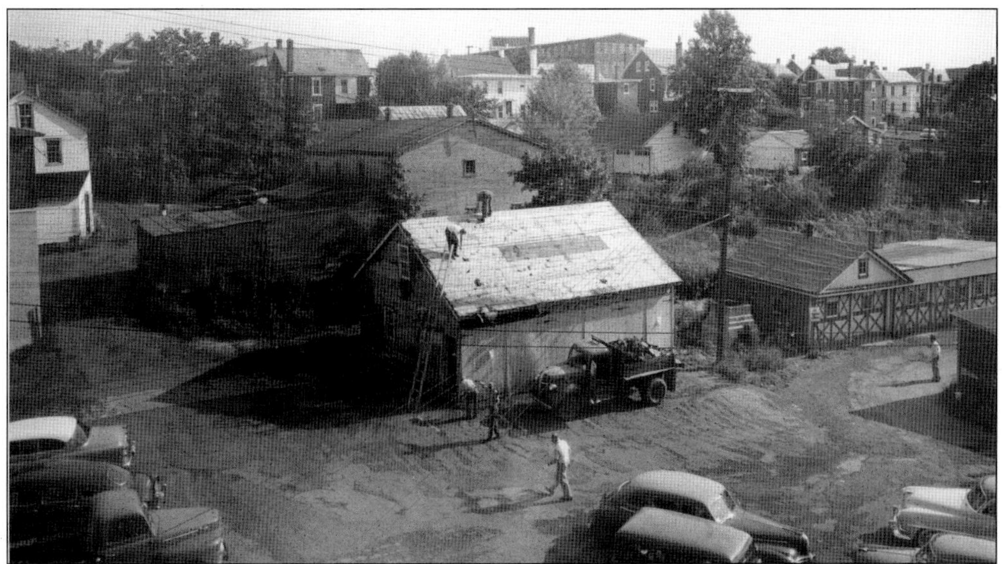

In 1957, the Souderton Parking Authority was formed when more people owned cars and the need for a municipal parking lot became apparent. On West Chestnut Street, located behind many shops on Main Street, these barns, out buildings, and two West Chestnut Street houses were removed (above). During the grand opening in the late 1950s, the new parking lot was being used to its full advantage (below). Stores along Main Street, to the left, opened up back entrances to the new parking lot for more convenient shopping. In the distance, on West Chestnut Street, is the well-remembered Cressman Motor Company. By the 1950s, Crouthamel's Flowers and John Boyer's Jewelry store occupied the space. (Both, courtesy of STMS collection.)

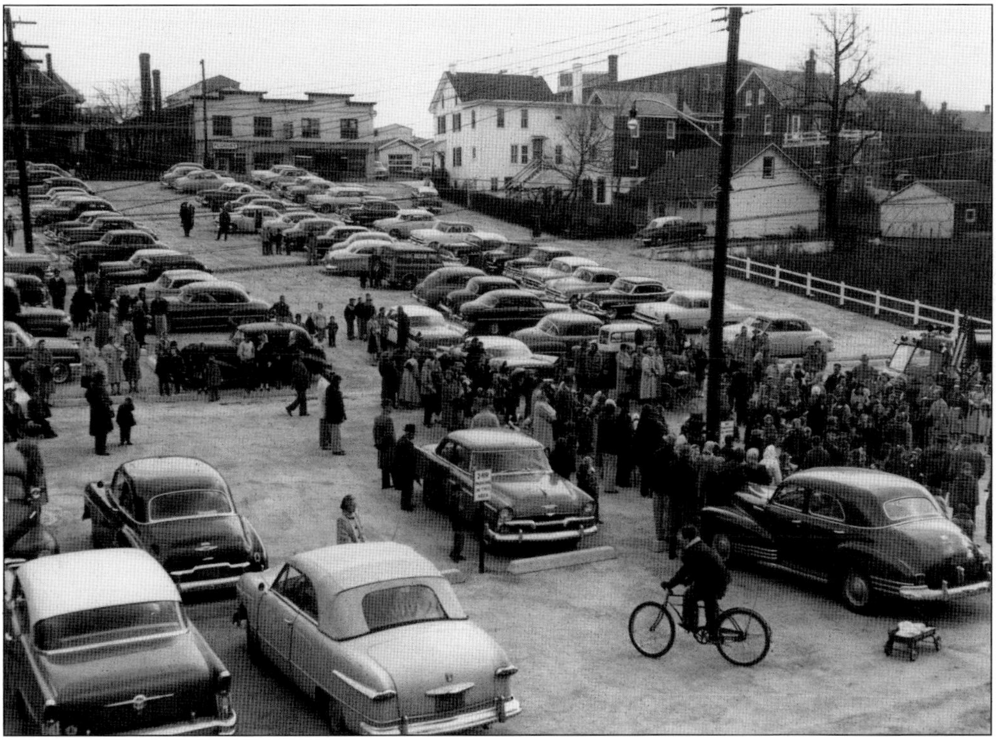

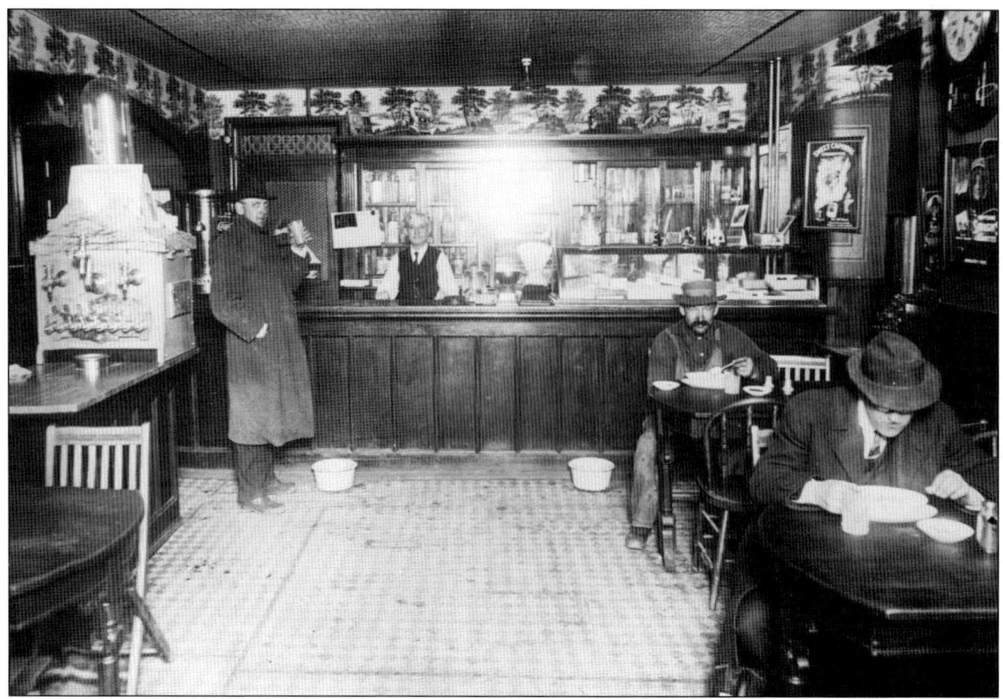

C.S. Freed's popular restaurant on Front Street served Souderton patrons for 47 years. Over time, the photographs taken of the interior showed changes in wallpaper and decorations. Eventually, the spittoons disappeared from the corners of the men's side of the restaurant after spitting tobacco juice in public was no longer considered an acceptable practice. (Courtesy of Gary Albright.)

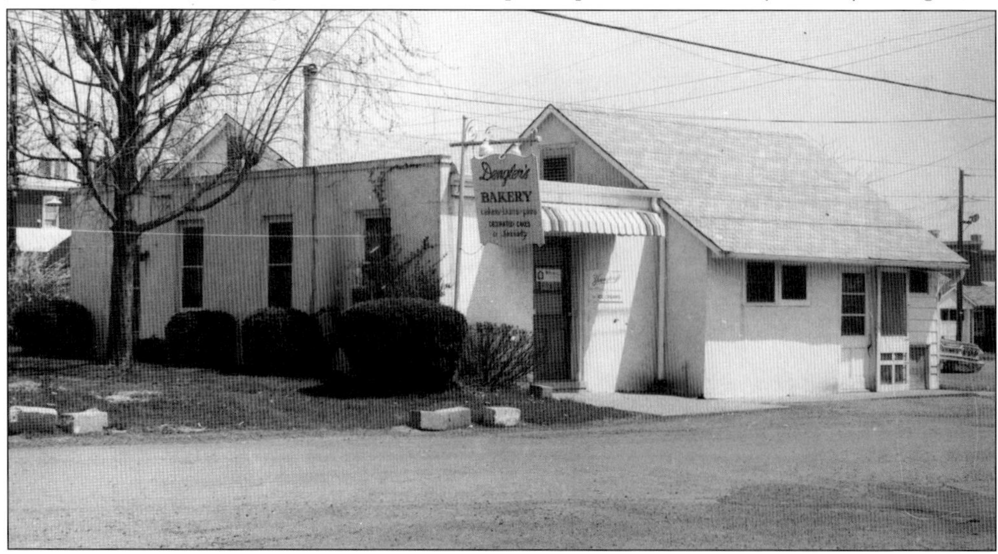

Herbert and Laura Dengler opened Dengler's Bakery on Summit Street in 1952, with son Harold and wife, Evelyn, joining them in 1960. They sold local Pennsylvania German favorites like shoofly pies, funny cakes, and sticky buns, and delivered many pies for firehouse dinners. The Denglers were proud to have baked the cake for Souderton's Centennial Celebration. Children often received a treat from the bakery after their mothers shopped at the nearby Souder Store. (Courtesy of Jessica Gillespie.)

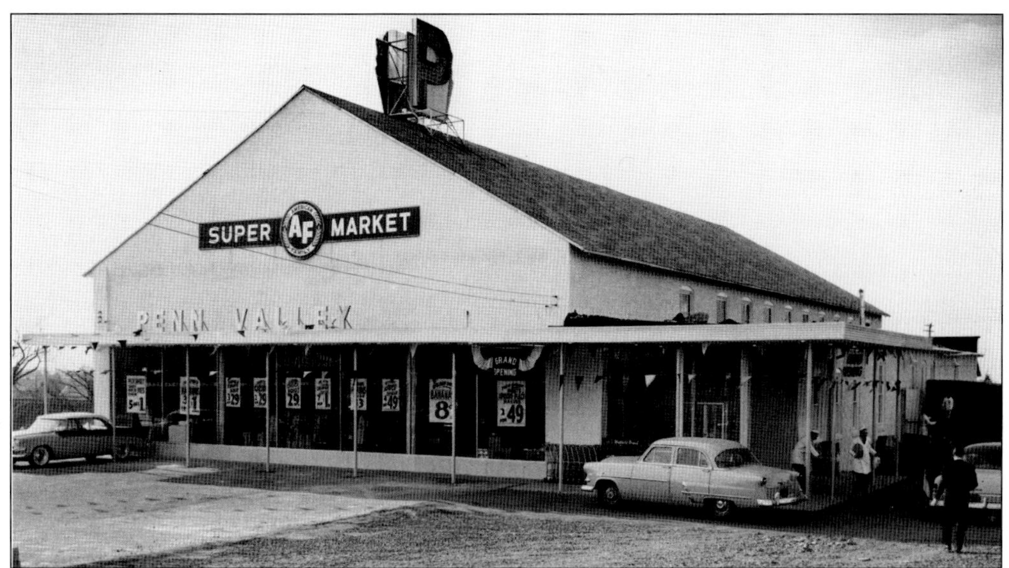

After trolley service was discontinued, the trolley barn, built by the Inland Traction Company in 1899 at Central and Second Streets, was transformed into the Penn Valley Supermarket, shown here. Business at smaller grocery stores declined, eventually closing, as customers enjoyed the greater variety of products and the convenience of off-street parking at supermarkets. In 1953, Clemens Supermarket bought out Penn Valley. Eventually, the building was vacated, and later burned. (Courtesy of Gary Albright.)

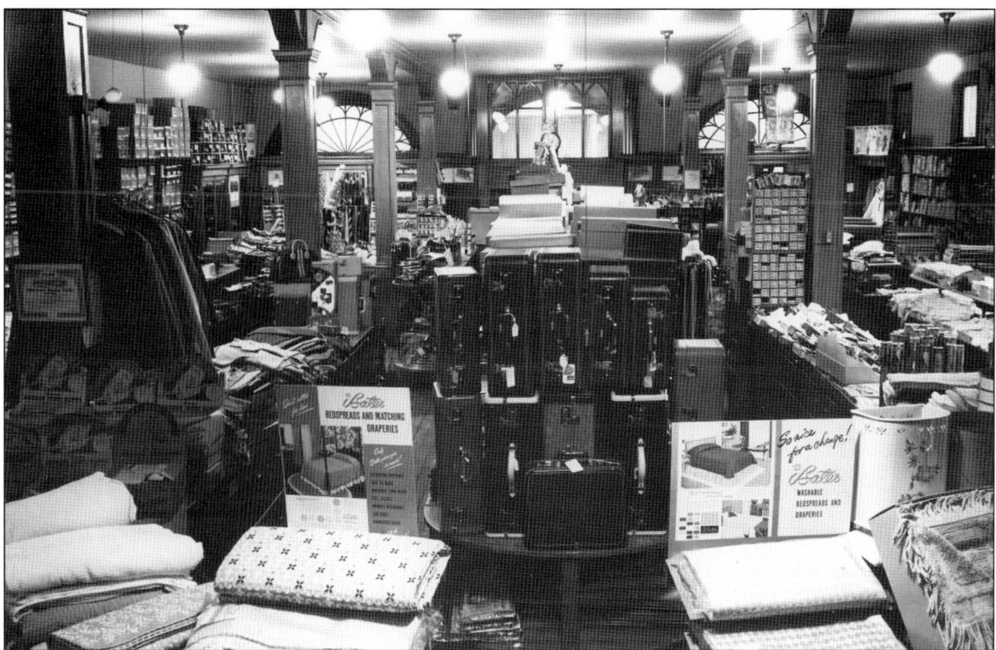

Yocum, Godshalk & Co. attracted many customers to its three floors of merchandise. Here, shoppers could buy clothing, scout uniforms, wedding gifts, household items, carpets, curtains, toys, and furniture. Old and young alike enjoyed the Lionel train display at Christmas, the greatly anticipated window displays, and the water fountain near the front door. In 1961, John Yocum's son Harold took over the management of the store until 1977. (Courtesy of Harold Yocum.)

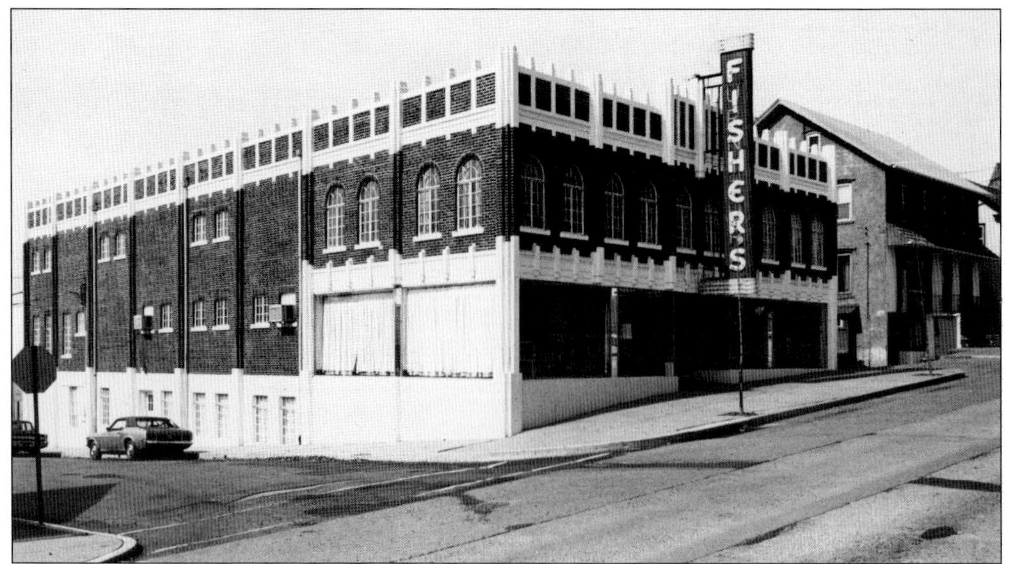

Astute businessman Paul K. "P.K." Fisher opened a furniture store on Front Street in 1924, moved to West Broad Street in 1927, and, in 1936, opened this store at Main and Green Streets, which is where the Central Hotel once stood. He introduced the idea of trading in old furniture for new, offered two-for-one deals, and gave Souderton High School graduates free miniature cedar chests, encouraging future customers. The store closed in 1984. (Courtesy of Gary Albright.)

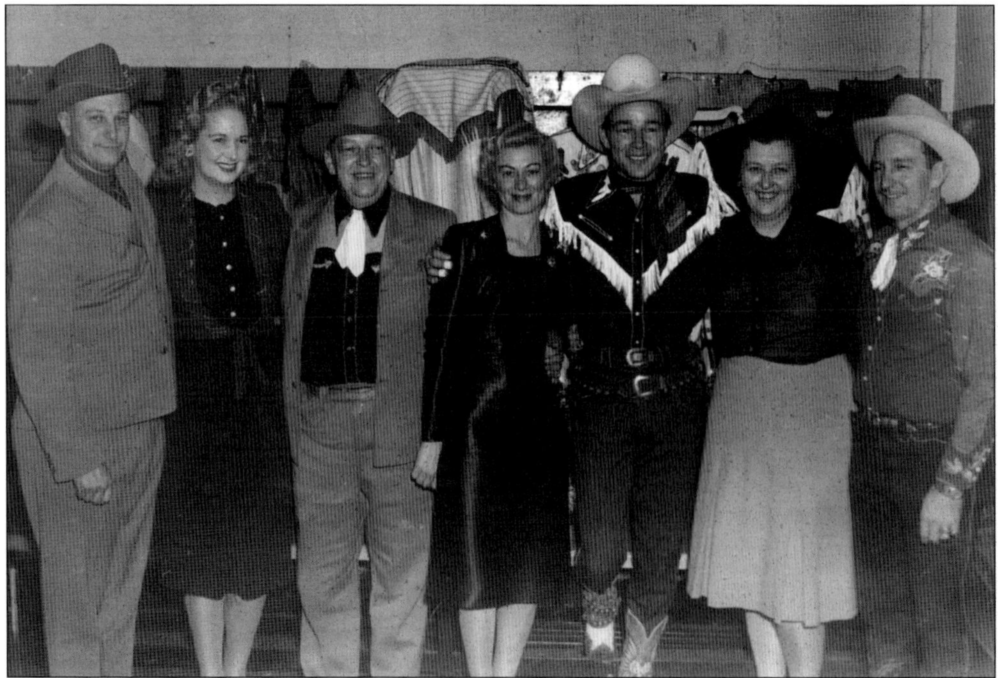
P.K. Fisher was interesting, charming, successful, and generous. He became the largest breeder of Palomino horses, Tennessee Walking horses, and Shetland ponies in the United States, operating out of eight farms in Franconia. Fisher's reputation as the "Palomino King" caused several "cowboys" to travel east to purchase horses. In 1948, Dale Evans, center, and Roy Rogers, third from right, bought the famous Trigger Jr. from Fisher, far left. (Courtesy of STMS collection.)

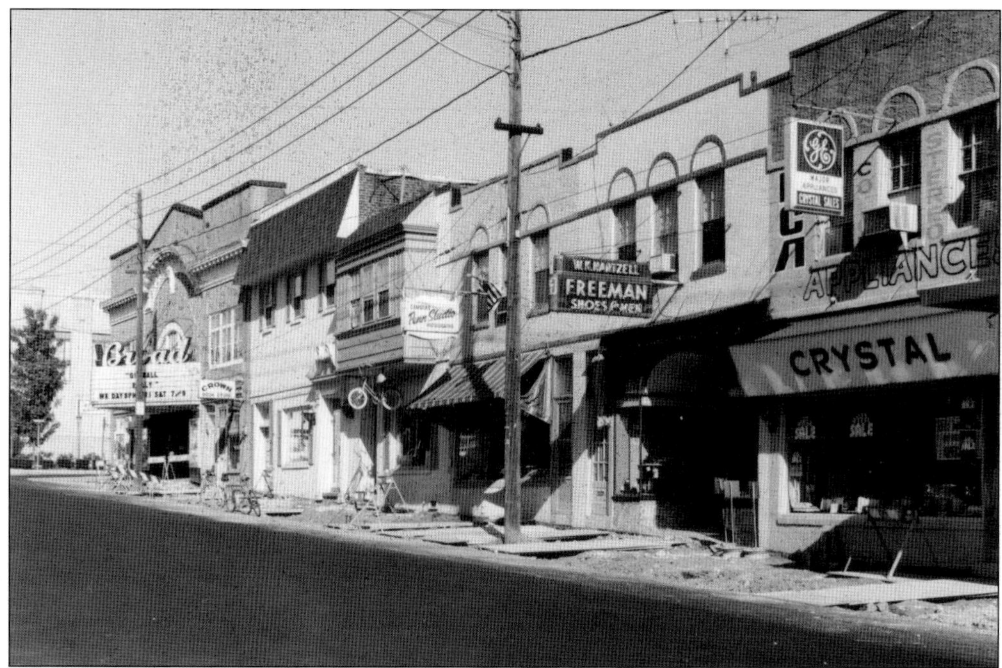

This Broad Street block of buildings has been home to many businesses over the years, including restaurants, beauty salons, and delicatessens. The photograph shows Crystal Sales (specializing in radio and television sets), Hartzell Shoes, Penn Studio photography, and Crown Bookstore. The sidewalk is receiving a much-needed face-lift. (Courtesy of Gary Albright.)

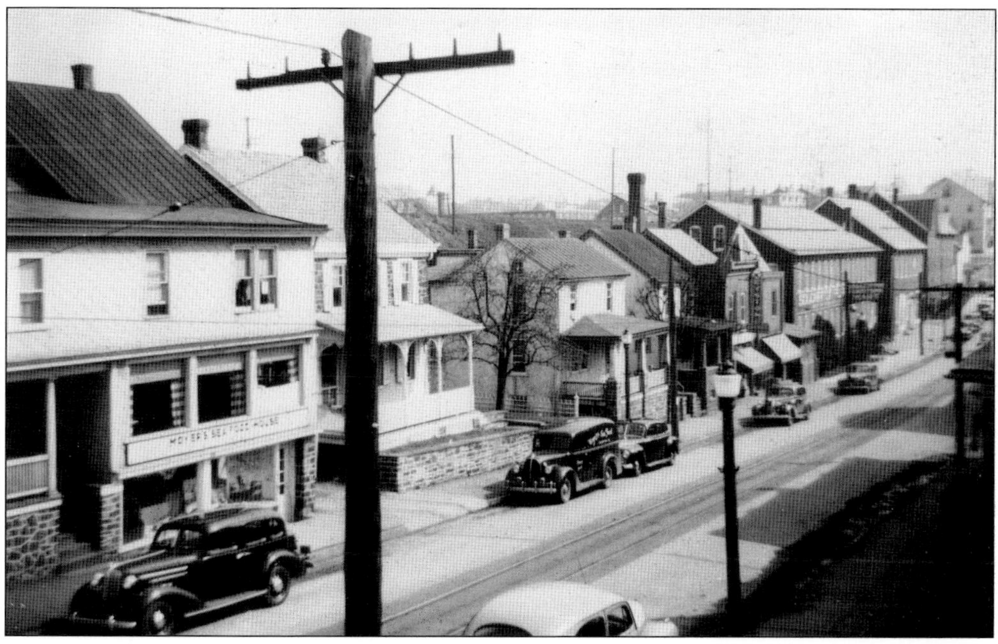

Photographed less frequently, the east side of the hollow on Main Street was home to many businesses, including Moyer's Seafood House, Marty's Dress Shop, and the well-known Souderton Furniture Mart. Some of these buildings were razed for a municipal parking lot. The three-story brick Furniture Mart, on the far right, was converted to office suites. (Courtesy of Gerald Hartzell.)

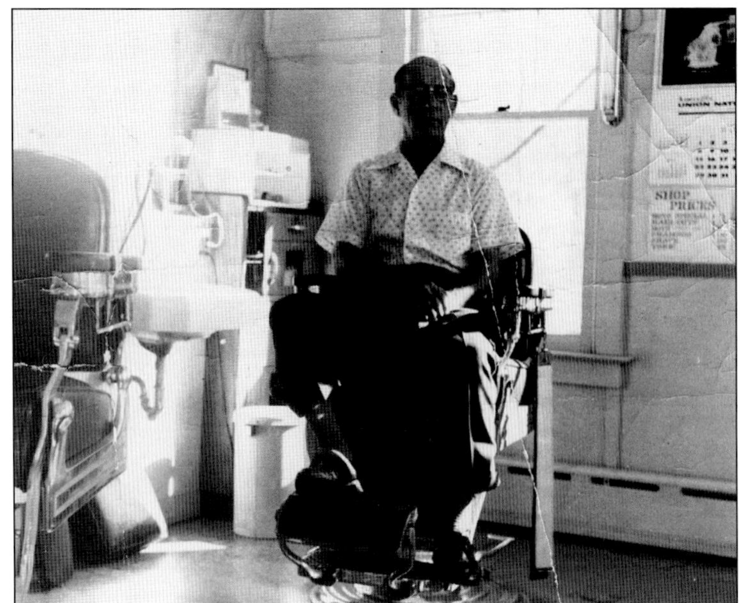

Linford Clemmer, seen relaxing in one of his barber chairs, opened his shop in 1925 on Wile Avenue in back of his house on Green Street. During the 50 years before his retirement, Linford trained many others in his profession and kept his customers handsomely groomed. (Courtesy of Vernon Clemmer.)

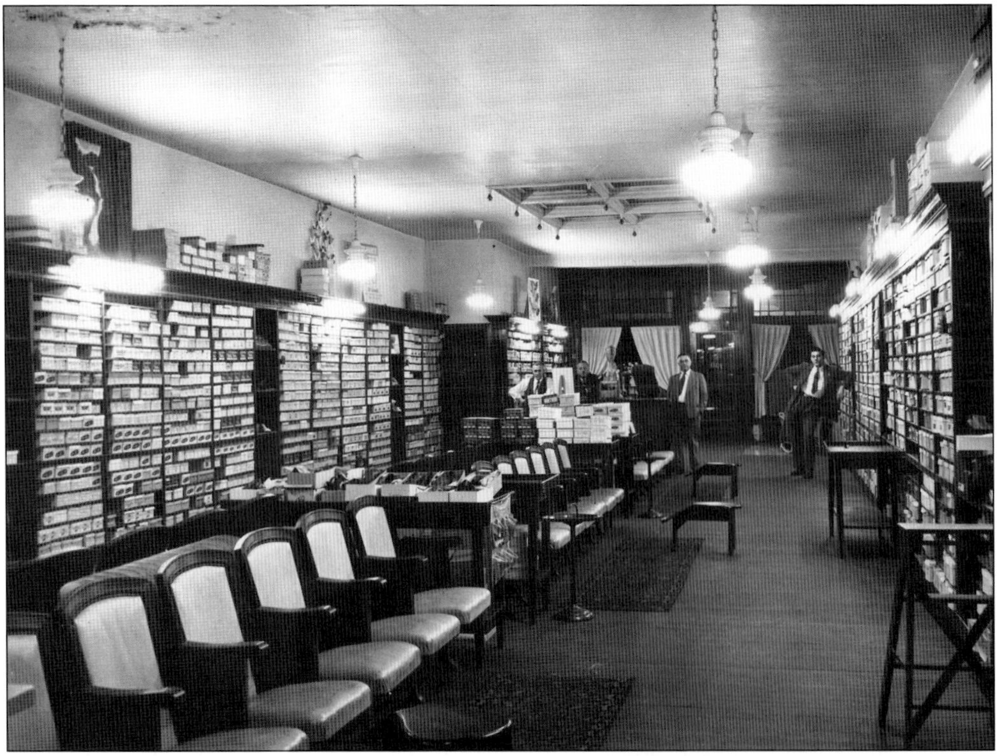

In 1920, Harvey Frederick moved his shoe store to the west side of Main Street where his sons LeRoy and Floyd "Jake" assisted him, eventually taking over the business. Jake Frederick, a fourth-generation shoemaker and salesman, was affectionately known as "Mr. Souderton" because of his involvement with many community organizations. Seen on the left with the staff of Fredericks Shoe Store, Jake supplied shoes for countless numbers of Soudertonians. (Courtesy of Scott Landes.)

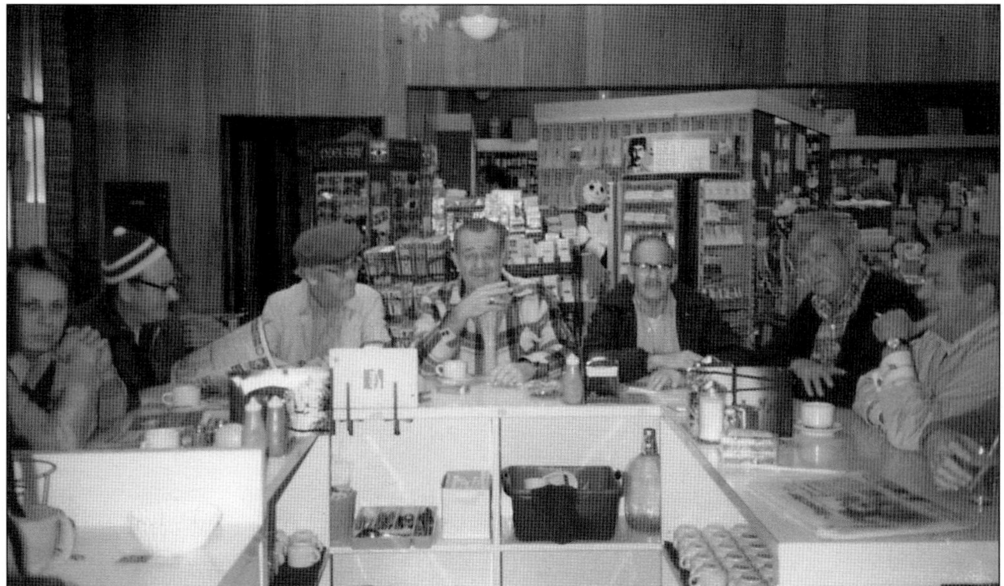

Irwin and Anna Hunsicker opened a pharmacy on West Broad Street in 1929, with their son Emerson as pharmacist. Their lunch counter became a popular meeting place. Patrons were given a coupon for a free Coca-Cola while their prescriptions were filled. Children waiting with parents had permission to read comic books from the rack if they promised not to bend the pages or get them wet! (Courtesy of Bonnie Freed.)

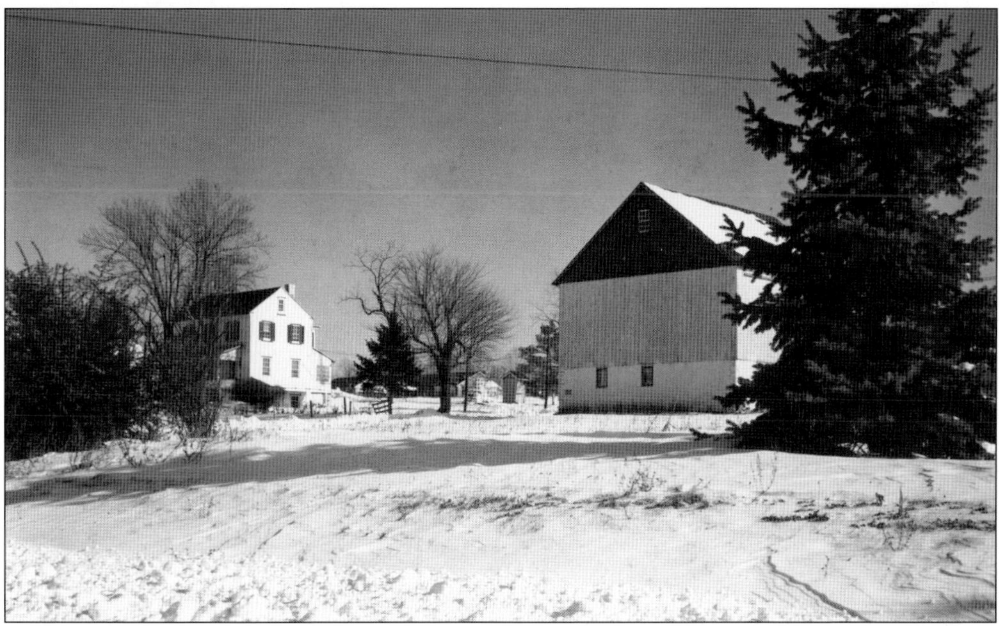

Granville and Blanche Moyer owned the last working farm within the borough of Souderton on West Broad Street extending to Highland Avenue. The Moyers exemplified the definition of "good neighbor" by sharing their produce with their surrounding neighbors from their yearly farm stand, a weekly stop for many town residents. All Souderton farmers had two occupations, and well-loved "Granny" was known to Penn View schoolchildren as their bus driver and maintenance man. (Courtesy of *Souderton Independent*.)

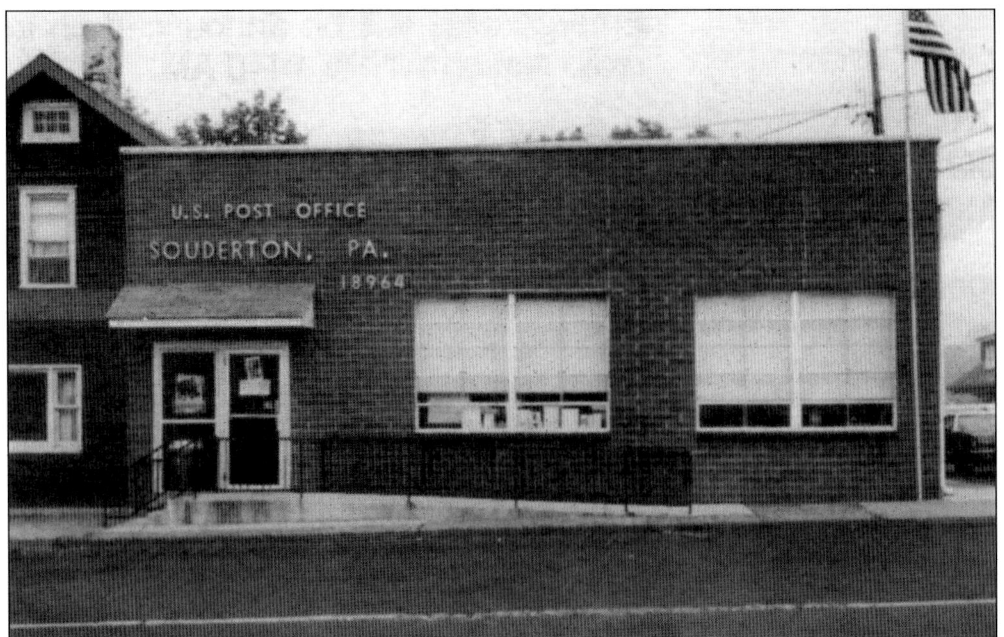

From 1860 to 1963, mail was delivered to Souderton twice a day by rail. Prior to 1901, the post office surprisingly operated seven days a week. Souderton Rural Free Delivery (RFD) began in 1902, first distributed by horse and, later, by horse and buggy. From 1912 to 1925, the Rumilla Post Office in "Reliance" hung its mailbag on a hook outside the Midway Train Station so that conductors could retrieve the out-going mail. In 1925, the government introduced village delivery service. Beginning in the 1950s, the post office was located for approximately 45 years behind the Hotel Souderton on East Broad Street, seen above. The blizzard of 1958 halted many things, but not mail service, as seen below. Eventually, most mailboxes disappeared from street corners, and the post offices of Souderton and Telford were combined in 2000. (Above, courtesy of STMS collection; below, courtesy of the *Souderton Independent*.)

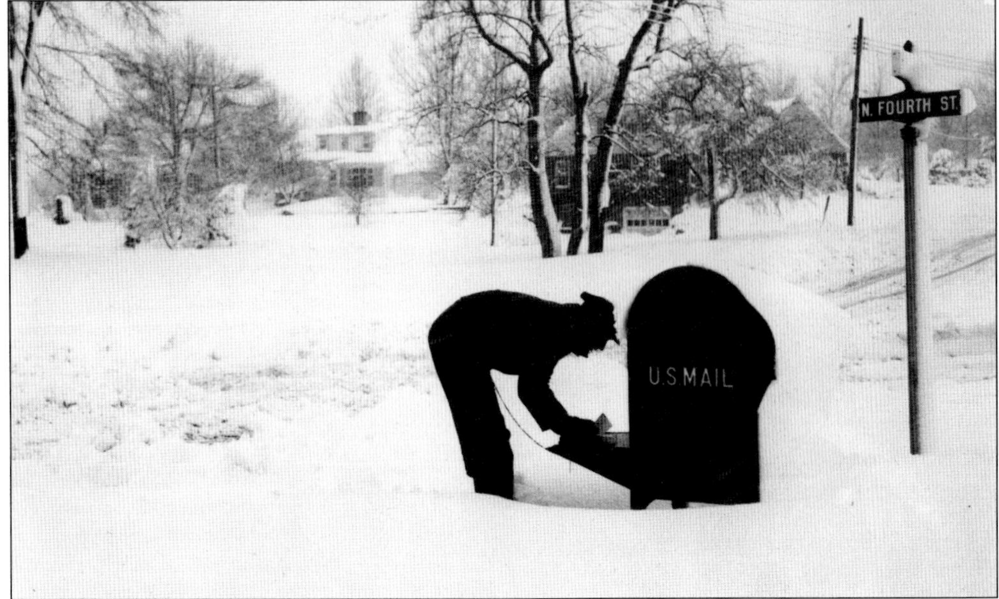

Every June starting in 1957, several thousand shoppers headed to Souderton to take advantage of the rolled-back prices at sidewalk booths during Old-Fashioned Days. Held to acquaint people with the shopping conveniences Souderton had to offer, the festivities included three days of varied entertainment. Parades, worm races, and pony rides were just some of the events. In later years, the popular Souderton Coaster Derby kicked off the annual event. (Courtesy of STMS collection.)

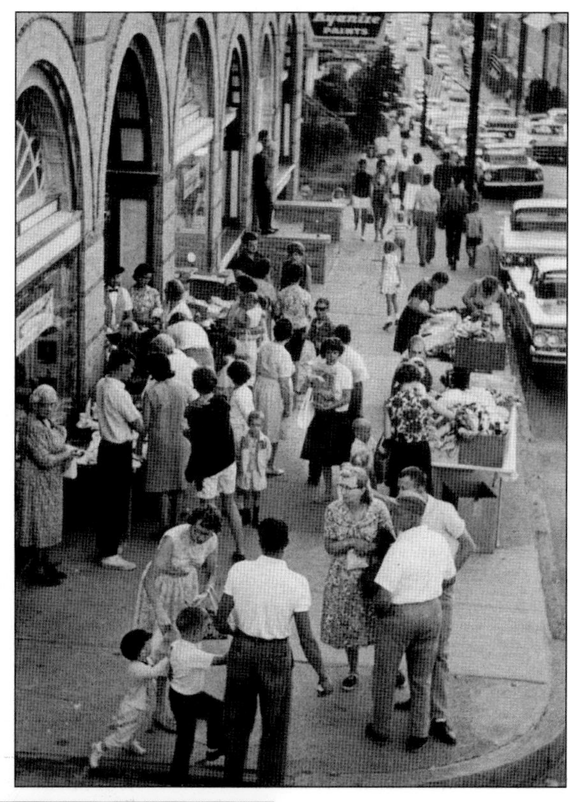

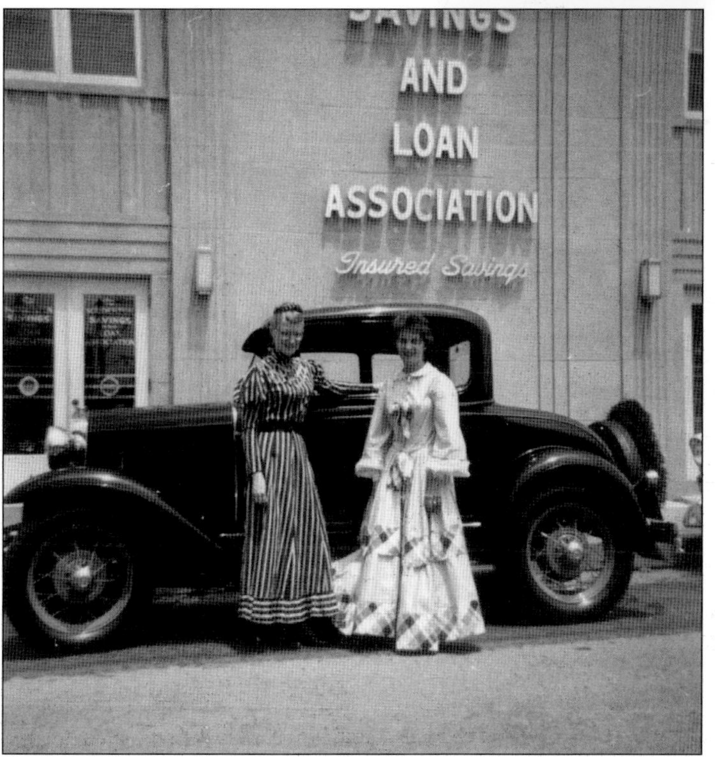

Employees Betty Hackman (left) and Marjorie Landis, wearing their Old-Fashioned Days costumes, pose in front of the Souderton Building and Loan Association. Started in 1896 to enable people to purchase or build homes, the newly renamed Souderton Savings and Loan Association opened an office on Washington Avenue in 1956. Employees visited classrooms to teach students how to set up savings accounts. (Courtesy of Betty Hackman.)

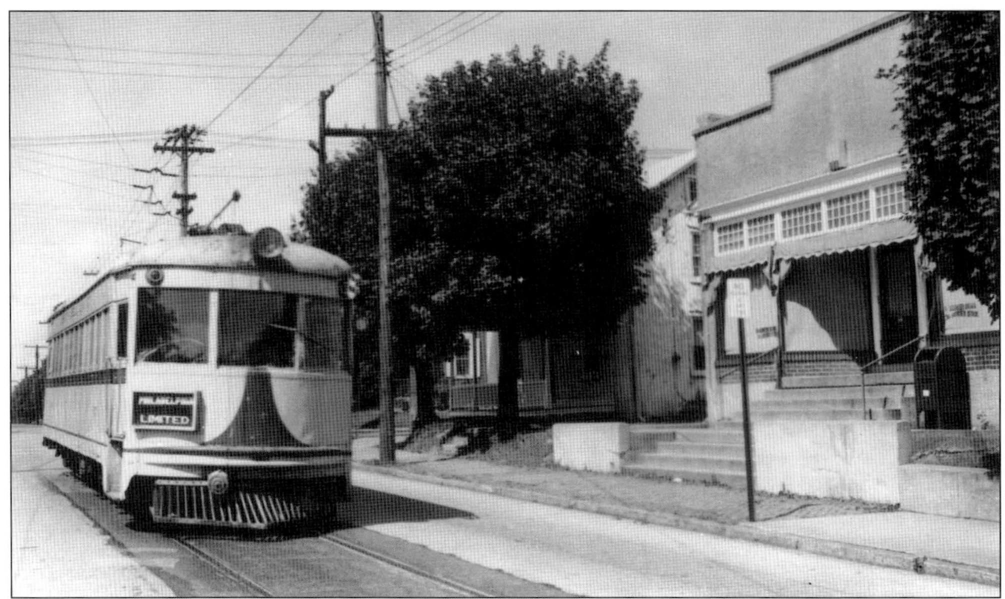

Trolley service provided by this Liberty Bell Limited 1000 series car was discontinued on September 7, 1951. On its right was the Alpheus K. Allebach and Elvin Souder clothing store on Main Street, specializing in plain suits, ladies prayer coverings, bonnets, and men's black broad-brimmed hats. Later as the Souder Store, this fabric and quilting center drew many customers. Sadly, both icons have disappeared from Souderton. (Courtesy of STMS collection.)

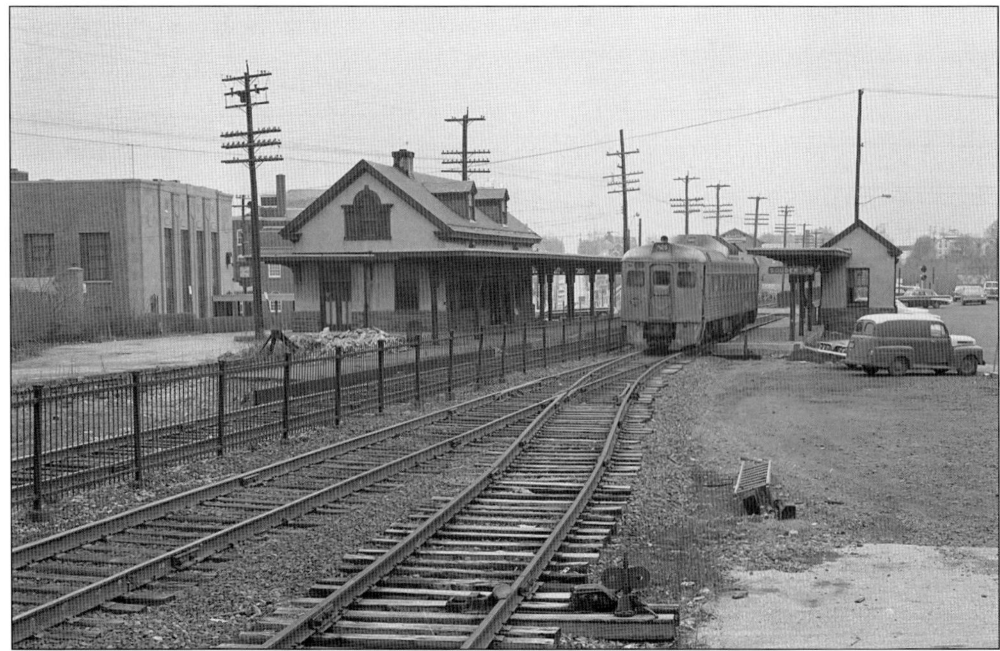

The once mighty steam engines gave way to rail diesel cars in 1961. In 1968, the Broad Street crossing was reopened, and the foot tunnel, which had become unsightly, was closed. On July 26, 1981, the last passenger train left Souderton for Lansdale with no fanfare. While an occasional freight train still rumbles through Souderton, the reason for the town's beginning is now mostly a nostalgic memory. (Courtesy of Heritage Conservancy.)

Eight

Reflections and Visions

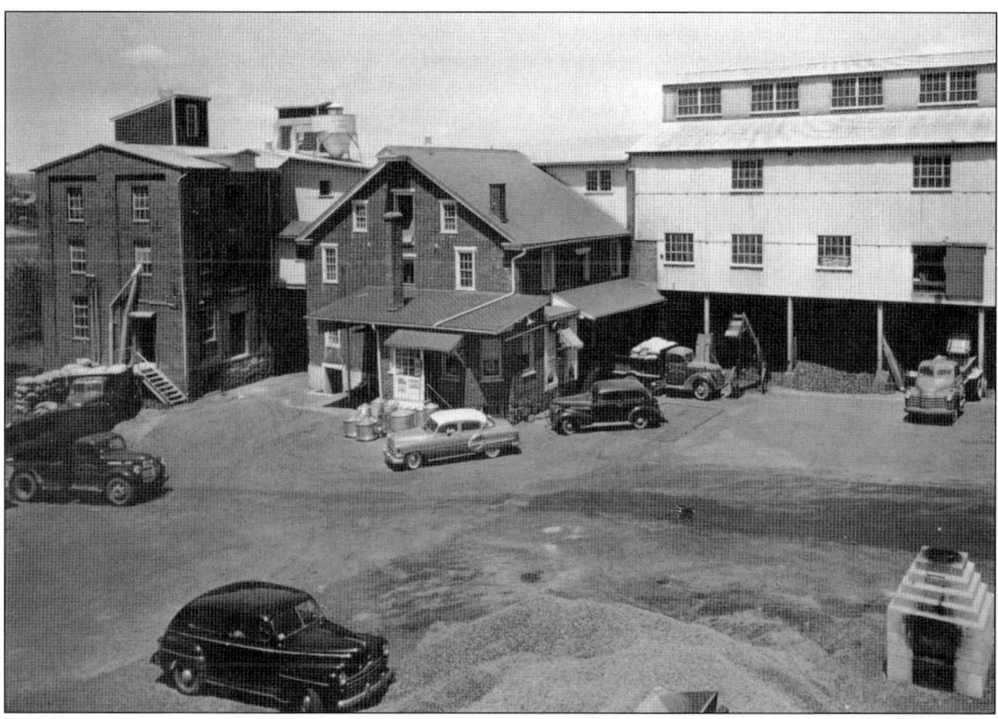

In 1887, a coal yard and feed store opened on Reliance Road, which was sold to Moyer & Son in 1892. In 1966, Moyer & Son, Inc., Souderton's oldest continuing family business, closed its Main Street store and mill, choosing to expand the Reliance Road location, seen above. The family has successfully adapted the business to meet the needs of changing times by maintaining its strong roots in the community. (Courtesy of Moyer Indoor/Outdoor.)

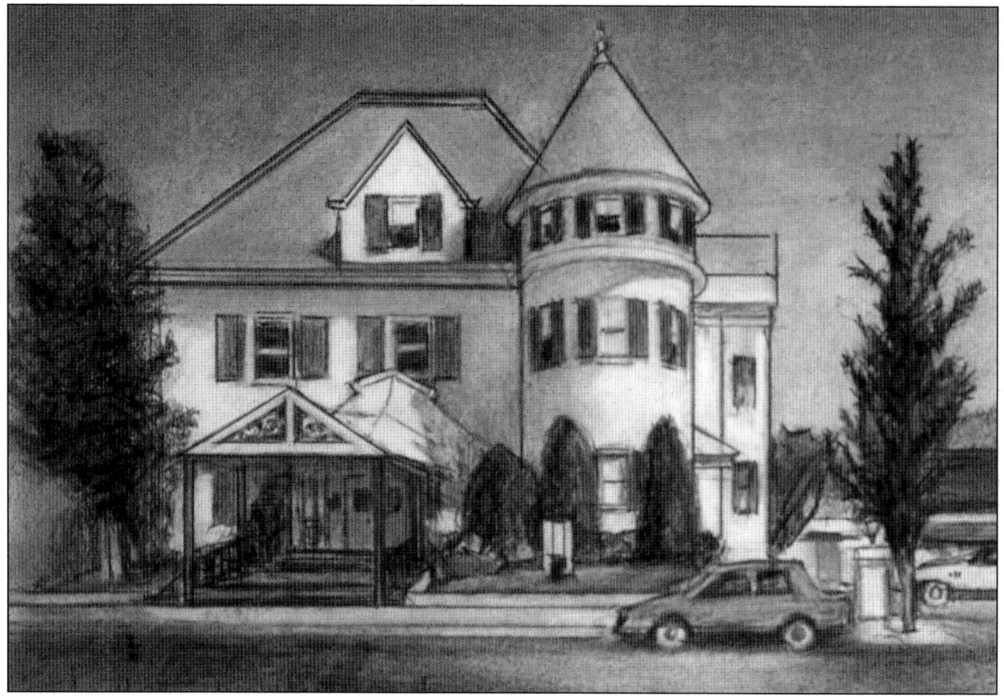

In 1933, Paul M. Hunsicker established the Home for Funerals on East Broad and Second Streets. This drawing by artist Theodore Hallman depicts the large Victorian building that was formerly the stately home of William H. Freed, owner of Hotel Souderton and Freed's Hall, which was diagonally across the street from the home. By the 1980s, Larry L. Anders, Dennis M. Detweiler, and others would join and expand the business. (Courtesy of Jeffrey Landis.)

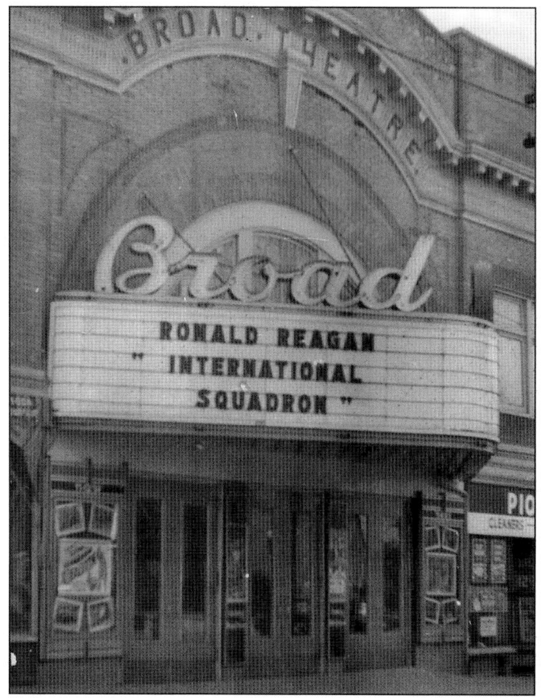

The planned Broad Street Theatre Restoration Project promises to revitalize the corner of West Broad Street and Washington Avenue, bringing back the ambiance of the 1940s in a state-of-the-art complex. The planned theater will show movies, accommodate live performances, and provide space for community use. Resplendent in period decor, the rebuilt theater complex will also include themed restaurants where patrons can enjoy several different dining experiences. (Courtesy of Broad Entertainment Group.)

Founded in 1993 by artistic director Tom Quinn and Hope de Frenes, the Montgomery Theater occupied the lower level of the 1926 Perseverance firehouse on Main Street. To spearhead a revitalization effort on Main Street, Souderton Borough bought the building in 2002 and encouraged renovations, resulting in a 122-seat main stage and an 85-seat project stage. Today, this professional Equity Theater maintains a distinctive reputation in the greater Philadelphia region. (Courtesy of Perseverance Fire Company.)

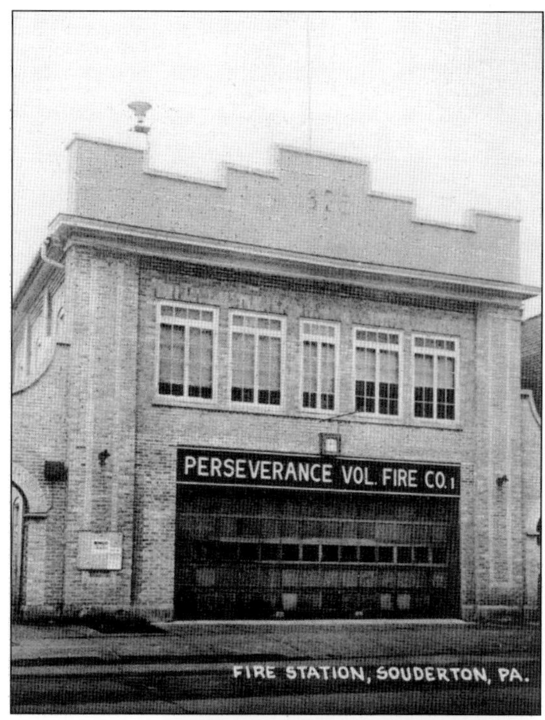

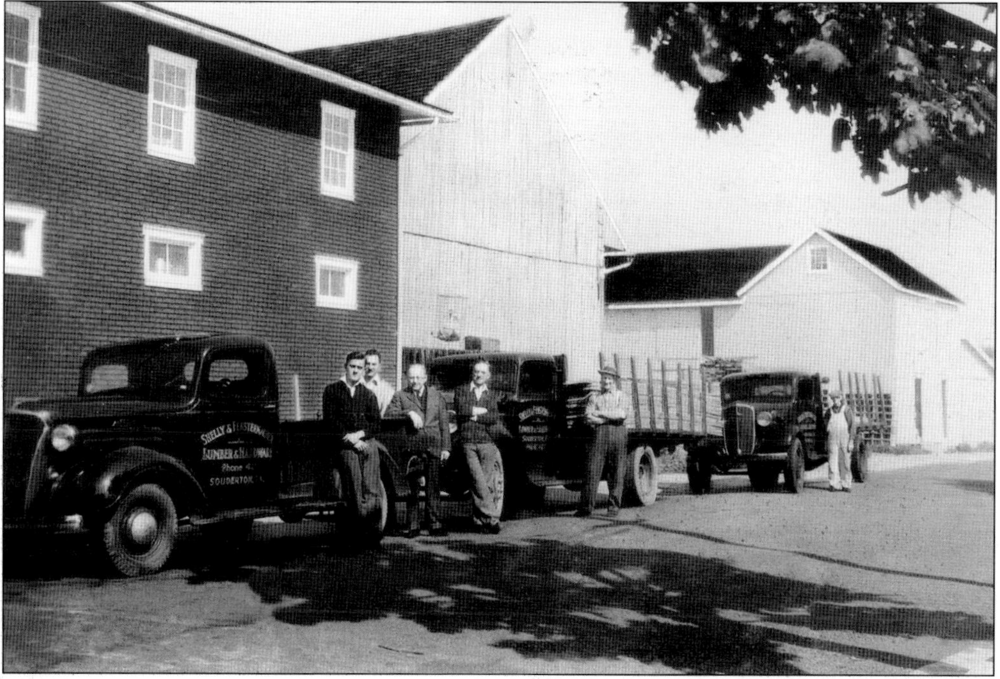

Harvey N. Shelly, fourth from left, and Frank H. Fenstermacher, third from left, formed a partnership, Shelly & Fenstermacher, in 1923 and bought the Delp Lumber Company, located at Highland and Franklin Avenues. In the early 1940s, Shelly's sons Paul and Willard joined the operation, buying out Fenstermacher's interest. Shelly's third-generation owner Greg Shelly recalls Franconia farmers still driving horses with wagons to pick up lumber. (Courtesy of Greg Shelly.)

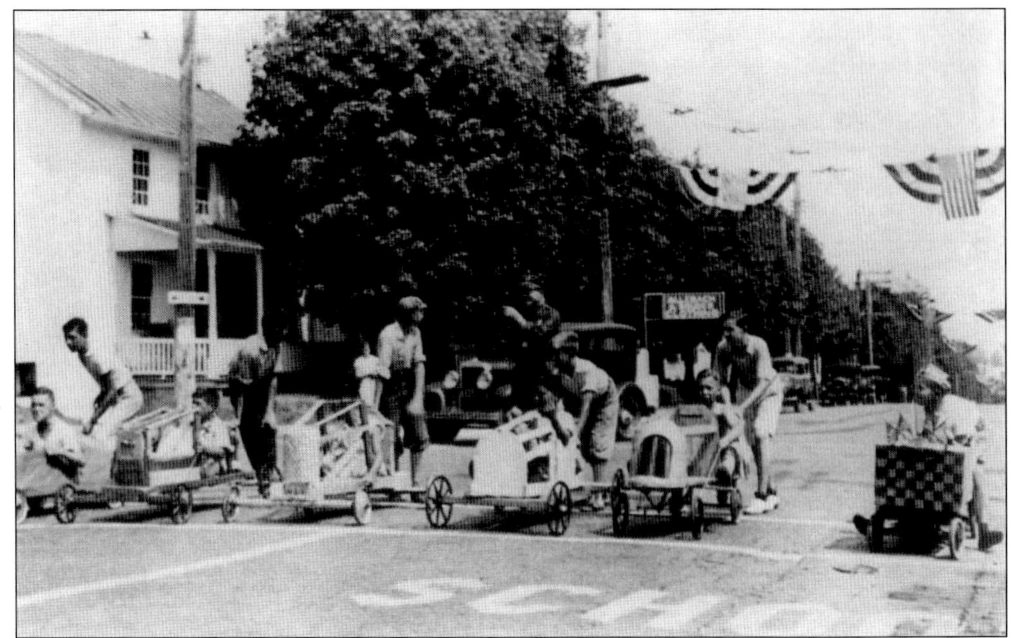

In 1998, the Indian Valley Soapbox Association revived an old Souderton tradition, finding that the combination of the hill and the hollow on Main Street was still a natural course for a race. No longer limited to just boys, about 60 racers in two different age and weight classes meet on the first Saturday of June to compete in the All American Soap Box Derby. Large crowds once again anticipate this exciting event. (Courtesy of Souderton Family Restaurant.)

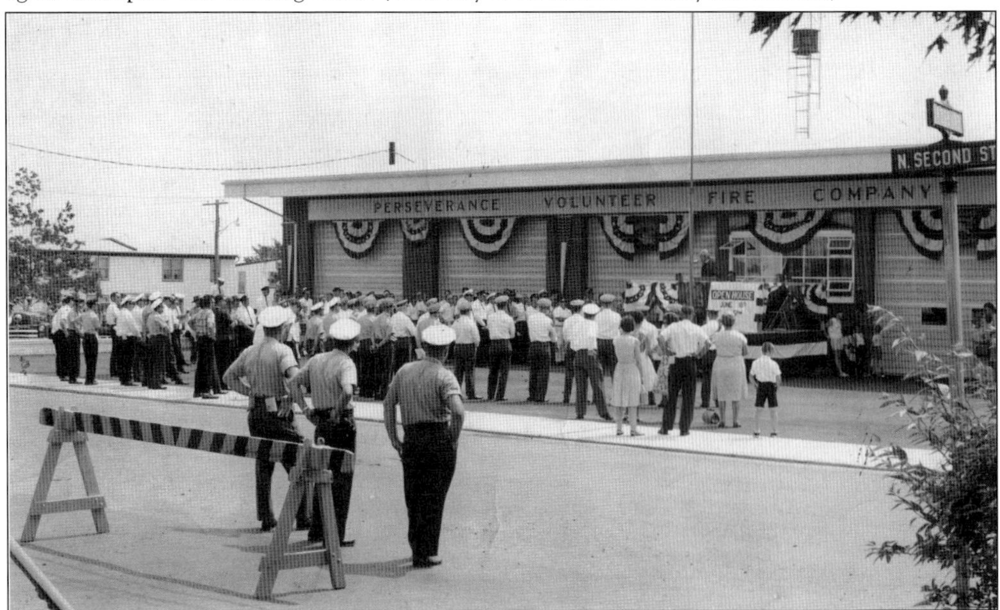

In 1950, land for a future firehouse was purchased on North Second Street, where a public ball diamond and skating pond were created in 1963. In July 1965, ground was broken for the new Perseverance Volunteer Fire Company Firehouse, and once again, firemen donated their own time to complete the project. Seen here is the dedication ceremony in 1967. (Courtesy of Perseverance Volunteer Fire Company.)

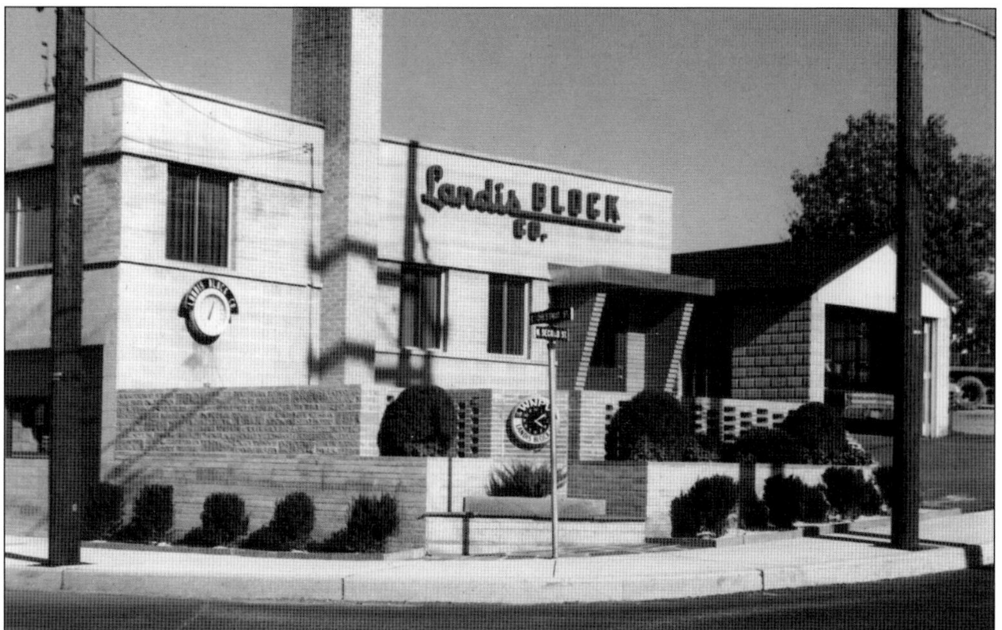

Allen M. Landis opened A.M. Landis in the 1930s, manufacturing cinder blocks and selling masonry supplies. In 1945, Landis wrote to his son Ernest, serving in Europe during World War II, asking him to join the business. In the late 1950s, they built this building on the corner of East Chestnut and Second Streets. In 1978, Landis Block Company relocated to County Line Road. (Courtesy of J. Rodney Landis.)

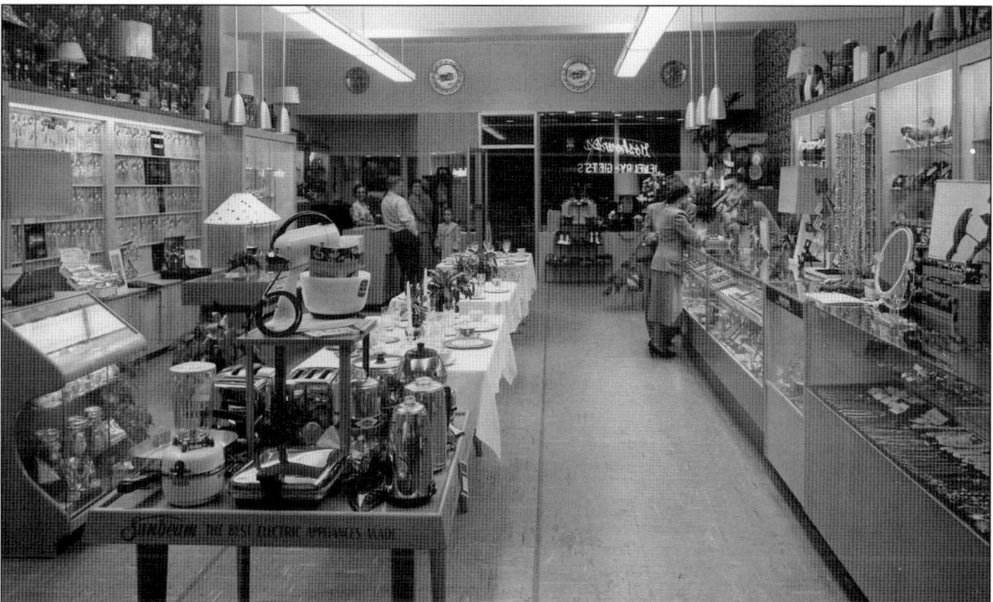

Floyd and Dorothy Goshow opened Goshow's Jewelry Store on West Broad Street in 1946, offering a line of fine jewelry and gift items. When a 1973 fire, started by a stove in an upstairs apartment, completely destroyed the store, Goshow's relocated to County Line Plaza. Although unfortunate, the loss provided an opportunity to increase their gift items to include an array of chiming clocks that delight noontime customers! (Courtesy of Dorothy Goshow.)

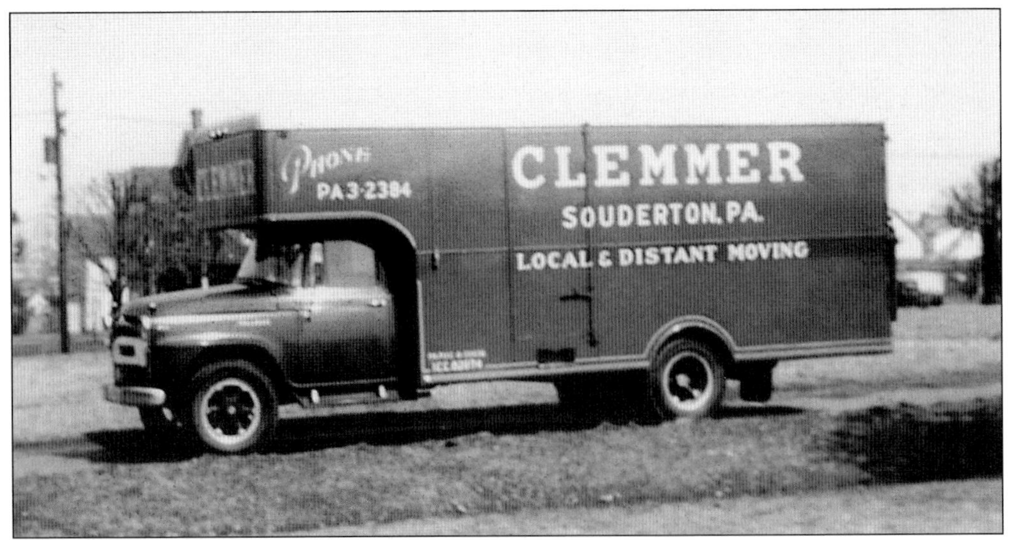

Norman C. Clemmer and his wife, Ruth, took over the moving and storage business from Norman's father, Norman H. Clemmer, in 1960, running the two-truck business from their home. Ruth carried out the administrative tasks while the children answered the phone. By the time they retired, Ruth in 1997 and Norman in 1998, Clemmer Moving and Storage had become the second largest moving company in Pennsylvania. (Courtesy of Norman L. Clemmer.)

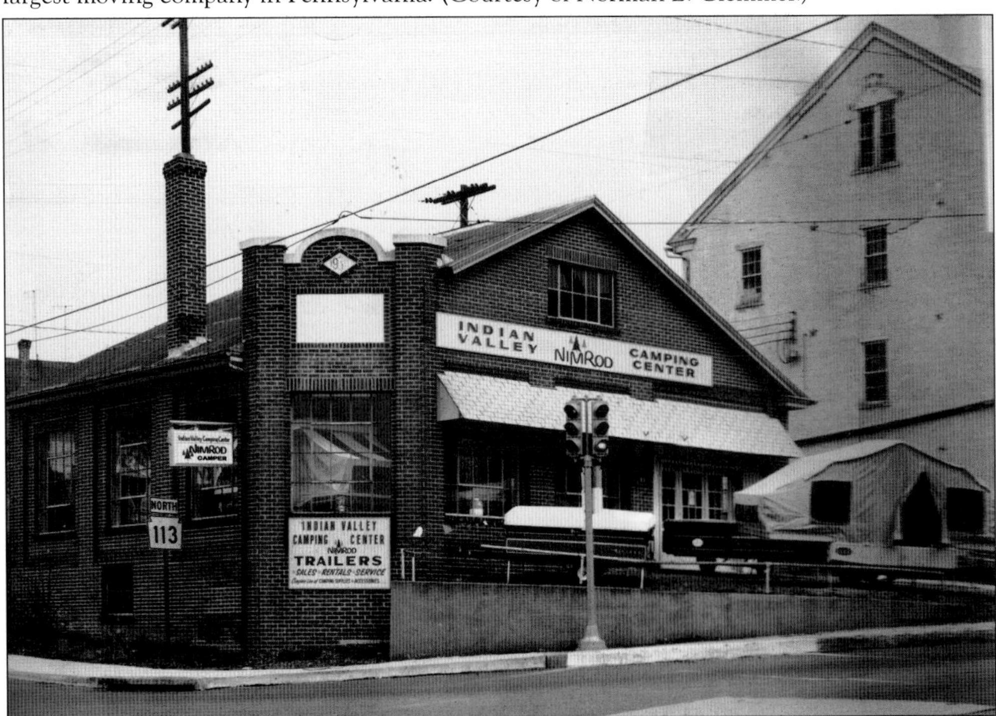

After the larger Main Street building was removed for the Chestnut Street underpass in 1931, E.W. Strasser built this smaller blacksmith shop on his remaining property. For years, it was best known as Jack Trappe's Sporting Goods. In 1968, Arden and Shirley Keller, owners of Indian Valley Camping Center, rented this space for one year to sell pop-up campers, as seen in this photograph. (Courtesy of Claire Keller.)

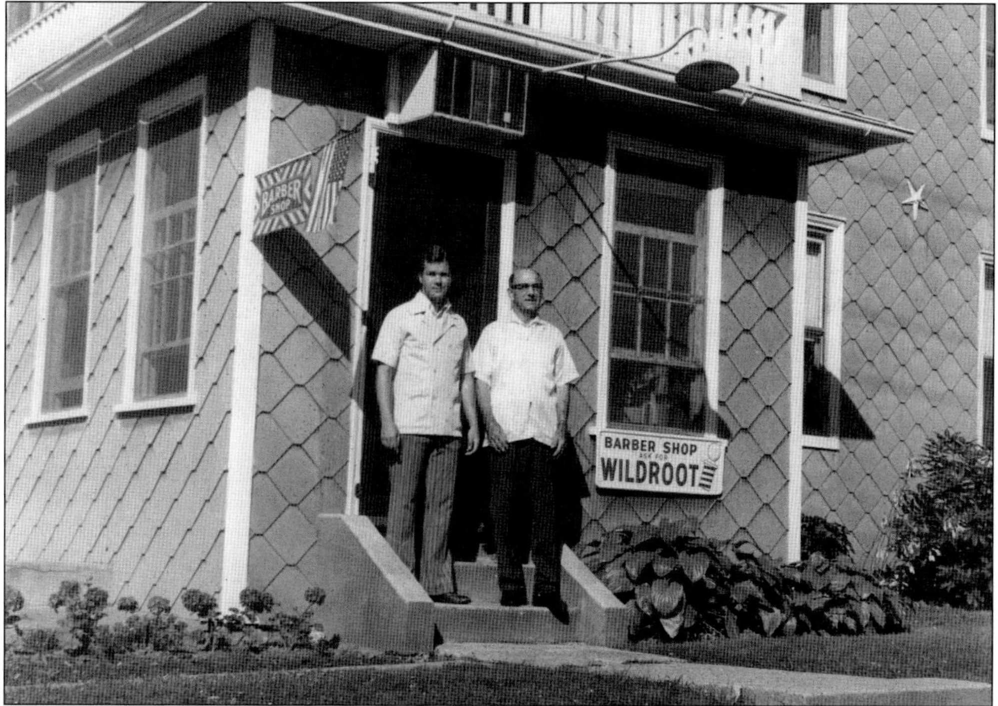

Helmut Schilling stands with Linford Clemmer outside their Wile Avenue barbershop in 1973. In 1965, Clemmer started training 15-year-old Schilling in the business. Schilling became a partner in 1969, buying the property in 1978. Helmut weathered the dearth of business during the long hairstyles of the 1970s, and by 1991, his son Blair joined him in Souderton's last remaining old-fashioned, walk-in barbershop. (Courtesy of Helmut Schilling.)

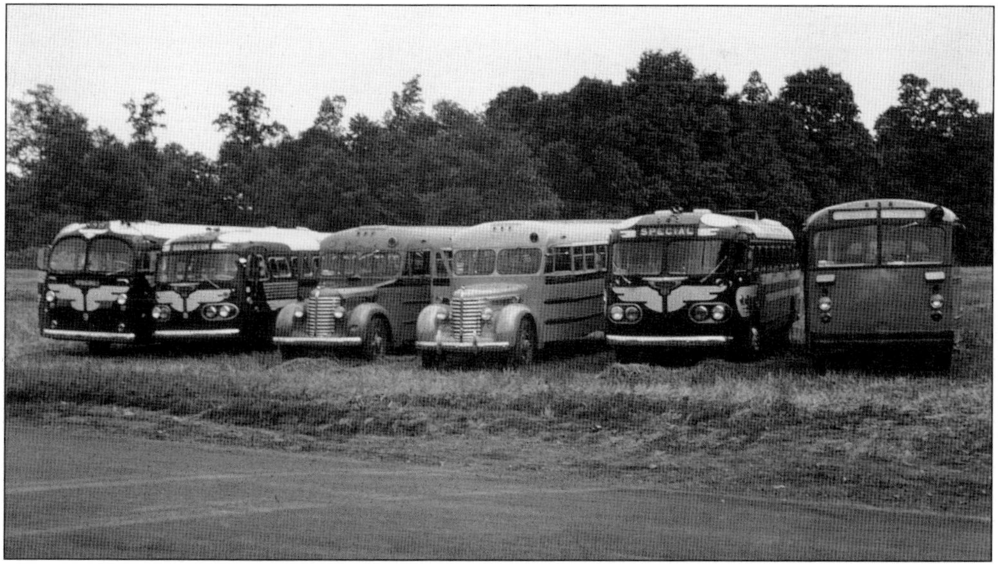

Clarence and Elsie Hagey began their business, Hagey's Bus Service, with one school bus in 1936. Two years later, they began shuttling factory workers from Souderton to nearby towns, and in 1947, they purchased their first deluxe tour bus. This 1949 photograph shows the entire Hagey fleet, which consisted of six vehicles, both tour and school buses. (Courtesy of Brian Hagey.)

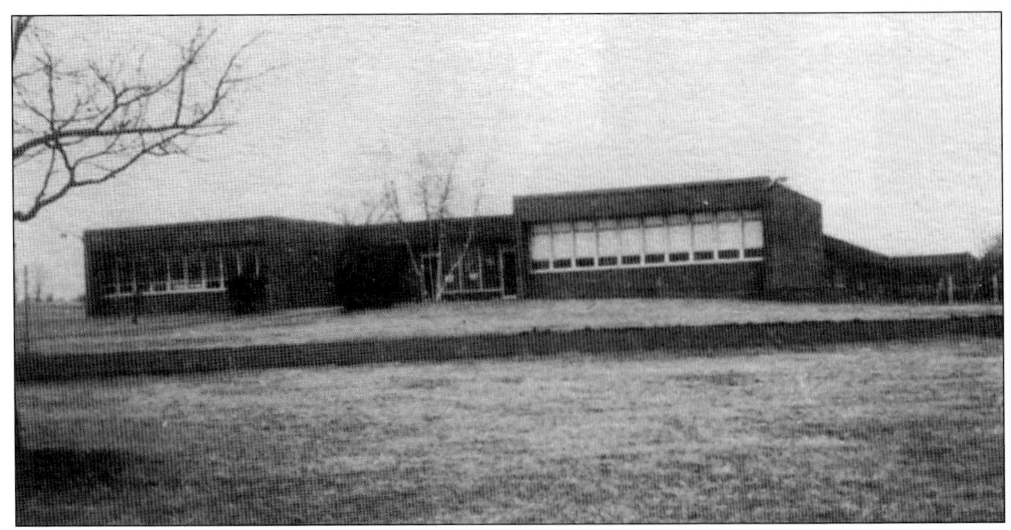

Within five years of each other, two elementary schools opened to serve the growing community. In 1962, E. Merton Crouthamel Elementary on School Lane welcomed students, and in 1967, West Broad Street Elementary (above) opened its doors. In 1966, the Souderton Area School District (SASD) was formed, again uniting schools in Franconia Township and closing nine one-room facilities. Currently, SASD has seven elementary, two middle, and one high school. (Courtesy of STMS collection.)

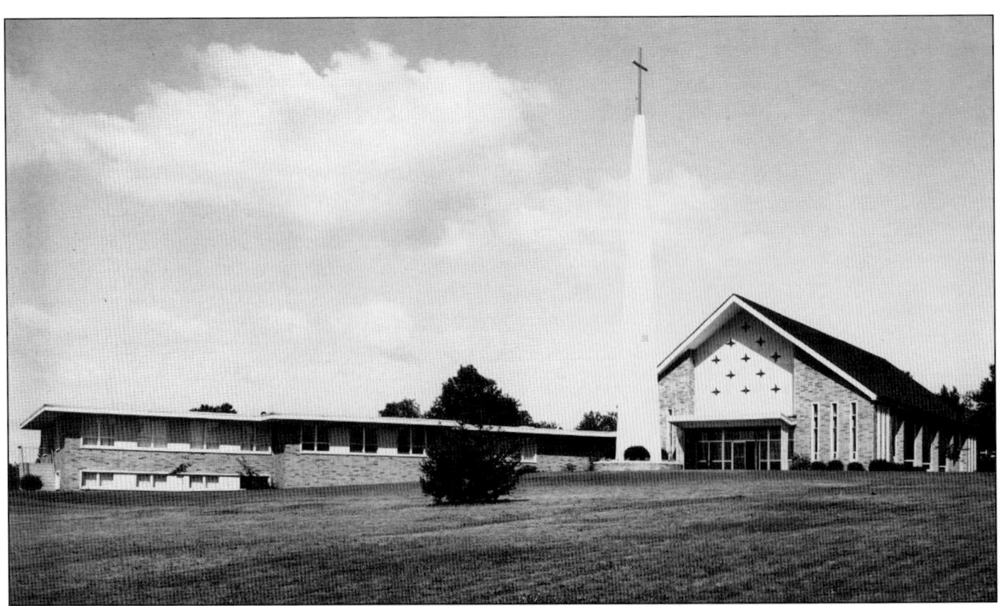

Faith has retained its place at the center of the community's value system. Founded with a respect for religious tolerance, Souderton has been home to many denominations and more recently new cultures, sharing churches or public spaces to worship. In 2008, Zwingli United Church of Christ on Wile Avenue, shown here in the 1960s, was heavily damaged by fire. The community rallied, lending support and offering space until Zwingli could rebuild. (Courtesy of Gary Albright.)

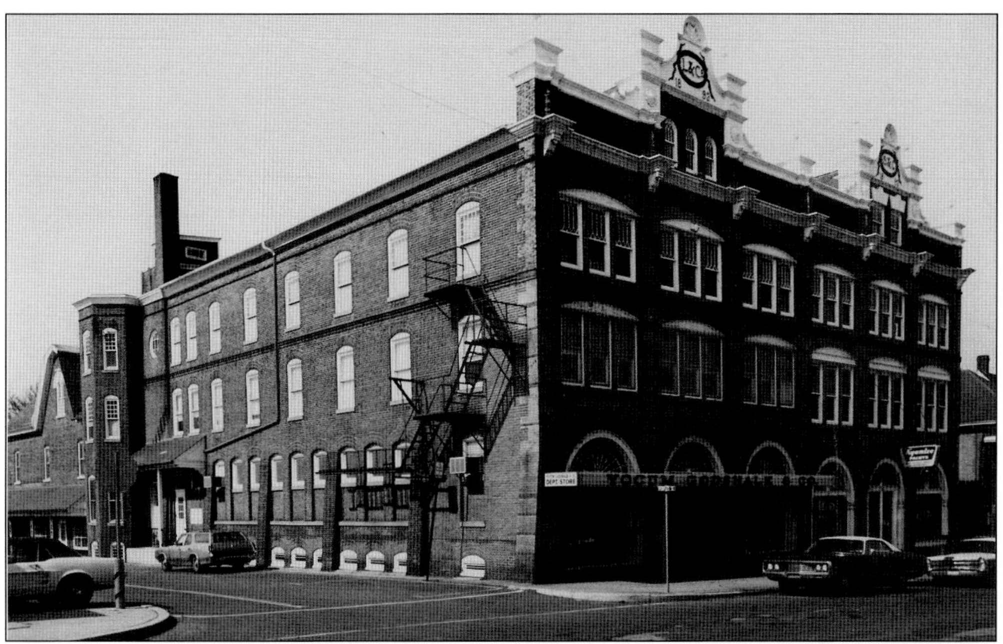

When the twin stores on Main Street that housed Yocum, Godshalk & Co. and Renreg Hardware closed in the late 1970s, bank officials from Univest Corporation of Pennsylvania purchased the buildings for their corporate offices, maintaining the character and memories of the stores, and finally connecting the buildings internally. Thanks to Univest, the building is eligible to be listed in the National Register of Historic Places, preserving Souderton's history. (Courtesy of Gary Albright.)

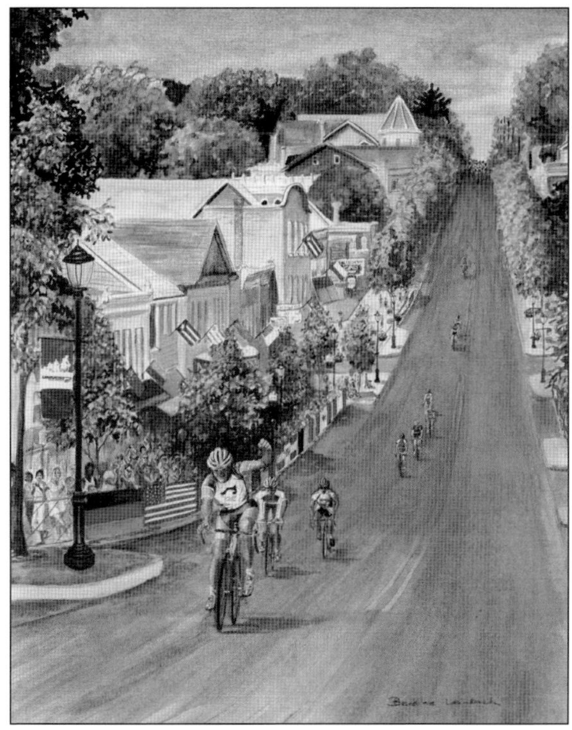

This watercolor by artist Berdine Leinbach for the 2007 Univest Cycling Grand Prix on Main Street captures Souderton's charm as the town welcomes the international cyclists. This top ranked race is proudly sponsored by local businesses and staffed by volunteers. Riders confront a challenging 6,000 feet of climbing through the hilly countryside of Eastern Pennsylvania. In its second decade, the race attracts another generation to Souderton's cherished landmark—the hill and the hollow. (Courtesy of Berdine Leinbach and Univest Corporation.)

www.arcadiapublishing.com

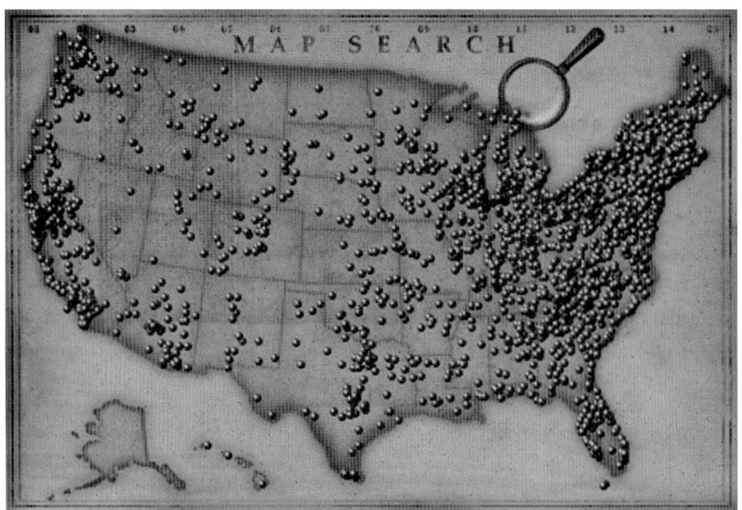

Discover books about the town where you grew up, the cities where your friends and families live, the town where your parents met, or even that retirement spot you've been dreaming about. Our Web site provides history lovers with exclusive deals, advanced notification about new titles, e-mail alerts of author events, and much more.

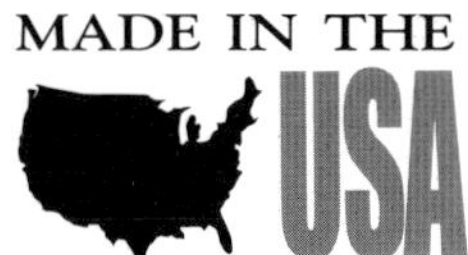

Arcadia Publishing, the leading local history publisher in the United States, is committed to making history accessible and meaningful through publishing books that celebrate and preserve the heritage of America's people and places. Consistent with our mission to preserve history on a local level, this book was printed in South Carolina on American-made paper and manufactured entirely in the United States.

This book carries the accredited Forest Stewardship Council (FSC) label and is printed on 100 percent FSC-certified paper. Products carrying the FSC label are independently certified to assure consumers that they come from forests that are managed to meet the social, economic, and ecological needs of present and future generations.

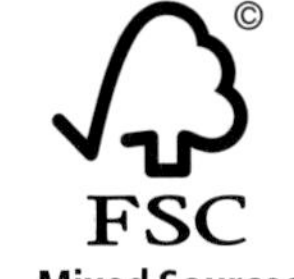

FSC
Mixed Sources
Product group from well-managed forests and other controlled sources

Cert no. SW-COC-001530
www.fsc.org
© 1996 Forest Stewardship Council

Find *Your* Place in History.